the

online writing
conference

the
online writing
conference

a guide for teachers and tutors

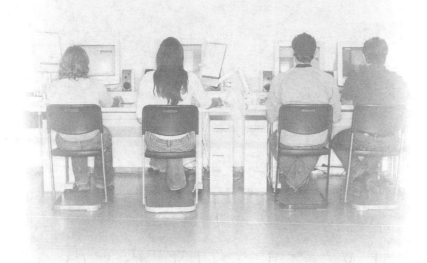

BETH L. HEWETT

foreword by **MICHAEL PEMBERTON**

Boynton/Cook
HEINEMANN
Portsmouth, NH

Boynton/Cook Publishers, Inc.
361 Hanover Street
Portsmouth, NH 03801–3912
www.boyntoncook.com

Offices and agents throughout the world

Library of Congress Cataloging-in-Publication Data
Hewett, Beth L.
    The online writing conference : a guide for teachers and tutors / Beth L. Hewett.
        p. cm.
    Includes bibliographical references.
    ISBN-13: 978-0-86709-601-9
    ISBN-10: 0-86709-601-2
    1. English language—Rhetoric—Computer-assisted instruction. 2. English language—Rhetoric—Study and teaching—Data processing. 3. Report writing—Study and teaching—Data processing. 4. Report writing—Computer-assisted instruction. 5. Online data processing—Study and teaching. 6. English teachers—Training of. I. Title.

PE1404.H48 2009
808'.0420285—dc22   2009044712

Editor: Charles I. Schuster
Production editor: Lynne Costa
Cover design: Night & Day Design
Cover photograph: Getty Images/Digital Vision
Typesetter: Valerie Levy/Drawing Board Studios
Manufacturing: Steve Bernier

Printed in the United States of America on acid-free paper
14   13   12   11   10   VP   1   2   3   4   5

This book is dedicated to the memory of Edward Gerard Berlinski, Ph.D., a scholar, teacher, and poet who showed me the way when my options seemed bare and bleak. As "way leads on to way," according to Robert Frost's simple wisdom, so did my friendship with Ed lead me to The Catholic University of America, to areas of fruitful and passionate interest, and eventually to this book that encapsulates much of my career as a postsecondary educator. Thank you, Ed, and rest in peace. †2009

Contents

Foreword

I'm writing this Foreword on a Sunday morning, so it seems only appropriate that I should begin with a confession:

Online conferencing has always frightened me.

It doesn't frighten me because computers make me nervous or because I have a problem with integrating online assistance into the services that my writing center offers. My center has a Web site and a computer lab, we use WCOnline for all of our scheduling and reports, we regularly refer our students to other OWLs (online writing lab) and online writing resources, and we're even looking into expanding our services by creating podcasts and incorporating Web 2.0 applications. In fact, as much as I like to complain about computers in moments of frustration, I have to admit that I'm a total geek. I spend far too much time on Facebook, eBay, Amazon, and YouTube. My daughters made a sign for my desk that proclaims me "Computer Guru and All-Knowing Sage of Ultimate Wisdom" (smart kids!), and one of my favorite TV programs is *The Big Bang Theory*, partly because I see aspects of Leonard and Sheldon, the show's quintessential uber-nerds, in myself. So why is it that the thought of online tutoring gives me—for want of a better phrase—the heebie-jeebies?

Several reasons, I think. First, because until fairly recently, the hardware and software necessary for successful online conferencing (and I define *successful* in terms of the degree to which online tutorials can emulate the f2f conference experience) have been seriously lacking. As Neal Lerner documents in "Drill Pads, Teaching Machines, and Programmed Texts: Origins of Instructional Technology in Writing Centers" (1998), until the 1990s, computers were fairly primitive, connectivity was poor, and software was exceedingly clunky. Even into the late 1990s, as Peter Carino (1998) points out, computer technology had not progressed to the point where online conferencing could be called anything but awkward. Though asynchronous tutoring (using e-mail and listservs) and synchronous tutoring (with MOOs and LANs) were used sporadically in 1998, Carino was less than enthusiastic about the results: "[W]e will need to assert what we know about live pedagogy," he says, "to prevent the mere placing of services online simply because they can be,

rather than because they should be" (192). For a long, long time, that
was my mantra. If f2f conferences worked so well, why would I want
to shift to a CMC environment that worked, as far as I could tell, pretty
poorly? Metaphorically speaking, it would be like moving the writing
center conference from an IMAX theater to a grainy, black-and-white,
thirteen-inch television screen just because I happened to own a TV.

Moreover, like many others in the field, I have been apprehensive
about what gets lost in virtual environments. I like people. I like *being*
with people in writing center conferences—seeing their faces, hearing
their voices, reading their body language, experiencing a strong sense
of *presence* as we talk. I enjoy being able to walk students to our reference library or get them a cup of coffee if they're thirsty, and somehow,
typing ":gives Becky some coffee" in MOOspace just doesn't feel the
same to me. I also wonder whether I can be an effective writing consultant online. When I talk, I feel freer. I can construct my thoughts
on the fly and spout ideas as they occur. I can ask quick questions
to stimulate conversation, and—even more importantly—I can be in-
terrupted easily by the person with whom I'm conferencing. When I
write, though, I feel more constrained. I tend to overthink what I'm
saying, even when I'm just chatting online or composing an email. My
conversational pace slows; I become less certain about what I should
say and how to say it. I feel somewhat like my non-Native English-
speaking students: vaguely uncomfortable, slightly embarrassed, and
often uncertain how to proceed.

These feelings, I think, point to the heart of my fear. I've been
afraid of online conferencing because I don't think I know how to do it
particularly well. Oh, I've done my homework. I've read a host of articles and manuscripts, from Hobson's *Wiring the Writing Center* to Inman
and Sewell's *Taking Flight with OWLs*. I've read descriptions of virtual
tutoring at numerous institutions using a diverse assortment of software tools, and I've read transcripts of synchronous and asynchronous
tutoring conversations that illustrate typical conference interactions.
But even so, these articles have raised far more questions for me than
they've ever answered. How do I get started with a student? How do I
establish rapport and a personal connection? How do we negotiate our
different platforms, resources, and tools? What's the best way to share
a text online? Given what many scholars have written about directive-
ness and the potential for plagiarism (by cutting and pasting a tutor's
words), how should I shape my remarks and advice? What problems
can I expect? What strategies should I rely on? How should I structure
the session? Help!

That said (complete with my barbaric yawp at the end), you can
probably understand why I regard the book you now hold in your
hands so highly. Beth Hewett manages in this brief volume to answer

a carload of my questions and alleviate an equal number of my fears. From the opening chapter in which she tackles the big question "Why do this at all?" to later chapters addressing matters of context, trust building, online discourse, tutor response, and assessment, Hewett stays focused on the practical matters of online conferencing. She does so impressively, incorporating not only her expansive knowledge of writing center theory (particularly in Chapter 4) but also a variety of assignments, specific examples, and tutorial transcripts. She provides strategies for interaction and response that are useful to online tutors and writing center directors but—equally important from my perspective—just as useful to teachers who wish to incorporate strong online components into their pedagogies.

It would be a mistake, though, to think of this book strictly as a training guide. Hewett's attention to the diverse and deeply embedded contexts of teaching—not just as points along a writing center/classroom continuum but as complex spaces at the nexus of intersecting discourses—is particularly striking. Rather than offer a series of tips and directives for teachers or a collection of "scripts" for tutors, Hewett challenges us to analyze the instructional environments in which virtual conferencing takes place and to interpret the sometimes subtle dynamics of our online conversations. She asks probing questions that often defy straightforward answers, but she never hesitates to explore the details, to tease out implications and possible consequences that might impact our decisions as teachers.

Many aspects of this book appeal to me, but one, perhaps, stands above the rest: Hewett's insistence that online conferences work best when teachers or tutors and students connect on a personal level. It is vital, she says, that we express our need to *care for them* while simultaneously ensuring that they can *care for us* as well. Some might be content to leave these as rather abstract goals, but Hewett does not. She explains in concrete, practical terms how we can accomplish them, even in a mediated virtual environment that writing center (and other) scholars have sometimes characterized as "isolating" and "impersonal." This deft refutation of a commonly held belief about computer mediated discourse will force many of us—myself included—to rethink our conventional, and possibly unfounded, understandings of online conferencing.

So on the one hand, *The Online Writing Conference: A Guide for Teachers and Tutors* is exactly the book that I—and others—have been waiting for. It's smartly constructed and deeply grounded in current theory. It answers nearly all of my questions about online tutoring and walks me carefully and thoughtfully through the process of teaching or tutoring effectively in a virtual environment. For that, I am profoundly grateful.

On the other hand, I no longer have any excuse not to begin on-line tutoring in my own writing center and online teaching in my own writing classes. For that, too, I'm grateful, if still a bit anxious as I begin to wade even more deeply into virtual waters.

Michael A. Pemberton
Georgia Southern University

Works Cited

Carino, Peter. 1998. "Computers in the Writing Center: A Cautionary History." Ed. Eric H. Hobson. *Wiring the Writing Center*. Logan, UT: Utah State UP. 171–93.

Lerner, Neal. 1998. "Drill Pads, Teaching Machines, and Programmed Texts: Origins of Instructional Technology in Writing Centers." Ed. Eric H. Hobson. *Wiring the Writing Center*. Logan, UT: Utah State UP. 119–36.

Acknowledgments

I truly appreciate Charles Schuster, my editor, who kindly and straight-forwardly helped me to reconceive this book, leading to its present state; I hope that my efforts have earned the trust he so cheerfully offered. I also appreciate Robert Brooks, who provided an editor's indispensible advice for—ironically, given the book's primary argument—owning and using my authentic voice. Over the years that this book has been in development, various colleagues have assisted by reading different portions and offering feedback: Cheryl Ball, Melissa Ianetta, Christa Ehmann Powers, Judy Lawton, Charlotte Robidoux, and Christina Lengyel. I appreciate their time and energies in helping me to articulate my thinking. I also thank Michael Pemberton, Rosemary Winslow, Bob Lynn, Gail Summerskill, Judy Davis, and Beverly Peterson -among other educators—who have all provided excellent advice for understanding various language, theoretical, and pedagogical concerns in the context of online teaching and tutoring. Burck Smith, Laurie Johnson, and Daniel Elkinson each were essential to my research processes, and I thank them deeply. My husband, Paul, and son, Russ, supported me in all ways throughout an invigorating, yet challenging, research and writing process. I could not conduct this work without them. The Pennsylvania State University provided funding to assist in some of the research in this book; I am grateful for this generosity. Finally, to all the students, teachers, and tutors who shared their work and consented for me to use it in this book, I thank you from the bottom of my heart.

Introduction

The Challenges of One-to-One Online Writing Instruction

Although many articles and books have helped me become a better writing teacher and tutor in online settings, I have read a few again and again—highlighting passages, marking them up, writing in them, and dog-earing them. Indeed, these few have articulated a coherent pedagogy of online writing instruction (OWI), but most articulations are rare nuggets in journal articles or edited book chapters. In particular, the text-based nature of most OWI interactions often is ignored in favor of less readily accessible audio-visual approaches that attempt to approximate traditional oral face-to-face, one-to-one interactions. Further, the dialogic nature of most interactions is addressed in terms of online peer groups and class discussions. In these peer activities, students teach each other and practice their writing through textual interactions. The one-to-one conference between instructor and student tends to be ignored or taken for granted. I have written this book to fill this gap.

Professional development opportunities for OWI are irregular; currently, there is no set of standards or best practices upon which to call. For example, some online writing programs offer extensive training, much of which addresses how to use the technology in pedagogically useful but not in disciplinarily specific ways; other programs offer no support at all. While many educators have gained some experience with OWI, when compared with our experiences teaching and tutoring writing in more traditional settings, we are still very new in our practices. Often, we can interact successfully with students, but we cannot say why what we did worked—or did not work. We can re-imagine our pedagogical strategies for online settings, but aside from the lack of face-to-face orality and body language, we cannot always say what is different.

In a course setting, OWI requires us to rethink both the instructor-to-class and the instructor-to-student interactions. However, our research, classroom strategies, and professional texts tend to address only the instructor-to-class relationship essential to networked and distance-based writing classes. The benefits of online discussions and the values of online peer response groups rightfully receive attention: these two peer-based strategies make strong use of the online setting for both classroom and distance-based students. And they can assist with developing critical thinking, reading, and writing skills. But the one-to-one nature of most instructor-based writing pedagogy is not often discussed, and the silence suggests that one-to-one teaching does not occur online, that one-to-one online pedagogy is transparent, or that one-to-one interactions are not considered teaching at all.

In the writing center setting, educators recognize that the ultimate pedagogy is one-to-one so that students can receive both reader response and time with more expert writers. Nonetheless, online tutoring often is likened to an occasionally necessary but substandard method for reaching students who cannot get to the brick-and-mortar writing center. Much of the literature and professional discussion privileges orality and focuses on making the tutoring experience as close to the oral face-to-face experience as possible, to include using the telephone and digital voice files instead of written feedback. Precious development dollars are committed to web cameras and audio equipment to avoid supposedly less "desirable" text-based interactions.

Online teaching and tutoring requires conscious and eclectic instructional approaches beyond peer-to-peer and oral interactions. And such instruction has both life and benefits of its own. OWI necessarily requires the teacher/tutor to use one-to-one computer-based teaching strategies: to teach deliberately and to intervene through online conferences using the student's text, instructional commentary, and other sources. Online conferencing is increasingly common, occurring during one-to-one virtual office hours, spontaneous virtual chats and journal interactions, online tutorials, and in the context of formative, or draft-based, comments written in response to students' developing work. Although of pedagogical value, I do not consider summative, or final, comments and grading to be conferencing unless teachers/tutors and students are interacting *about* them.

This book is my articulation of how to be successful when using one-to-one conference-based online pedagogy. It is written both for novice teachers/tutors and for experienced teachers/tutors new to online settings. Collectively, I call teachers/tutors "instructors" except when the instructional context specifically addresses either classroom or tutorial strategies. Even traditionally oriented educators are included in this audience as more often they are finding themselves communicating with students through email, trying to resolve an immediate problem that cannot wait until class time, or addressing a draft on the fly hoping that students can interpret their comments as intended.

These communications may not always be recognized as the online conferences that they are.

Ever since my first experience with online courses in a networked writing class in 1994, I have been passionately curious about how technology-based writing instruction works at the nuts-and-bolts level. So I have empirically studied and experientially enacted OWI in a variety of settings: in networked classes, tutorials, and professional contexts from the perspectives of teachers, peer response groups, administrators, trainers, coaches, and managers. I have learned that educators are excited to talk about their peer-based, social strategies for teaching online but are less forthcoming about their one-to-one textual teaching interactions, possibly because they do not view online conferences as teaching or tutoring of a special nature. Because most interactions occur textually—a major consideration in this book—educators often express a longing to conduct online teaching and tutoring through audio-visual methods like web cameras and voice recorders to simulate the supposedly superior face-to-face interaction.

This book guides instructors in reconsidering OWI as text-based instructional commentary and looks to student feedback and revision for proof of learning. OWI provides us the opportunity to reconceive response and commentary, to relearn our skills, or even to learn them consciously for the first time. These skills are applicable to both traditional and online commentary and instructional feedback but are especially critical to OWI. In traditional settings, for example, written feedback is provided in the context of previous or future face-to-face instruction. In online settings, however, such feedback often occurs outside any face-to-face opportunities for clarification or further instruction. Indeed, it is the *textual nature* of OWI that provides teachers/tutors both impetus and opportunity to hone and reflect on these skills.

Teaching with Semantic Integrity

Many of the theories we call upon to guide online instruction are based on traditional experiences of writing development, and our practices tend to be culled from traditional classroom strategies—both of which imply a straightforward application of traditional instructional theory and practice to online settings. Yet, the fundamentally textual nature of teaching and learning in the virtual environment is at odds with such a one-to-one transference. For example, Gail Hawisher and Charles Moran argue that "as a medium email is so different from handwritten comments-in-the-margins that as we begin to respond online, we may be forced to rethink our assumptions about responding to student writing" (cited in Moran 2001, 211; see also Hewett and Ehmann 2004, xiii, 46;

Cooper, Bui, and Riker 2000, 92). Christa Ehmann Powers reports that online instructors indicate frustration when they know how to address a problem in face-to-face settings, yet they struggle with transferring that ability to a completely textual setting: "Individuals noted in great detail the difficulty experienced in moving from the identification of particular student weakness to the *written instructional expression* of how to address said weaknesses" (Appendix 1). It seems, then, that the convergence of traditional instructional theory and related pedagogical practice in online settings brings to specific relief some disconnects between contemporary composing theory and practice, and they can be found in a lack of what I call "semantic integrity" in online written commentary. As such, this convergence actually can be helpful, forcing us to realize and address these disconnects by developing composition instructional theory specific to online settings and by adapting practices to this theory.

By semantic integrity, I mean creating writing commentary that accurately addresses what students need to know in order to develop and improve their writing—on a case-by-case, problem-centered basis. Thoughtfully written interactions can convey instructional intention and students can interpret it with accuracy. It requires instructors to own their expertise and authority as educators—not to abuse it but to use it freely in support of student learning. Ideally, online commentary that has semantic integrity does not hint or ask students to guess at what they are supposed to be learning; it is not evasive nor does it poorly address the subject matter. Rather, it demonstrates respect for students' intellectual capabilities by explicitly addressing a session's expectations and goals. The result of semantic integrity is instructional language that provides sufficient information to students, offers clear guidance about potential next steps (which includes teaching students how to make choices and encouraging them to do so), and works to prompt new or different thinking—all through textual commentary. To teach through text—which includes but goes beyond holding online discussions, lecturing by means of digital handouts, or providing summative evaluation of writing—is a challenging task. *The text becomes the instructional voice.* Thus we need to express instructional intentions as transparently as possible.

Intervention into the Writing

Contemporary composing theories typically were developed in traditional instructional settings. When applied inappropriately to online settings, certain beliefs connected to these theories can choke the instructor's voice, while a consciously held eclectic theoretical approach can liberate the instructional voice and empower it to do the work that will most help students—to *intervene* in their writing at the point of need.

In particular, OWI difficulties emerge from privileging three pedagogical interpretations of contemporary theories. The first derives from expressivist theory and suggests that students must retain authorial ownership of their writing at all costs, which calls into question the instructor's ability to teach overtly since the very act of instruction might be interpreted as co-opting student writing. The resulting pedagogy becomes blatantly noninterventionist. From social constructionist theory, the second interpretation is that although students need opportunities to collaborate with experienced writers like teachers/tutors as well as peers, students may not use or "appropriate" the product of collaboration at the risk of "plagiarism." Pedagogically, this line of thinking suggests that to prevent such appropriation, instructors should avoid "giving the answer" or "doing the student's work," and this thinking limits the range of instructional response. From postprocess theory, the third interpretation is that writing processes or activities cannot be taught because there is no such thing as a codifiable writing process. Pedagogically, this belief leads to teaching and responding to idea-based content—critical, political, cultural, ideological—over writing processes. Hence, in classroom settings, peer-to-peer discussion is privileged over teacher-to-student instruction. The pedagogies that stem from these theoretical orientations are especially significant in online settings because what is digitally recorded is the sum total of the interaction. Without the sounds of phatic language and the unspoken messages of body and facial language, digital intervention is the only way to teach writing and revising.

Using illustrations from research, practice, and literature relevant to instructional commentary and student revision, this book urges readers to re-examine their theoretical preferences when applied to online settings. Indeed, it argues for the "liberating potential" of a consciously held eclectic theoretical grounding that can free online educators to teach students without unnecessary hindrance (Hewett and Ehmann 2004, 54). It argues in favor of intervening into the student's writing—content, process, or product—as well as for providing explicit instructional response language that uses direct rather than indirect syntax. It does so because we need to select the most helpful practices from various instructional theories in order to address student writing in a problem-centered context, a context that challenges students to work in collaboration with teachers/tutors to improve their writing. We can honor a student's individual voice and prize the collaborative process in idea development while acknowledging when students need more directive instruction, taking advantage of specific teaching moments to address the student's writing with language intended to guide future writing. In doing so, the instructional voice will remain intact, potentially improving semantic integrity.

Many instructors already call on a variety of strategies to work with a student's writing (see, for example, Welch 1997, 163–64). Indeed, even those online writing programs and writing centers guided explicitly by expressivist, social constructionist, or postprocess theories often practice a more *implicitly* eclectic approach to teaching writing. Yet, this book proposes that implicit practice is insufficient in OWI because unconscious applications of traditional instructional theory to online settings can lead to tension between what one thinks ought to occur online and what likely does occur. In such cases, the semantic results of that tension may negatively affect student learning. Consciously held, explicitly eclectic practice *overtly* addresses the common concerns of writing instruction like authority, collaboration, process, audience, purpose, and correctness. Among others, this book will emphasize three such eclectic practices: modeling writing and revision, consistently using targeted mini-lessons that require student action, and listing next steps that explicitly guide students toward future drafts.

How This Book Is Organized

The Online Writing Conference consists of eight chapters with figures and examples that illustrate concepts and potentially strong or weak online instruction.

Chapter 1: Benefits of Online Teacher/Tutor Conferencing addresses why online conferencing can work well, such as by forming connections among instructors and students, and how conferencing can provide a necessary sense of immediacy in online settings. It also discusses what teachers worry about and the challenges of conferencing well. Finally, the chapter outlines the key concept of problem-based teaching, which involves doing *with*, but not *for*, the student.

Chapter 2: Practical Matters illustrates what online conferencing looks like in both "non-real" time (asynchronous) and "real" time (synchronous) environments, with a focus on how to use the two environments as different tools for teaching and learning. Because digital text can seem flat when compared to spoken language, it considers how instructors can provide dimension to textual interactions. It also discusses how to balance time spent with students online in order to meet both institutional and individual needs, as well how to make pedagogically-sound use of online media.

Chapter 3: Establishing Trust focuses on how creating a learning environment and laying the groundwork for trust can establish a productive relationship among instructors and students. The chapter addresses preparing and orienting students to online conferences, setting realistic teaching and learning expectations, and helping students to become independent online learners. By addressing affect in terms of trust, it provides specific ways that instructors can show caring for students and—vice versa—how students can be encouraged to recognize instructors as teachers, professional colleagues, and fellow writers.

Chapter 4: Theories for Writing Response in Online Settings uses current research and theory to help instructors with understanding their online communications as one-to-one conferences. It outlines what students can learn in a conference that they might not otherwise learn in an online setting and discusses the vital importance of clear communication.

Chapter 5: First Steps for Writing Response in Online Settings provides practical, hands-on support for online writing instructors including vocabulary usage, issues of tone and register, learning outcomes, and creating mini-lessons within problem-centered instruction.

Chapter 6: The Orneriness of Language considers what students say they need and what they say is and is not helpful in a conference. It addresses why instructors send mixed messages, how such messages block learning, and how to avoid them, with an emphasis on how to write messages that convey instructional intention straightforwardly.

Chapter 7: Using What Works discusses where to comment, how to format comments, and how these decisions may affect students with certain kinds of cognitive challenges. It illustrates what too much and too little commenting look like in terms of time spent and length of the conference. This chapter demonstrates the importance of modeling the key writing strategies of proofing and editing and illustrates the need for straightforwardly addressing sensitive issues.

Chapter 8: Having Effective Conferences discusses the need for online audits of student learning—whether daily or weekly, mid-term or end-of-term. It also addresses how to get students to self-audit and help themselves to improve their own learning. Finally, this chapter urges instructors to conduct self- and other audits to help improve teaching skills in one-to-one settings and shows how instructors can assess their conferences' effectiveness.

Postscript: Toward a Theory of Conference-Based Instruction stresses what research has yet to address regarding instructional language and revision, which are the primary concerns of this book's advice for conferencing one-to-one. It suggests how instructors can use their knowledge and understanding of online conferences to develop a working theory of text-based teaching as it emerges in online conferences.

This book does not attempt to cover even minimally the basics of writing instruction, especially basics typically found in the traditional classroom or writing center environments. For timeless teachers' rhetorics that address such issues, see, for example, Barbara Walvoord's *Helping Students Write Well*, James D. Williams' *Preparing to Teach Writing: Research, Theory, and Practice*, or Erika Lindemann's *A Rhetoric for Writing Teachers*. For a useful compendium, see such works as Robert Tremmel and William Broz's *Teaching Writing Teachers of High School English and First-Year Composition*.

Summary

The one-to-one online conference is an increasingly popular, vital, and viable way to teach writing. In addition to composition teachers/tutors, I hope that both English studies and writing across the curriculum-based (WAC) educators will see themselves as potential online instructors who can apply this book to their online instruction. Because of both varied roles and settings, I do not see or promote one single "right" way of conferencing with students about their writing in online settings. I also do not promote one composing theory over another, preferring instead an eclectic approach. Although my research and experiences point to some trends that seem generally applicable, each instructor must find his or her own effective voice and approach. In fact, a genuine instructional voice increases the likelihood that the communications will positively intervene with students and their writing where needed.

Chapter One

Benefits of Online Teacher/ Tutor Conferencing

What an Online Conference Is

An online conference, as discussed in the Introduction, occurs as a one-to-one interaction between a course teacher and student or a tutor and student.

Between course teacher and student, the conference may occur during or outside the class session. Online writing courses typically are either:

- Distance-based, where participants communicate from separate locations and are connected only through Internet technology;
- Hybrid, where participants may meet one day in the traditional classroom and another day may be co-located in a networked classroom or separated by distance; or
- Blended, where participants meet both face-to-face and via networked computer for each class.

Any traditional or hybrid/blended course setting can become distance-based when a teacher-to-student conference occurs online outside of class hours. It is less likely, though not impossible, that distance-based courses will lend themselves to co-located or face-to-face conferences. The primary difference may be in where and how the initial teacher-to-student relationship is developed and then maintained: face-to-face or online. Thus, course teachers who read this book should consider how its advice can be used in their particular institutional and classroom settings. For example, a conference with a student whom one has met only through an online biography and photograph may require different greeting strategies than one where the teacher and student have begun to develop a face-to-face relationship.

Between tutor and student, a conference usually is not course-based—but it can be as with writing fellows—and it similarly is affected by location, as well as by whether the tutorial relationship will be a one-time event or ongoing. When a tutor and student meet completely online, the greeting again may differ from a traditional face-to-face relationship. Additionally, if the online technology does not enable the same tutor and student to meet again except by chance, the singular nature of the encounter may guide some of the tutor's goals and responses as well as the student's.

Who Conferences Online and Why

More instructors conference online than we might guess. For example, we may respond to questions via email; we may type and asynchronously return feedback to students through their documents; we may contact students through instant messaging (IM), whiteboards, and discussion forums. Because teaching and tutoring students are our primary jobs, I first want to examine some student scenarios for engaging in online conferences. Then, I will switch focus to instructors.

Students

The following vignettes suggest that some students are more technologically savvy than their instructors, but that using computers for educational conferencing is still foreign to others.

HYBRID COURSES

Stan's writing course is taught in a blended classroom at his small liberal arts college. Sometimes the class has a fairly traditional oral discussion where they sit together at a conference table, but often he and his classmates use computers at separate workstations for the entire day's session. They draft, read each other's writing, and comment on discussion topics. Although a printer is available, Stan's writing is always turned in as a digital file. His instructor's response is always provided digitally as comments within and appended to his document. When he has a question in class, he signals his instructor and she meets him at his workstation. But when he has a question outside of class, Stan writes an email or looks for her on IM. One of Stan's friends introduced the instructor to IM since she'd never used it before.

DISTANCE LEARNING

Amalie is a working mother of two toddlers. Although she has a decent job, she realizes that she needs a college degree to get promoted. So, after the babies are asleep (and sometimes before), Amalie takes her distance-based writing course from a well-known university. All her interactions among classmates and with the instructor occur online although her instructor has indicated he'll phone students if needed. Amalie knows her classmates and instructor from their posted biographies and photographs. So far, all of Amalie's communications with the instructor have been conducted through email, the course discussion board, IM, and—of course—through her written assignments.

ONLINE TUTORING

Janine and Fritz are community college students who like to hang out and study together. Janine is taking a writing course that Fritz has already passed, and he is in a business writing course this semester. Both courses take place in traditional brick-and-mortar classrooms. Sometimes Fritz reads Janine's essays, but he also guides her to the school's online writing center, which is a partnership enterprise between his school and another institution. He also sends his writing there for feedback. Usually, they send their papers asynchronously; in about twelve to thirty-six hours, they receive responses—often from different online tutors. If they don't understand the responses, they can sign up for a synchronous whiteboard-based conference with an available tutor. They like getting the online help because it suits their work schedules and everything is written down for them to think about later.

ONLINE FEEDBACK AND GRADING

Although Shakira takes her writing class in a traditional classroom setting, her instructor asks everyone to post assignments through email. Shakira isn't very comfortable with email attachments because she fears they won't work. Although the instructor started the class by providing handwritten comments on a hard copy of students' papers, now she's typing the comments in an email. Shakira doesn't like this change. She feels confused and sometimes the comments don't make sense to her. Shakira wonders whether she has to make the changes the instructor notes. And when she makes those changes, why doesn't she get an "A"? She talks on Facebook and IM all the time, but Shakira's not used to interacting with instructors this way.

What these scenarios illustrate is that it is becoming increasingly common for traditional-age college students to have used some form of computer technology for social interactions. Even when they must visit friends' homes or use a public library's computers to do so, many adolescents and younger adults use email, IM, and the Internet. This group tends to be avid web-surfers who publicly journal using weblogs (blogs) and venues like Facebook, and they talk with others in chat rooms and on discussion boards. They know what a wiki is and use the latest web browsers. Some accomplish these communications through the convenience of their cell phones and personal digital assistants (PDA). They are what Marc Prensky calls "digital natives"—members of the first generation to "have spent their entire lives surrounded by and using computers, videogames, digital music players, video cams, cell phones, and all the other toys and tools of the digital age" (2001, 1). Although I am not convinced that such "students *think and process information fundamentally differently* from their predecessors" (2001, 1), characteristics like a preference to parallel-process information, a developed ability to multitask, an appreciation for graphics over text, and a desire for instant gratification and frequent rewards easily could describe many postsecondary students (2001, 2). These students are open to conferencing with their instructors online, yet they need text-based response that addresses them at a linguistically appropriate level. For example, given the short, chunk-like paragraphing common to web texts, students may not be strong readers of longer text, suggesting a need for shorter, chunked conference text since the goal is to communicate clearly rather than to stretch students' reading skills.

Like Mary's little lamb of nursery rhyme fame, technology has followed its users into school. Even in less-affluent colleges, it would be unusual to find students who have not experienced some form of computer-based educational technology: computer-accessible grades, course-based web pages, online library and other Internet-based research, online peer discussions, or instructor-to-student online conferences. Technology has changed education by varying instructional interactions from the traditional fifty- or seventy-five-minute class or tutorial to a few minutes or more nearly any time of day or night —a potential 24/7 educational opportunity. Technology also has affected the notion of educational place, moving it from the traditional brick-and-mortar environment to any intranet- or Internet-accessible computer. Thus unbounded by traditional notions of time and space, many students interact flexibly with digital material, each other, and instructors. Similarly, while universal access certainly has not been achieved, an increasing number of students have experienced school-based writing instruction using some form of educational technology.

Nonetheless, students who participate in OWI conferences have not necessarily had equal access to technology in their social and school lives. Going to the public library to surf the Web is not remotely the same as doing it from one's own home. Indeed, some students will not even have used computers socially when they reach college. Others own slower computers or use older technologies like dial-up access to the Internet, or have no Internet access at all. And although some institutions are eliminating their computer labs, many students still need them. Unfortunately, even when it is available, institutional lab space is often inadequate, overcrowded, and frustratingly slow. Usage rules may impose time and other limits (for example, no food, drink, or music; restricted printer access and lab hours) that are not friendly to students' writing needs. Moreover, there is often a marked difference between the kinds of institutional access that, for example, a community college and a better funded small private college might have (Moran 2001, 217–18).

Understandably, students quickly lose ground if they "don't know how to use computers: students who come to college with little training in technology struggle to keep up with peers who have been raised with it. If you have neither digital access nor literacy, you risk being marginalized even further in this increasingly digitized society" (Sidler, Morris, and Smith 2008, 89). Thus, it is important to assess students' technological skills when conferencing. Students can have varied comfort levels with:

- Hardware, especially when using institutional computers;
- Software, particularly during the first weeks of school; and
- Learning curves like talking online with instructors and using the appropriate register (formal versus informal) and dialect (standard written English versus IM-ular or slang writing), as well as understanding text-based instruction.

The last set of issues is particularly challenging for students who meet an instructor in completely online settings. Even students who are digitally fluent may find themselves unfamiliar with educational text-based talk and may need considerable support from observant instructors. Sometimes, only a voice interaction in person or by phone can help a student to address such problems. However, clues to these problems often can be found in the student's textual response to the conference, as later chapters discuss.

Instructors

While students come to the interactions with differing skill and experience levels, educators have their own contexts and struggles with the technology, as well as the pedagogy.

HYBRID COURSES

Andy, a twenty-year veteran of English studies in higher education, teaches his first-year composition course in a hybrid classroom. He talks with students both digitally and orally, but the class conducts most of the writing instruction and practice online. Andy responds to drafts and grades his students' writing digitally. He has attended online instructional training offered by a nationally known scholar, and in turn he has provided similar training to his colleagues at his home college.

DISTANCE LEARNING

Juanita teaches three writing-intensive classes for her institution's distance-learning program, but she originally worked as a history professor in WAC courses. Beyond online group activities, she conferences with her students digitally, using text both to discuss the course content and to review and respond to their writing. Having learned to use IM with her own teenage children, sometimes she uses it with students to check in or discuss their writing in "real time" during online office hours. Otherwise, aside from rare phone calls, they communicate by email and through the course management system (CMS).

ONLINE TUTORING

Reese supplements his adjunct income by tutoring part-time for a commercial online writing and learning center. He reads and responds to students' asynchronously submitted essays in a non-real time, web-based setting. He contextualizes his instruction to their drafts, to what they write about their assignments, and to what he knows about effective writing instruction. Occasionally, he also works with individual students in a synchronous whiteboard setting. As an adjunct at a small comprehensive university, he teaches in traditional settings, but sometimes he thinks about how to make his responses to traditional students' writing more like the conferences he has with the online students.

ONLINE FEEDBACK AND GRADING

Virginia is a graduate assistant at a land-grant research university where new teachers learn to teach writing through various methods, one of which is to provide asynchronous online response to student writers in a variety of writing classes. She grew up with computer technology and is eager to put it to work educationally. Because she's not the instructor for the students to whom she responds, her responses occur outside the classroom context; but because all teachers work from a common syllabus, her commentary might be considered highly contextualized. Her responses sometimes receive critical feedback from her own mentor because the program gives serious attention to professional development.

Except for Virginia, these vignettes reveal educators who might be called "digital immigrants," those for whom digital interaction is more a second than a first language, complete with an "accent" of the analog world (Prensky 2001). But most online writing instructors began teaching with the expectation that they would meet with their students face-to-face, and they composed their responses to student writing with that meeting in mind. Now, however, they instruct partially or wholly by conferencing digitally. Whether their primary pedagogy involves critical (idea-based) feedback, reader response, peer discussions, modeling, or correction—or all of these strategies—they all ask one question: *Does what I do help students?*

Like the educators in these vignettes, online writing instructors hail from a variety of backgrounds and teach in various settings. Only a few would consider themselves to have strong backgrounds in writing instruction. Often they are English literature teachers and scholars, some with master's and others with doctoral degrees, whose duties include writing instruction. Increasingly, more online instructors are rhetoric/composition scholars who specialize in teaching and researching writing or specialize in teaching with technology. Some are WAC-based educators who value writing about their subject matter as a way to induce comprehension and retention. Some have had specific training or professional development in online work, while others have been left to learn on their own. Finally, in addition to classroom teachers, some are tutors who work online.

The idea of the tutor as online instructor may cause some readers to hesitate. Aren't there differences between the roles of teacher and tutor? Certainly. A course teacher has the authoritative responsibility to structure a course, develop assignments, and assess student writing for grades, while a tutor's job is to listen, read, and provide formative feedback uninvolved with grading. Writing center tutors often separate themselves from writing teachers as having different, somewhat higher, purposes of "produc[ing] better writers, not better writing" (North 1984, 438). Eric Hobson explains: "Without the onus of having to grade writers' efforts in specific texts, writing center practitioners have long argued that the writing center tutorial is a unique pedagogical space" (2001, 166). While their primary roles differ, their tasks frequently do not. Given the popular pedagogies of conferencing and portfolio writing, both course teachers and tutors provide formative feedback, although tutoring practices especially resist direct intervention into the writing. It is likewise true that writing center staff contribute to the work of online course teachers. Writing centers often are staging areas for technology in the course-based setting: "Writing center staffs have traditionally been in the vanguard of writing teachers exploring, implementing, and adapting technology for sound pedagogical use" (Hobson 2001, 172).

Yet the roles of teacher and tutor naturally intersect. Among scholars who identify themselves as writing center educators, Therese Thonus suggests that the notion of "tutor as peer" is somewhat mythological since tutors often enact the role of teacher. She suggests "a continuum of roles stretching from teacher to peer, negotiated anew in each tutorial" (2001, 61, 77), and believes one goal of tutor training is to prepare "writing instructors of a different sort, supportive yet independent of the classroom" (2001, 77). George Cooper, Kara Bui, and Linda Riker allow that some "teaching" by a tutor can be effective if "the tutor is striking a balance by holding corrections to a minimum . . . and supplying them with explanation" (2000, 96). They suggest teaching a few sentence-based issues to allow more time to "address more global issues" (97). Among scholars who identify themselves as teachers, Thomas Batt believes that a teacher plays the roles of mentor, "fellow writer, evaluator, editor, coach, and responsive reader" (2005, 211); tutoring seems implicit in the coaching role. Webster Newbold (1993) explains that one of the key skills an instructor needs in an OWI-based course, where a great deal of online conferencing occurs, is the ability to tutor one's students effectively in the computer environment. Clearly, the role of an online teacher/tutor involves *both* critical feedback *and* interventional teaching—*both* supportive *and* critical instructional commentary—as explicit tasks.

Indeed, where one-to-one OWI is concerned, there is good reason to blend the roles of tutor and teacher. In arguing for mainstream scholarship that acknowledges the shared ideals of writing centers and composition programs, writing center professionals Elizabeth Boquet and Neal Lerner stress: "Our field can no longer afford, if it ever could, to have forged a separate peace between classroom and nonclassroom teaching. There is no separate but equal" (2008, 186). It is important, they suggest, to "find an emic theory or model, one developed by research that is conducted in writing center settings that could act as a lens to examine other teaching-learning contexts" (182). Their call for an emic model is partially fulfilled in the research grounding this book, where the online writing lab (OWL) intersects with classroom-based OWI. Classroom-based OWI involves both assessing student writing and strategies that engage peer group work and discussion, which are not common to the OWL or traditional writing center, although group work certainly is possible. The OWL's specialty is a dialogically focused one-to-one conference with writers, but, grading aside, classroom-based online teaching also shares this strategy—or, it should. In fact, while they are not the subject of this book, both venues also share the use of group-focused static materials and/or lectures, which are made available for students to use in self-teaching and writing development. Figure 1.1 illustrates the vital intersection of one-to-one conferencing in online teaching and tutoring.

Figure 1.1
The Intersection of Conferences in OWI

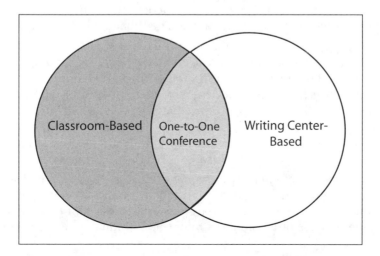

Classroom-Based   One-to-One   Writing Center-
                         Conference   Based

Nonetheless, undergraduate/graduate peer tutors in particular may not yet have the knowledge base needed to teach online with semantic integrity or to engage in genuinely eclectic pedagogy. Further, they often are encouraged to own their peer status as one that is incompatible with teaching fellow student writers (Ascuena and Kiernan 2008). Their currently understood position in the academy suggests that, should their administrators adopt a more theoretically eclectic practice as this book suggests, these tutors will need additional training and support to help them develop more diverse instructional strategies and to successfully teach student writers. This book provides a starting point for peer tutors, as well as novice teachers/tutors.

When and Why Conferencing Online Helps

Instructors can conference with students at almost any time. Although facial expressions, body language, and vocal tone are lost in most online settings, a conference can be initiated whenever a need arises using tools like email, virtual classrooms, and IM chat. Conferences occur for various reasons, among them relationship building, problem solving, and writing formation. Let's take them in order.

Relationship building is an important first step. Often, a greeting and initial informal chat establish one's interest in the student and vice versa. Ways that instructors can build relationships include:

- *Influencing affect by offering reassurance that the student is a valuable individual.* For example, recently I noticed a student was online in my distance-based classroom. Not having "met" her, I "pinged" her on IM to say hello. Her response was warm and excited: "How are you, Dr. H.? I've never had a teacher talk to me on IM before!" My simple act of checking in conveyed that I saw *her* and not just a *class*.

- *Creating immediacy and a sense of presence by speaking in the first person about an issue or writing.* In a tutorial setting, for example, tutors can signal or create immediacy by responding to a draft with positive language that conveys the instructor's presence: "I just finished reading your draft, and I can see how hard you're working to clarify a complex point. I think your next draft will be even stronger as you work out your thoughts."

- *Clarifying by softening or hardening a message.* In a recent distance course, one student harshly critiqued another's draft. I emailed him to praise his critical awareness and to ask him to change his tone because other students might be intimidated or offended. In the next critique, he was similarly sharp, so I pinged him to chat the next time I saw him online. Expecting a possible confrontation, he surprised me by greeting me warmly and raising the issue himself: "I think I did it again, Dr. H. I'm even harder on myself though. How do I change my tone?"

Other relationship-building opportunities include using conferences to address apparent misunderstandings and to model register, tact, tone, interest, and other communication strategies.

Problem solving is another reason for engaging in online conferences. Often students initiate these interactions when they want answers to questions about grades or assignments. Such conferences can occur via email, through the CMS, or using chat. Problems that may be addressed include:

- *Technology malfunctions or misunderstandings such as how to post a draft for review.* For example, in a recent distance class, a student wrote in her journal (private to student and instructor) that she had sent her draft to the online writing center three times with no response. I responded both in her journal and in an email message that connected the student to the writing center director so they could address the problem together.

- *Peer interaction guidance.* For example, a student emailed me to say that he had not received peer response from his online study group and that none of his peers had posted drafts for his review. We determined that he felt comfortable directly emailing his peers to see whether and when they would be posting an essay.

- *Clarifying instructions.* Once in a tutorial setting, a student began a brief synchronous chat with me to learn whether it was acceptable to post both an earlier draft of an essay and its final form for comparative review.

Chapter 3 further considers relationship building and problem solving in terms of preparing the learning environment and direct interactions among participants. Chapters 4, 5, and 6 particularly address how conferences can help students with such writing challenges as idea and content development, essay and genre instruction, organization, audience and purpose, revision, and editing.

Why Conferencing Online Is Hard to Do Well

Conferencing can solve a number of problems, but it is not always easy to do well given that participants may have competing interests. In online course settings, for example, teachers worry about how much time and effort their online interactions will take, how to communicate clearly, how to handle individual conferences in often-large classes, student (and their own) preparedness for online education, and changes in everyone's notions of time and virtual time, such as the idea that teachers might be available 24/7 or that students might be writing and interacting daily instead of only on the due date. In tutoring settings, tutors worry about similar issues of time and effort relative to their workload, communicating well, what to say, and how to apply their traditional tutoring beliefs online. Similarly, students worry about time constraints, overscheduled lives, and course requirements—as well as inconsistent or nonexistent communication with teachers/tutors and what to call them online ("hey, professor"?). Student expectations may vary: Some may view asynchronous conferences about writing formation as time off and away from the project (analogous to hiring someone to clean the house), while others may expect to be in constant email, phone, or IM contact. Students may believe that online courses equal "easy credit"; instructors, too, may fall into that myth by worrying that they are doing *for* students rather than *with* them.

As this chapter's earlier vignettes show, quite often online conferences are asynchronous, which can give the appearance of being somewhat one-sided, hardly a conference at all. Yet whether asynchronous or synchronous, there are always at least *two* participants struggling to communicate about an activity that feels of great consequence to each. Students want feedback on their writing—certainly because grades ultimately are in play—but also because they want to know, to learn, to be better writers, and especially to be understood. Instructors—even when tired, frustrated, or uncertain about how to proceed—also care about the interaction. They want to help, to support and guide, to teach writing, and especially to be understood.

Nonetheless, with the relative newness of OWI, it is not unusual to hear teachers/tutors contrast traditional and online settings by saying: "At least in my face-to-face class, I can sit with my students, explain my comments, and make sure they understand me" or "In the face-to-face writing center, I can establish a real writer-to-writer relationship." Interestingly, even those who specialize in online writing conferences have expressed skepticism and doubt about their work. For example, in her study of Smarthinking online instructor attitudes toward the instruction they provide, Ehmann Powers notes:

> Despite claims of enthusiasm about working online, the majority of respondents approached OWI with skepticism. . . . These attitudes were characterized by: (1) concerns about the pedagogical validity of OWI itself and (2) politically focused concerns about the use of online instruction within educational institutions more generally. (Appendix 1)

Their concerns about the pedagogical validity of OWI apparently relate to a misguided belief that efficacy emerges from the apparent intimacy of face-to-face instructional interactions:

> Nevertheless, all respondents save two stated that they believed OWI was an inferior teaching medium for writing. Their primary reason was the perceived lack of in-person, human touches that most considered could not be conveyed online. Despite respondents' detailed statements about steps they took to create personal, human touches in asynchronous conferencing, the majority of respondents characterized OWI as overall less personal and intimate than face-to-face writing instruction. For this main reason, respondents perceived OWI to be overall less effective than teaching writing face-to-face. (Appendix 1)

As Chapter 5 suggests, efficacy likely is related more to students' decisions to use the conference in their writing and in how instructors semantically phrase their commentary than on issues of lost body language—although the lack of body language has an effect, to be sure. Pedagogically, for example, instructors cannot "wink" and "nod" students into agreement in online instruction; they cannot nudge them through facial and body language to journey intellectually with them or to accept a particular implied path as the logical or best next step. Instead, online instruction requires quick thinking and clear, purposeful communication. With writing formation particularly, instructors must know both how to provide reader feedback and how to *teach* using precise vocabulary and explanations that help students proceed primarily from instructional text—of which they might be suboptimal readers.

Lack of familiarity with online conferencing strategies may cause some skepticism or anxiety about using various OWI methods with student writers. Natural concerns about the unknown in education may be compounded by abundant, sometimes confusing choices regarding modality (for example, asynchronous or synchronous) and platform (such as email, bulletin boards, listservs, IM, and whiteboards). Quite simply, traditional oral instruction in brick-and-mortar classrooms remains more familiar. Established on-the-ground environments can function without the additional costs, maintenance, and learning curves that good online education necessitates. Traditional oral instruction easily can appear to be more educationally advantageous than OWI, which is newer and less-comprehensively studied. Indeed, on some levels, a lack of full understanding about OWI makes it seem an iffy proposition. While such skepticism is natural and understandable, *OWI, by virtue of its widespread use, already is an accepted means of teaching writing, and teachers/tutors need to learn how to conduct their instruction in this setting.* OWI needs its own strategies based in strong online and traditional pedagogy, so that even where such online pedagogy also applies to traditional writing instruction and conferences, it can be discussed from the online education perspective.

Chapter Two

Practical Matters

The Nature of the Writing Conference

Writing conferences are common to all educational levels—from elementary through graduate school. But people do not need to be in school to conference. Professional writers and scholars often conference about their writing. Few books are published without extensive conferencing among peers and editors.

In the genre of writing conference advice, the most universally applicable description I have found is from Carl Anderson's *How's It Going?* Anderson, who writes about elementary and middle school–based writing conferencing in traditional settings, explains writing conference roles from the instructor and student's perspectives. These roles and their responsibilities also fit postsecondary levels and can be adapted for classroom and tutorial settings in face-to-face or online asynchronous and synchronous modalities. Because this chapter considers the basics of teaching and tutoring online, it is helpful to review Anderson's outline in Figure 2.1.

Anderson separates the conference into two parts of a conversation about writing. In the first part, the student leads while the instructor listens; then the instructor connects the writing to the student's agenda and thinks about what to teach. In the second part, the instructor takes the lead, using both the student's set agenda and writing as the impetus for providing critical feedback and a specific mini-lesson related to the student's writing; the student listens, responds, and tries to implement the instructor's suggestions.

According to Anderson, there are at least two purposes for a writing conference: (1) to provide critical feedback, and (2) to teach, which involves not only identifying and teaching a skill but also getting the student to practice that skill (2000, 58–62). Thus, we might understand the

Figure 2.1

Anderson's Teacher and Student Roles in the Writing Conference

The Teacher's Role in a Conference
In the first part of the conversation: • Invite the student to set an agenda for the conference; • Get on a line of thinking about the student's writing work by asking research questions and reading the student's writing; and • Decide what to teach the student.
In the second part of the conversation: • Give the student critical feedback; • Teach the student; • Nudge the student to have a go; and • Link the conference to the student's independent work. (2000, 26)
The Student's Role in a Conference
In the first part of the conversation: • Set the agenda for the conference by describing her writing work; and • Respond to her teacher's research questions by describing her writing work more deeply.
In the second part of the conversation: • Listen carefully to her teacher's feedback and teaching; • Ask questions to clarify and deepen her understanding of her teacher's feedback and teaching; • Have-a-go with what her teacher taught her; and • Commit to trying what her teacher taught her after the conference. (2000, 83)

teaching aspect of a writing conference as one that develops naturally in problem-centered teaching. Often described as a method for "introducing concepts to students by challenging them to solve a real world problem" (Duch 1996), problem-centered teaching is used purposefully and fruitfully in mathematics, physics, chemistry, and other sciences studies.[1]

Although such learning often occurs online collaboratively in group-based document- and chat-sharing venues like whiteboards and chat rooms, it also can occur in one-to-one conference-based settings. The greatest challenge of problem-centered teaching and learning is to find

---

[1]See also Kenn Martin, "Problem-Based Learning"; Tony Greening, "Scaffolding for Success in Problem-Based Learning"; and Mike Kestner, "Why Problem-Centered Learning?"

the actual problem to be taught. For an economics student, the problem might be in an issue of international economics connected to euro/dollar exchange rates. However, for a writing student, the problem most likely resides in the student's own writing, which is contextually connected to an assignment. The problem might arise from the discomfort of writer's block, confusion about a classroom lesson, a critiqued essay in a formative stage, or the writer's own knowledge that something is not clicking. Once the problem emerges, however, it becomes the natural point of engagement—the teaching moment—for a writing conference. Students can genuinely progress in their writing from such problem-centered instruction if they are taught strategies for dealing with the problem.

Writing Conference Characteristics

Aside from relationship building and problem solving, the primary task of a writing conference is to intervene in the writing activities, and it can be initiated by one or both parties. Typically, these conferences occur with respect to some kind of formative writing concern, although they certainly can occur after a summative experience regarding a final or graded essay. Such draft-based conferences may occur more than once in a writing cycle and, ideally, would benefit the writer when moving into a new writing assignment. As Figure 2.2 shows, formative conferences feed directly into the student's decision to revise or to end

Figure 2.2
Conference Intervention Cycle

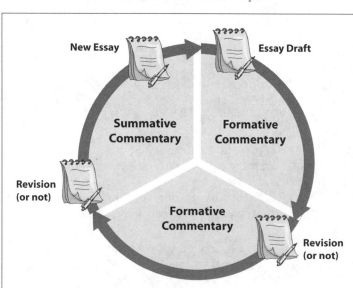

writing on an essay. A conference's potential to intervene in the student's writing process exists in both traditional and online settings.

A conference can be summative regarding a completed assignment, of course. In such cases, critical and response-based feedback may more often be the content, but even summative conferences can be used for problem-centered instruction. For example, because portfolios for end assessment are popular, often students can revise papers that have received summative feedback and a grade. More important, what students learn in one instance should be applicable to future writing, making a summative conference an intervention into a new draft's early stages.

In this intervention cycle, conferences inevitably are infused with power relations. Laurel Johnson Black, who studies conferences through sociolinguistics, addresses the inherent differences between conferencing that occurs as *conversation* and that which occurs as a *teaching interaction*. Black cites Kenneth Bruffee, agreeing with him that, "[c]onversation with members of another community is always somewhat strained" and "performance"-like (1998, 22; see also Bruffee 1985, 4). This point is important because writing conferences—whether face-to-face or online—have a transactional nature, and the participants—each from a different community (teachers or tutors and student writers)—have their own objectives. They are goal-driven interactions (Black 1998, 31), not merely social exchanges, which removes them from the realm of most common conversations and even of "critical" conversations about the content of one's writing. Such transactional interactions require language adjustments that can work to minimize the strain that Bruffee notes, although those adjustments naturally may affect the apparent freedom of the conference as instructional strategy (Black 1998, 30). In other words, to make the writing conference a conscious transaction between instructor and student removes any pretence that the conference is merely a conversation. It is, in fact, a goal-oriented conversation that strives to accomplish something specific with respect to a student's writing, knowledge, and skills.

Asynchronous Conferences

According to Hewett and Ehmann, all asynchronous writing conferences involve three or more phases whether they occur through email or a website:

1. A writer emails or electronically posts an essay to an online instructor.

2. The instructor reads the essay and provides feedback and instruction.

3. The writer reads the instructor's response and revises the essay (or not).

4. The writer desires further feedback and submits a new essay draft. (2004, 70–71)

These phases are not much different for relationship development or problem solving and may be initiated by either party.

Asynchronous text-based conferences are a hybrid between talk and writing, as Lester Faigley (1990) states, with elements both of oral talk and text. Understandably, the time lag between the initiating written "talk" and response can cause difficulties: Participants may talk past each other by failing to address each other's main points and talking, instead, about other points of interest (Hewett 1998). Equally, however, participants who attend carefully to the communication usually can converse effectively about each other's writing and commentary.

The asynchronous interactions in this book engage text rather than voice to communicate, and they are removed from the oral nature of talk and the spontaneity of synchronous interactions because they occur over a longer, less immediate period, with unspecified time gaps between the participants' speaking (writing) and listening (reading). Instructionally, these interactions are part of a sustained and long-term dialogue: Students "speak" by asking questions and submitting writing; online instructors "listen" and "reply" by reading and responding to the questions and writing; students "listen" by reading the comments and "reply" in turn by (a) revising or not and (b) resubmitting the writing or not (Hewett and Ehmann 2004, 69). Depending on the instructional context, the interaction can continue through multiple draft submissions of one piece of writing or through submission and response to subsequent assignments.

These asynchronous conferences resemble handwritten marginalia and global commentary, with similar goals of addressing strong and weak writing ideas, processes, and products. Contextually, however, they may represent a singular or especially significant contact between an online instructor and student. This context can create a high-stakes environment for the instructor, who may be tempted to address every problem in the writing; the context also lends immediacy to the feedback and instruction—possibly encouraging longer replies and greater specificity, as well as more focused teaching and guidance than in a traditional oral teaching setting and probably more so than with traditional handwritten marginalia. Of course, the instructional environment for students also tends to have high stakes. Experience suggests that students respond to asynchronous instruction with serious purposefulness.

The following is an example of asynchronous conference in a tutoring setting where the instructor (Tom) teaches the student (Christina) through both global, or overarching, responses and responses embedded in the draft that point to local issues

Example 2.1
Asynchronous Instructional Interaction

Description of the assignment: In this assignment, we are to state our position and provide logical evidence and good reasons to support this position. It has to include intro paragraph, paragraphs supporting my position, counter-arguments, field research, case studies, and a conclusion paragraph.

Help requested: My teacher has critiqued my paper and asked me to send it here with my revisions. I would like to know if my assertion and argument is strong enough to convince the reader that television violence contributes to violent behavior in children. I would like to also know if my transitions are good enough and cause no confusion.

General Comments: Hi, Christina. My name is Tom, and I'm happy to be working with you on this essay. I've made a few comments in the body of your paper, and you should know that they refer to the sentences that come before them. Also, they appear in bold print and brackets so you can locate them easily.

Specific Markup Comments: Christina, this is a really strong paper, and I felt engaged throughout the essay both by your writing and by the facts you included. I think that all the sources you've used were well chosen, and really helped you make your points. Also, the writing itself, sentence by sentence, is clear, direct, and interesting.

Content Development: For the most part, Christina, your essay is very effective in its ability to persuade. Here are just a couple of suggestions I have as far as ways to make the content even more effective: First, I notice that you've used the same few sources repeatedly in this essay. Because I've written and read a bit on this subject myself, though, I know that there are literally hundreds of scholarly and non-scholarly reports on television violence and its effects on children. Also, it seems that you can't help but make some mention of the school violence that has taken place over the past couple of years; school violence has often been linked to television violence. Do you think that including more and more recent and topical research and sources could improve the persuasiveness of your argument? Second, I want to play devil's advocate for a moment and suggest that maybe you've let parents too easily off the hook here. An essential part of any argumentative essay is the refutation of counter-arguments, and one of the first counter-arguments your essay will provoke is that of parents being to blame. You've raised this argument near the end of your paper, but I'm not very convinced by your handling of it. To say that parents don't have time to monitor what their children watch doesn't release them from blame, does it?

Organization: Christina, this seems like a well organized essay to me. I do have one suggestion, though, that you might want to think about. Generally, in an essay such as this, it's effective to mention a few solutions to the problem before concluding the essay. This way, you're not simply pointing out the problems, but are calling your readers to act upon them because you've shown them that something can be done. Would it be a good idea to spend a paragraph or two on possible solutions to the problem of violent programming for children?

Introduction/Conclusion: Your introduction is very effective, as is your conclusion. I do want to mention, though, that I think the concluding sentences at the end of each paragraph are unnecessary. You end most of the paragraphs with the same line, but I think you can simply move from one paragraph to the next without "wrapping it up" each time.

Advice for further work: Primarily, Christina, I'd focus on broadening the scope of your sources. Your arguments are well organized and have the potential to be very strong; I think you just need a little more backing-up from some of the abundant authority that's out there on this subject. Thanks for submitting your essay, and do stop back with another draft if your time allows! Good luck to you! Best, Tom

Student Essay:

Violent television programs are often blamed for contributing to the aggressive behavior of today's youth. Although there are other forms of media such as video games and music lyrics that may cause this violent behavior, television violence seems to have a stronger impact, both long and short term. Most of the programs children watch contain some type of violence. The programs glamorize these acts of violence, which cause children to imitate the most admirable characters. Violent characters are too often portrayed as *heroic*, which causes children to believe acting aggressively is an acceptable way to solve problems. Over exposure to television violence is another reason for aggressive behavior because it seems to desensitize children to the consequences of their violent actions. Children are exposed to violent programming everyday, which makes me believe it has an affect on their behavior. The television violence to which children are exposed may have an effect on the violent behavior of today's youth. **[Do you think it might be more effective if your thesis statement was more precise? For instance, rather than saying "have an effect," would it be stronger to say exactly what the effect *is* in your thesis statement?]**

The glamorization of violence on television causes children to imitate the violent actions they see. The programs children watch show admirable characters acting violently to overcome some type of evil. They do not show the real consequences of acting violent. When exposed to television violence at a certain age, children begin to pay more attention to violent programs without actually understanding the meaning of its content. Dr. Donald Cook, president of the American Academy of Pediatrics and clinical professor of pediatrics at the University of Colorado School of Medicine, states: "Children do not become full-fledged 'viewers' until around the age of two-and-a-half. As toddlers, they begin to pay more attention to the television set when it is on, and they develop a limited ability to extract meaning from television content. They are likely to imitate what they see and hear on television" (Cook 2000). **[This is a good, effective use of a source. Well done!]** The characters the children see are not punished or show little visible pain which causes them to believe that if they act in the same manner no pain or punishment will come to them either. Joanne Cantor states in *Television Violence Contributes to Violent Behavior of Children*: "They are most vulnerable, both because they are in the process of forming their own sense of right and wrong,

and because they are not yet adept at distinguishing between fantasy and reality" (Cantor 18). Without this distinction, children may believe that what they see
is acceptable and may begin to imitate the violent actions from television. Two
surveys of young American male violent felons found that 22–34% had imitated
crime techniques they watched on television programs (Beckman). Children learn
visually which is why they *learn* violent behavior from the programs they watch.
They also learn to believe that violence is the only way to express their anger
and get what they want. Television violence contributes to the violent behavior of
today's youth. **[I think it's all right to end this paragraph without the "concluding sentence." It may be stronger to simply end with the previous sentence,
and move straight ahead into the next point.]**

The way violence is portrayed causes children to act more aggressive. The
characters in the programs children watch are often honored and praised for acting violent. Studies by George Gerbner, Ph.D., at the University of Pennsylvania,
have shown that children's TV shows contain about 20 violent acts each hour and
also that children who watch a lot of television are more likely to think that the
world is a mean and dangerous place (Lees 1994). The actions of these characters
are portrayed as "heroic" whether the character is the "good guy" or the "bad guy."
If the violent character's actions seem to be honorable, the child may adopt the
aggressive behavior thinking he will also be honored. Cantor states in *Television
Violence Contributes to Violent Behavior in Children* that "Research shows that the
way violence is portrayed can make it more or less likely that a child will adopt
violent attitudes or become violent" (Cantor 18). The violent character is usually
the "good guy" whose actions are performed for the good of the country; however, the villain may seem to be the *hero* if he is praised for his actions. **[In my own
tv-watching experience, the violence is just as often coming from the "bad
guy"; where is your source for this statement about good guys most often
being the violent ones? I think it's a source your readers will need in order to
believe this statement.]**

Children then believe that the aggressive acts committed by the character
are acceptable since the character was rewarded and not punished. For example, in Spawn, the main character was an assassin until his murder. He was
sent to Hell and sold his soul to be able to see his wife again. The devil granted
him this request but also made Spawn the general of Hell's army where he
could avenge his death. However, he not only got his revenge, but also pro-
tected those on his street from drug dealers and other enemies. While on his
mission for vengeance, Spawn came across an abused little boy, whom he began to love and protect. Although this character was vengeful and technically
evil, Spawn's actions were considered honorable and praise worthy. **[Using an
actual example has really made this argument more effective. Could you
locate more places in the essay to use specific examples from tv?]** Since
broadcasters do not show the severity of the consequences of a character's
actions, children do not know the seriousness of acting violently. Joanne Cantor states in *Violent Children* that "the young perpetrators seem surprised at
the severity of the consequences to themselves and their victims…violence on

television usually underplays violence's negative effects" (Cantor 19). Many of the programs children watch are also meant to be humorous. For example, in Problem Child, the violent acts were performed by a child of about eight years old, Junior, and acted out on adults and children his own age. For example, at a neighbor's birthday party a little girl teased Junior, so he turned on the sprinklers and ruined all of her presents. Since he did not like the idea of his father remarrying, Junior would also sabotage his father's dates. Children could very easily perform these acts, yet they were meant to be funny. Since they thought the violence on this movie was humorous, children believe that if they act the same way others will think that they are funny as well. Children tend to mimic the actions of characters or persons that they believe are admirable, such as violent characters on television. The violence on television to which children are exposed has a strong effect on the behavior of today's youth.

Over exposure to violent programming causes children to act more aggressive. Often children watch programs that contain some type of violence. Children's television programs actually contain five times more violence than the average prime time hour of TV (Beckman). **[That's a really powerful fact! It's also really troubling!]** For example, the Power Rangers and the X Men are popular but violent programs that children find entertaining; the characters in the Power Ranger fight evil villains to protect the earth and the X Men use their "special mutant powers" to attack their enemies. By being exposed to this violent programming over a long period of time, children become desensitized to the consequences of violence (Cantor 18). A study performed by the American Psychological Association (APA) shows that children might become less sensitive to the pain and suffering of others, be more fearful of the world around them, and are more likely to behave in aggressive or harmful ways toward others ("Violence" 1992). Continuous viewing of violent programs has a long-term effect on a child. Leonard Eron, Ph.D., and his associates at the University of Illinois, found that children who watched many hours of TV violence when they were in elementary school tended to also show a higher level of aggressive behavior when they became teenagers ("Violence" 1992). Children are exposed to violence everyday from their school and home to the programs they watch on television. Therefore, the aggressive behavior of children may be caused by their exposure to television violence.

Many studies have been done to prove that there is a connection between television violence and youth violence. In one study done at Pennsylvania State University in March of 1991, about 100 preschool children were observed both before and after watching television; some watched cartoons that had a lot of aggressive and violent acts in them, and others watched shows that didn't have any kind of violence. The researchers noticed real differences between the kids who watched the violent shows and those who watched nonviolent ones. They noticed not only a change in some of the children's behavior towards others but also their lack of attention (Lees, 1994). In several studies, those who watched a violent program instead of a nonviolent one were slower to intervene or call for help when, a little later, they saw younger children fighting or playing destructively ("Violence" 1992). Violence is everywhere on television today which makes it hard for children to avoid. The excessive amount of violence on television may actually be the cause for the violent behavior of children. Cantor states: "Only 4% of violent programs portray a theme that promotes non violence. Moreover, more than half of the violent interactions on television shows no pain, and almost 40% of violent interactions show good guys behaving violently" (18). Violent programming is a main contributor to the aggressive behavior of today's youth.

During my field research into the issue of television violence, I surveyed five parents all of whom have children from the ages of two to five. I have found that three out of the five surveyed believed that violent programming has affected the actions of their child. Also, everyday these children viewed programs such as Powerpuff Girls, Looney Toons, Power Rangers, and X men. The male children seemed to be more affected by the violent programs than the females. A parent of a four-year-old said that her child "acts more violently after watching his favorite program, Power Rangers, than he does any other time." Also, she stated that her child was more apt to imitating reality shows since Power Rangers is his favorite. She noticed her child would not share his toys and was often fighting with the other children his age. On the other hand, the mother of a three-year-old girl said that her child would watch the Powerpuff Girls every time it was on and would not act differently after watching the show. She also said that her child would share her toys and hardly ever fought with other children. However, this parent mentioned that her daughter often watched Blue's Clues and Dora the Explorer which teach cooperation, understanding, and problem solving. Although some children are not affected by violent programming, it appears that the majority of those exposed to violence are affected. Violence on television often causes children to act in a violent manner.

There are some people who would place the blame on parents instead of television for a child's aggressive behavior. They believe parents should be able to control what their children watch. These people believe that parents can encourage their children to watch programs that demonstrate helping, caring and cooperation. Studies show that these types of programs can influence children to become more kind and considerate ("Violence" 1992). However, many parents do not have time to examine the shows their children are watching; therefore, do not understand the excessive amount of violence to which their children are being exposed. Broadcasters put violent programs on television without taking into consideration the severity of violence on the influential minds of children. These programs entice children to mimic the actions of the heroic characters not knowing the seriousness of the consequences. "The young perpetrators seem surprised at the severity of the consequences to themselves and their victims…violence on television usually underplays violence's negative effects" (Cantor 19). Some of the programs children watch do show blood and gore from shootings and other horrific events but they do not show children the severity of the wounds. Violence on television is a main contributor to the violent behavior of today's youth.

Many people believe children imitate their parent's rather than characters on television. Since children are exposed to domestic violence more than television violence, these people think that "real- life" violence has a stronger impact on a child. **[I'm not sure if I understand this sentence. Are you saying that children are more often exposed to domestic violence than they are to violence on television?]** James Baldwin wrote in *Nobody Knows My Name*, "Children have never been very good at listening to their elders, but they have never failed to imitate them" (Males 21). However, children may not mimic the actions of their parents because they felt fear and anxiety when they experienced this violence. Nevertheless, the characters in the violent programs children watch get rewarded and praised for acting aggressive causing children to mimic the character's actions instead. Two surveys of young American male violent felons found that 22-34% had imitated crime techniques they watched on television programs (Beckman). **[I think you've already used this fact above, haven't you?]** Children tend to imitate those whom they admire and if they are not proud of their parents, children will not mimic their actions. On the other hand, the violent characters children see on television are very admirable making it easier for them to act in the same manner. Therefore, the violent programs children watch contributes to the violent behavior of today's youth.

Children are exposed to violence everyday in the programs they watch. These programs contain many violent acts that are glamorized, and over a period of time will affect a child's behavioral patterns. The glamorization of violence causes the child to imitate the character he admires most and continuous viewing of violence causes the child to become desensitized to the consequences of aggressive behavior. Although a parent's supervision and control over the programs their child watches can prevent violent behavior, television violence still seems to have a major impact on a child's actions. The violence on television to which children are exposed is related to the violent behavior of today's youth.

Works Cited

Beckman, Jeanne. "Television Violence: What the Research Says about its Effects on Young Children." 1996. Homepage. 15 Sept 2000. <http://www.jeannebeckman.com/page18.html>.

Cantor, Joanne. "Television Contributes to Violent Behavior in Children." *Violent Children*. Bryan J. Grapes, Ed. San Diego, CA: Greenhaven P, 2000. 17-20.

Cook, Donald. <u>Media Violence.</u> 13 Sept 2000. American Academy of Pediatrics. 15 Sept 2000. <http://www.aap.org>.

Lees, Mary, Deen, Mary, Parker, Louis. <u>Research Review: Child Abuse and Violence.</u> Online posting. Winter 1994. 17 Sept. 2000. <http://www.coopext.cahe.wsu.edu>

Males, Mike. "Television Does Not Contribute to Violent Behavior in Children." Violent Children. Bryan J. Grapes, Ed. San Diego, CA: Greenhaven Press, 2000. 21-25.

"Violence on Television: What Do Children Learn? What Can Parents Do?" Online posting. Feb. 1992. 17 Sept. 2000. <http:www.apa.org>.

This asynchronous conference has two distinct parts: (1) a global, somewhat generalized response and (2) a local, focused response to distinct parts of the writing. It includes targeted praise of Christina's efforts, contextualized comments that demonstrate close reading, critical feedback of the content development and organization, and a short mini-lesson about counter-arguments. Tom did not provide a fully developed mini-lesson or series of next steps as described in Chapter 5, but he did encourage her to broaden "the scope of your sources" and to provide "a little more backing-up from some of the abundant authority that's out there on this subject." Those weaknesses aside, Christina likely found this to be a helpful conference session because it generated her question in Example 2.3 (p. 29), a synchronous tutorial.

Synchronous Conferences

Synchronous online conferences have four or more phases; may involve relationship building, problem solving, and/or writing formation; and may be initiated by either party:

1. Either the student or instructor begins the interaction by asking a question or posing a problem.
2. The respondent assesses the question or problem.
3. They engage in the conference.
4. The online instructor guides the conference to a conclusion.
5. Depending on the technology, participants save the interaction for future reference. (Hewett and Ehmann 2004, 117–18)

Hewett and Ehmann believe that synchronous conferences can be especially "tricky" (2004, 116). In a typical face-to-face conference, the give-and-take of dialogue guides the process. Participants engage primarily in oral interaction, sometimes aided by such textual activity as note taking. On the other hand, although they may use text alone, synchronous online interactions resemble oral interactions in that they tend to involve turn-taking, spontaneity, and relatively high degrees of interactivity. When conferencing via chat, IM, whiteboard, or other platforms, participants know who is present and involved. Yet, these conferences are more complex than at first is apparent because the instructor must have "highly developed verbal teaching skills and vocabulary about writing along with strategies for encouraging students to commit to writing out their thinking as part of the conference" (Hewett and Ehmann 2004, 116–17). While novice instructors certainly can learn such skills, they require both writing facility and pedagogical flexibility that typically come with experienced, metacognitively reflective writing teachers/tutors. Finally, while synchronous conferences are a way to conduct discussions about ideas (Moran 2001, 211–12), they also are powerful teaching environments for idea development specific to particular writing. Moreover, such conferences are not limited to content discussions and may well lead to global or local writing improvement (Hewett 2006).

A synchronous interaction might look like Example 2.2, an IM-based chat, which features an online instructor and a student in a discussion on developing transitions for counter-arguments.

Example 2.2
Synchronous IM Chat About Transitions

Student: Hello?

Instructor: Hi. I'm Shane and I'll be talking with you tonight.

Student: My name is Deene and I am working on an essay for my English class. We have to argue a point, then present the counterarguments, I am having problems transitioning from my argument to the counterarguements. I would appreciate any help you can give. Thanks. Done

Instructor: Hi Deene. Sometimes transitions can be tough, but there are some ways to make them smoothly. One way is to write a couple of sentences that show how two ideas are related to each other. Can you give me an example from your paper of an argument statement and one of the counterarguments that we can work with? Done

Student: I will try…*Although a lot of support goes for revenge as the stronger motivation for the killings, the stronger evidence supports that the killers of Columbine committed the murders to gain celebrity status.* Done

Instructor: Okay. Now, where is the transitive word (the word that makes a transition)? Done

Student: There really isn't…it transitions at, the stronger – wait….would it be "although"? Done.

Instructor: You've got it exactly. Words like "however," "although," and even "but" can make transitions. These words show the reader that they are "turning around" the subject matter. Do you see how that works? There are also phrases such as "on the other hand" that can be transition-makers. Done.

Student: Yes I do. My main problem is when I have finished my argument, I have to transition over to the counterarguments, and I am having problems starting that. That which I gave you is my assertion. Done.

Instructor: Okay. Let's see: you are saying that some people believe revenge was the motivation, but others believe it was done for fame. So, you could simply say,

"However, others believe…" to introduce the counterargument, or you might want to write a couple of sentences to say how there are others who have differing opinions. In arguments, you'll often see constructions such as "on the other hand," or "opponents to this argument state…" or even, "while this argument is strong, some disagree." What you are doing is saying, "here is the other side," but you want to move into it gradually. What do you think about this? done

Student: This really helps a lot, I never thought about using more of a couple sentences to introduce. It kind of helps keep my reader with me. Done

Instructor: Yes! And it helps your reader know you are changing the subject. Is there anything else you want to discuss about your writing right now?

Student: No, I think I'm good. I want to work on the transitions while doing it is fresh. Thank you. Bye

Instructor: Bye, Deene.

In this example, the online instructor (Shane) focuses first on understanding the student's (Deene) problem and then on teaching ways to resolve it. While the give-and-take of synchronous chat enables the instructor to learn exactly what the student needs, it relies on the student being sufficiently forthright and able to articulate her needs. This example features participants who make efforts to be clearly understood and who want to teach and learn. There is a particular weakness, however, in that the mini-lesson does not require any action on the student's part. Deene is not invited to test the lesson by creating her own transitional sentences before the conference ends. That invitation would involve an instructional strategy of helping the student to commit herself to writing out new ideas and to using new skills. From Deene's attempt to use the skill, Shane could then identify useful "next steps" that naturally emerge from the mini-lesson. An invitation to practice a new skill is critical to problem-centered instruction, and it will be discussed and demonstrated at various points in this book.

From the length and depth of this interaction, which developed over fifteen minutes, we can see one critical characteristic of a synchronous interaction: It is an ideal venue for detailed focus on one or two specific issues rather than on numerous aspects or on an entire essay. These issues could involve higher-order concerns like developing or refining ideas, thesis, topics, and organization; or they could involve lower-order concerns like style, grammar, mechanics, proofreading, or editing. Although both parties might read a student's writing online prior to talking, it is likely that the conference will naturally focus on the most critical aspects of either party's agenda.

Another characteristic of a synchronous interaction is that the feedback and teaching will occur only as quickly as either participant can think and type. Slow typists might be less verbal or "quieter" or even less clear than faster typists. Similarly, dysfluent or uncomfortable writers may type or "talk" less than more fluent ones. Fast typists, who can be equally unclear if they do not think carefully about what they are writing, generally can say more and provide more detail and depth to the conference. In synchronous venues, mistypings and misspellings tend not to be problems as they are recognizable hybrid traits of online talk. Indeed, any lack of clarity can be corrected immediately if either party raises a question. For this reason, experienced instructors who have a variety of instructional strategies at hand may address writing problems in this modality more quickly and fluidly than novice instructors.

Example 2.3, another synchronous example, is from a whiteboard conference, where graphics tools enable an instructor to identify and emphasize key lessons. Student writer Christina, from Example 2.1, and a different tutor (Judy) talk about thesis development. Her conference with Tom in Example 2.1 seems to have sparked Christina's question for Judy about her thesis: "The television violence to which children are exposed may have an effect on the violent behavior of today's youth." In the asynchronous interaction, Tom had asked Christina: "Do you think it might be more effective if your thesis statement was more precise? For instance, rather than saying 'have an effect' would it be stronger to say exactly what the effect is in your thesis statement?" This example suggests that Tom's feedback encouraged Christina to learn more about the effect of her thesis on readers.

This example demonstrates another characteristic of synchronous interactions: They enable students to participate actively in the mini-lesson by responding immediately and receiving instant feedback and additional instruction. They also enable students to try the lesson, practice the skill, and demonstrate what is learned. In fact, beyond the general look and feel of a chat versus a whiteboard interaction, Example 2.3 differs from 2.2 primarily in terms of the level of student activity. Except for the graphical insertions of highlighting, boxes, and arrows that appear on Example 2.3's whiteboard as a finished lesson, the whiteboard interaction and synchronous chat enable the same kind and quality of conference. In other words, the platform differs, but a skilled online instructor can use similar strategies to make either one work for students' benefits.

Example 2.3
Synchronous Whiteboard Interaction About Thesis Development

Hi my name is Christina and I was wondering if you could help me create a stronger thesis
Hi Christina. My name is Judy and I will be happy to help you. Would you explain to me just a little about your
assignment and what you hope to accomplish in your essay? done
Hi. Are you still there, Christina? done

yes. sorry
In my essay i have to state my opinion on television violence and strongly support it. My
opinion is that television violence causes violent behaviour in children
Ok. Would you write your thesis statement below? done

The violence on television to which children are exposed
is related to the violent behavior of today's youth. ←
Working
Thesis

I have been working on it and that is my final thought. Im not toally sure if it is
good enough.

Ok. I'm going to place something on the board that might help. One minute, please . . .

A thesis statement performs a combination of four functions. It: 1. Identifies and
narrows the subject; 2. Makes a claim or an assertion about the subject; 3. Sets the
tone of the writing; and 4. Often indicates the order of main points.
Functions
of a
Thesis

Now, I'm going to ask you to evaluate your thesis according to the criteria in this list.

1. Does your thesis identify and narrow the subject? (Please write your answer here.) done
          yes I believe it does
     **It seems rather broad to me. Violence on television is broad; so is the concept of "violent
     behavior of today's youth."**
     **Can you limit one or both of these in some way? What violent behavior are you referring to in
     particular? done**
Evaluation
of Current
Thesis

          the violent behavior of today's youth
          I don't really know how else to write it
               Ok. Let's go to the next point. Maybe we'll come back to this one.

2. Does your thesis make a claim/assertion about the subject? done
     Well it states that television violence is a contributor to a child's violent behavior

     Actually, it does not state that at present. It says only that TV violence "is related" to . . .
          so maybe i should state that it contributes to violent behavior
          That way it will be more clear.
               I think so . . . and more specific, too (even though it remains somewhat general.)

3. The issue of tone does not seem relevant to our discussion.

4. Does your thesis indicate the order of main points? done
          No it doesn't. Maybe I should put how the violence is portrayed on television and
          over exposusre to the violence in my thesis, because those are my main points.

Example 2.3 *continued*

Please write your revised thesis here:

> Over exposure to and the glamorization of violence on television contributes to the violent behavior of today's youth.

Wow! That's quite a different thesis. What is your opinion of this one?   done
> It actually has all of the guidelines a thesis should have and still states my opinion.

Does your essay (including topic sentences and body paragraphs) fit your thesis?   done
> yes they do.

Does your paper show a clear and compelling relationship between the two?   done
> yes

Great! Is there anything else I can help you with tonight? Would you like to talk about your thesis some more?   done
> I think that is all the help I need right now.
> Thank you very much. My thesis is alot better now.
>> You're welcome. Best wishes with your assignment. I hope to see you again in the future, too. Good night!   done
> Thank you. Goodnight

Identify the Strengths of the Tools

As we have seen, online asynchronous and synchronous modes of communication have different kinds of attributes in regard to temporality, connectivity, and uses of speech and text. They differ, as well, regarding interactivity, which is the degree of interpersonal interaction one might expect from each. Figure 2.3 (Hewett and Hewett 2008, 458) reveals a continuum where the most interpersonal interaction appears to the left with more synchronous interactions, and the least interpersonal interaction appears to the right with more asynchronous interactions. Email, one kind of asynchronous conference described in this book, appears adjacent to IM, which represents synchronous teaching conferences. Indeed, "both are located mid-continuum because they are similar in their hybrid, interpersonal natures" (2008, 458).

In other words, although asynchronous and synchronous instructional conferences are different, their common digital, hybrid, interper-

Figure 2.3
IM-inclusive Communication Interactivity Continuum

Casual Conversation ↔ Telephone ↔ IM ↔ Email ↔ Fax ↔ Radio ↔ Text

sonal natures are much alike when compared with casual conversation or conventional books and web pages.

To use an analogy, it is disturbingly easy (and debatable) to suppose that face-to-face oral interactions are always better than digitally mediated ones. Similarly, it is easy to assume that digitally recorded oral interactions must be better than text-based ones. Instructors certainly can use technology to offer voice-based instruction. However, any digitally recorded oral instruction has all the properties of asynchronicity (including language hybridity) and offers its own set of benefits and challenges. For an instructor-to-class lesson, for example, voice files may complement existing text materials, assisting students with mixed learning styles. Yet, while students may like to hear the instructor's voice, some find it is harder to remember or to review particular sections without replaying the whole lesson while others may experience excessively long download times or may not be able to play an MP3 file at all. In the one-to-one conference, voice files can encourage instructors to indulge in too many corrections and too much information, rather than reasonably focused global and local issues, as I will explain in Chapter 7. Time also may become problematic as—for some—talking about writing issues can take as long as or longer than writing about them, and when reviewing revisions against earlier oral conferences, instructors may have to listen to their entire files to recall what they had asked writers to consider.

The point is that neither voice nor text is better or worse. Similarly, neither asynchronous nor synchronous is a better modality. When faced with the choice about which to use, it is important to decide based on the qualities and strengths of the available modality and platform, as well as what needs to be accomplished. The rest of this chapter considers how to determine which tool to choose from the digital toolbox.

Asynchronous Modality Qualities

- Allows for varied time schedule; both parties do not have to be present simultaneously.
- Enables either long or short messages from responding instructors.
- Provides respondents (instructor or student) time to think, draft, and proof the message, while requiring a high level of care to ensure clarity and good communication.
- Offers instructors time to read drafts carefully and students time to read and reread the commentary.
- Enables conference interactions to be either discretely or broadly focused to multiple topics.

- Usually can be saved by both parties, and may be archived automatically by the platform or software.
- Tends to be private to students receiving the comments, which helps them in their one-to-one relationship with the instructor.
- Depending on its purpose, may require between fifteen minutes to an hour (thirty minutes average), so one or both parties should monitor time and set appropriate limits.

Synchronous Modality Qualities

- Requires both parties to be logged into the computer platform at the same time.
- Enables immediate feedback between instructor and student, allowing either to immediately check understanding of specific messages or points.
- Tends to limit the topic to one or two discrete issues due to the complexity of talking textually about a topic.
- Usually can be saved by both parties, and may be archived automatically by the platform or software.
- May enable group viewing or participation in the interaction, leading to a more collaborative experience.
- Depending on its purpose, may require between fifteen minutes to an hour, so one or both parties should monitor time and set appropriate limits.

Instructional software tends to be pre-selected by an institution's administrators for their academic uses. Such software includes Blackboard or WebCT, which enables a mix of modalities and platforms (for example, asynchronous file sharing, email, and group and private discussion lists or synchronous chat and/or whiteboard). Sometimes instructional platforms are developed in-house by technologists, while other times they are leased or purchased from tutoring-focused software providers. Experiential, practical teaching simulations on all the tools can assist teachers/tutors in understanding what is available; then it becomes easier to decide whether to use the non-real-time or real-time modality for a particular student, class, lesson, or assignment. In terms of platforms, we will briefly consider chat, whiteboard, email or web-based essay exchange, and a mix of these three choices.

Earlier in this chapter, we looked at three example online conferences. Example 2.1 showed an asynchronous conference where instructor Tom did the talking and commented on various higher- and lower-order concerns of Christina's essay. He offered a reasonable response to the writing at its current stage. Although the platform allows for doing so, he did not present the student with a problem-centered mini-lesson. Strengths inherent in this conference include those general qualities listed above, as well as:

- The conference can be repeated multiple times to account for various iterations or drafts of an essay.
- Online instructors can take their time to develop a mini-lesson tailored to the student, which includes the potential to save, reuse, and personalize it.
- Archived essay conferences can be made available to all online instructors (whether teachers or tutors) for easy reference, allowing students to receive more seamless feedback and instruction from multiple instructors.
- Such essay conferences provide students with the distance necessary to choose whether to follow, disregard, or otherwise incorporate the feedback differently.

Challenges inherent to an asynchronous platform include:

- There is lack of immediacy and dialogue for correcting misunderstanding or uncertainty of messages.
- The aspects of the writing on which the online instructor chooses most to focus may not be the same ones that the student would choose (which, most educators know, also can be an advantage).
- It is seductively easy to try to address every concern that a particular draft presents, leading to a too detailed, too lengthy, too time-consuming interaction that may confuse or overwhelm students and poorly use both individuals' time (see Chapter 7).

Example 2.2 showed a synchronous conference in a chat style where online instructor Shane and student Deene talked through the problem of when and how to use transitions. From this example and the general qualities listed above, we can intuit some strengths inherent to an IM or chat platform:

- Most often, writers type and press "enter" or click "send." The usually slight time lag between typing and sending enables writers to check the message before sending.
- When messages are complex, mistyped, or otherwise unclear, the dialogic quality of chat enables both participants to ask questions and clarify meaning.
- The text box size varies, but often it is big enough for up to 500 characters, enabling one to paste a chunk of text into the box for mutual consideration.

- Various font sizes, colors, and markings are available to enable text differentiation, variation, and emphasis.
- It is an easy-to-use and familiar type of software with a mild learning curve.

Challenges inherent to a chat platform include:

- There is a potential to be writing about a different aspect or question than the one to which the other party is responding; in other words, one person may be finished with one message thread and moving ·on before the other one is ready, requiring signals like "done" or "finished" to indicate completed messages.
- Unusually small text boxes may not allow for complete messages, which require extra care from both participants to be patient, to signal for more time to finish a message, and to ensure that the entire message is clear to the other party.
- There are no graphics capabilities in most chat platforms, which means that any drawing or pictorial working out of a concept or problem must be accomplished through a different medium and somehow shared.

Finally, Example 2.3 showed a second synchronous conference, this one developed on a whiteboard between online instructor Judy and student Christina from Example 2.1. In this conference, not only did the discussion appear on the board, but Judy also planned and provided the space for Christina to write out a revised thesis and to consider her essay in light of that thesis. Strengths inherent in a whiteboard platform include many of those dialogic and group qualities inherent to chat, but differ in these ways:

- The board resembles the physical space of a familiar teaching tool, the chalkboard, enabling familiar kinds of shared space instruction.
- In some whiteboards and CMS, an entire essay can be shared and discussed collaboratively, which can enable either a broadly or narrowly focused interaction about the text.
- The whiteboard space can be used in various types of mini-lessons where students can participate instantly and learning can be corrected and solidified immediately.
- In some whiteboard settings, there are minimum time lags whereby letters appear as they are typed, offering students the opportunity to watch the instructor's own writing process (which often includes mistypes beneficial to understanding a mature writer's writing process).

- Generally, a whiteboard affords graphics capabilities, to include changing font size and color; adding boxes, circles, arrows, lines, symbols; and cut and paste potential—these may be especially valuable for visual learners or for learners with some reading disabilities.
- There is a mild learning curve for some operations such as deleting text on the board.

Challenges inherent to a whiteboard platform include:

- There is potential for some students to freeze or feel uncomfortable with their typing skills or writing ability due to the immediate view of typed letters.
- Some software may not archive the boards automatically, requiring that one or both parties save and archive the board for future use.
- Online instructors need to think especially quickly to use the board's full capabilities beyond that of simple chat.

It becomes obvious that either modality has its advantages. Perhaps for some instructors the best option, when available, is to use both modalities when allowable by mixing and matching them to particular purposes. For example, regarding Example 2.2, if Shane had been more aware of the instructional capabilities of the chat method for his work with Deene, he might have used it to greater advantage by copying and pasting material into the chat window. He could have asked Deene to paste the last line of one paragraph and the first line of the next paragraph into the window, allowing him to see what kind of transition problems she was experiencing. Then, he could have coached her through trying out various transitions. Or, in a whiteboard setting, he could have created a box or special space for Deene to write in some new transitions and then highlighted her best options from his perspective. Had he responded to her whole essay alone, he might have isolated the issue of transitions and then addressed her transitions in the context of each paragraph using a commenting function and highlighting. Engaging all three possibilities, as some software allows, Shane might have asked for a file share of Deene's essay and read quickly through parts of it while Deene presented her problem in chat. Then, he could have pasted part of the essay into the whiteboard and taken Deene through a lesson whereby she edited her own writing. Such a planned and focused interaction could take about thirty minutes, which is about average for any of the three platforms discussed in this section.

Conferencing Action Plan for *identifying the*
strengths of the tools

1. Learn about the modalities available at your institutional setting, and consider their unique strengths and challenges.

2. Using the platforms available to you, practice online instruction with other instructors, switching between student and instructor roles.

3. Practice with various writing problems, from idea development
   to organization to standard mechanical/grammatical errors to
   determine which modality and platform works best for you as
   an instructor and potentially for different kinds of learners.

Chapter Three

Establishing Trust

Creating the Learning Environment

Establishing a trusting relationship with students in online settings involves a wide variety of activities that both build relationships and solve problems. Some of these activities require distributing information to all students in order to address the individuals' needs. Before any one-to-one conferences are attempted, it is first necessary to create a learning environment that provides students with the means to access the learning venue and materials independently. In this sense, preparing students for the technological idiosyncrasies of any online instructional platform is a relatively straightforward and obvious responsibility. We cannot expect students to function using any technology—asynchronous or synchronous—without orientation, practice, and follow-up to ensure that everyone can operate the software and platforms at least minimally. With practice and time, skill levels and comfort factors tend to improve, which provides learners with grounds for trusting their online teachers/tutors.

Beyond technology orientations, trust building occurs from practical orientations that help to mitigate potential student resistance or anxiety about using even familiar technologies like email, file-sharing media, and IM for educational purposes. For example, when students are to post any piece of writing for an asynchronous conference, they minimally need to know:

- When to submit their writing;
- Where and how to submit their writing;
- How to express their own needs and expectations for the writing and the conference;

- When they can expect a response;
- What form they can expect that response to take;
- Where to find the completed response; and
- Whether they are to respond directly to the conference with a revised submission or through other online, telephone, or face-to-face conferencing.

On the other hand, conferencing in synchronous online settings may seem less straightforward because these settings require more coordination. Minimally, synchronous settings require that students know:

- When they are supposed to meet, especially if there is more than one time available;
- With whom they are supposed to meet, particularly if there are multiple teachers/tutors involved;
- Who is expected to initiate the interaction;
- On what platform they are to meet, which may include knowing IM nicknames, a URL (and any username and passwords necessary), or the specific forum of a discussion board or chat room;
- How long the interaction may be expected to take;
- How long one should wait if the other party is late; and
- Whether one or both participants are expected to save or archive the interaction, as well as where to find the archives later and how long they will remain available.

In both modalities, students need a basic understanding of whether the response they will receive will be summative and, thus, more or less "final," or whether it will be formative, with idea development, revision, and editing anticipated as follow-on activities.

Additionally, for both kinds of conferences, students need to understand the degree to which their instructors view the interactions *as a conference with two fully functioning participants*. I hope that this book will encourage online teachers/tutors to see all one-to-one interactions as potential conferences regardless of modality, but certainly some instructors may consider the asynchronous conference to be more one-sided than the synchronous. Because the idea of educational dialogue is familiar in a face-to-face conference setting, it is not difficult for most students to view themselves as engaged in conversation when writing synchronously with an online instructor. However, students might see themselves as in a less relational interaction when conferencing asynchronously. Thus, just as online instructors need to decide how and where they will present their advice, students need to be oriented to the form and format of an asynchronous interaction.

One way to orient students is for the instructor to show them an essay that has received traditional handwritten response and the same essay with typed or digitized response. Among the similarities will be placement of any local and global commentary. Among the differences may be length, completeness, and general organization of commentary, as well as the depth of the teaching in a formative conference. Additionally, because online instructors are enabled and may be tempted to write quite a bit more feedback when providing commentary digitally, students need to see and discuss how the longer feedback may differ from traditional handwritten response. Guiding questions for discussion might be:

- What does the global commentary look like to you? Where it is longer than handwritten feedback, what is the substantive difference in terms of advice or explanation? Are more writing issues addressed overall or are a few issues addressed more completely?

- What separate sections or type of transitional methods are used to connect and separate the commentary?

- In the local commentary, there may be more full explanations of a common problem or a pattern in the essay. How are these embedded comments connected (or not) to the global commentary?

- What differences are there between critical commentary and mini-lessons? How does each type of response help with potential revision? What actions might one take based on these types of response?

- How should students interpret the weight of longer commentary? In other words, does the response mean more because it is longer?

- How is the commentary presented (spontaneously or organized systematically)? How is it organized? By least to most important concerns? By the writing's strengths to weaknesses? By opening global to embedded comments, or by local to global end comments, or by a combination of opening global, local, and end commentary?

- If there is a mini-lesson, where is it? How does its placement affect the conference as a whole?

By raising such questions and comparing the traditionally generated with digital commentary, instructors can help students navigate a less familiar feedback format. Doing so may reduce their anxiety, prevent them from feeling overwhelmed, and increase the benefits they receive from the conference.

Many teachers/tutors worry that students are not sufficiently aware that their learning will occur online and what that venue means for them technologically and educationally. From this standpoint, those who administer an online writing program or writing center should work with their information technology (IT) partners to develop student-friendly introductory materials that use the technology, explain how instruction will be accomplished, and address writing-related expectations. The sample script in Example 3.1 uses text and video shots, as well as audio clips to communicate with students about how to use a university's online writing center.

Example 3.1
Sample Script for Tutorial Video (directed to students)

(1) Video opening page: [view of the portal through which the online conference will occur]

Audio: *Hello and welcome to the University of ABC's Online Tutoring Center. The purpose of this demonstration is to show you what an asynchronous online tutorial looks like and how you can use it to your advantage as a student writer.*

At the Online Tutoring Center, we read and comment on your writing as part of a writing process: You develop your ideas, draft your writing, receive our feedback, and then you redraft. We call this process an online writing conference, or tutorial. If you want a second round of comments, then you can resubmit your writing to the Online Tutoring Center.

We hope that our feedback will be helpful to you in your writing process. Our job as online tutors is to read your paper, comment on your writing strengths, and offer you both general and specific suggestions for developing your ideas and improving your writing.

It's important, though, that you take responsibility for using that feedback as you redraft and edit your paper. We don't correct your writing or mark all of your errors. And we don't edit or proofread for you. That's your job as a writer.

When you're ready to move on to the next view, click "Next."

"Next"

(2) Video: [Advance to sample paper and focus on the top where there is a greeting.]

> Hi, Paul. My name is Ann. I've read your essay today and I really learned a lot about your vision for yourself as a music teacher. Below there are *writer's strengths*, *general comments*, and *next steps*. Within your paper, I've embedded a few specific comments using a "comment balloon."

Audio: *What should you expect to see in a tutorial? Here's what your tutorial might look like:*

Your online tutor will start by greeting you.

"Next"

(3) Video: [Advance to sample paper and focus on the Writer's Strengths.]

Writer's Strengths:

Your writing seems really strong in several ways:

- You write with vivid, clear detail.
- Your examples paint a picture of how music relates to academics for people who don't know that about music.
- Your transitions are great; you use keywords from the preceding paragraphs to lead your readers into the next ones.
- Your conclusion takes your personal experiences and thoughts and applies them to life, tying your paper together.

Audio: *Your tutor will explain some of the strengths that your writing shows.*

You may wonder why we talk to you about your strengths rather than simply give you suggestions for changes. We do this for two reasons. First, it's important to point out what's working in this piece of writing so that you can make similar choices as you redraft the paper. Second, it's important to know what you're doing well or where your writing generally is strong because that will help you to make good choices in this and future papers.

In this example, you'll see that the tutor (Ann) is telling the student (Paul) some of the ways that his paper is especially strong. These strengths will help Paul to think about how to improve the weaker parts of his essay.

"Next"

(4) Video: [Advance to the "General Comments."]

General Comments:

I see that you have lots of ideas for teaching. However, I wonder if you feel really confident talking about your teaching skills. Or, it seems that maybe you're not quite certain whether you are writing about your future as a teacher or what you know how to do now. I say this because in paragraph two, you say: *"In addition to making helping students find an outlet of interest, I could assist the students in relating music to help areas of study including math, sciences, and even literature."*

The use of the modal verb "could" makes it sound like you feel less confident in yourself or that you aren't sure whether you want to talk about your past, present, or your future. Before this sentence, you use present and past tense and the sentences sound more confident because they are clearly placed in time. So, if you have done the assisting before, you could say: *"I have assisted students...."* If you haven't done that assisting before, but you want to do it when you teach, then you could say, *"I want to assist..."* or *"I can do XYZ...."*

Audio: *In the "General Comments," your tutor most likely will give you an explanation of where your writing needs improvement. You should expect to find at least one example of a problem area and some kind of specific suggestion for how to improve it.*

In this example under "General Comments," Ann is teaching Paul about his use of the modal verb "could" and the way it influences his readers. In a mini-lesson, she provides Paul with some sample changes that depend on the effect Paul wants to have on his readers. Paul's job is to try out these strategies in his paper, deciding on which one or ones work best for his subject and writing style. Ann hasn't "fixed" his paper for him because the choice is Paul's to make. But she has given him some specific strategies for revising his paper. These are strategies that Paul could use in writing future papers, as well.

"Next"

(5) Video: [Advance to the "Next Steps."]

Next Steps:

For your next steps, try this:

- Read your paper carefully for similar verb tenses where you may be showing a lack of confidence in your teaching ability or a lack of clarity about what you want to say here.
- Use the examples that I've written above to change any verbs that need to be revised in order to clarify your meaning.

- Check your thesis. Is it the last sentence of the first paragraph or the sixth sentence of the second paragraph? I've highlighted both in yellow. Think about where you want the thesis to be. It might be helpful to talk to your teacher about it.
- Carefully proofread by reading this paper aloud and making sure that your sentences each say exactly what you want them to say and that your spelling and grammar are accurate.

Audio: *The "Next Steps" are the tutor's way of suggesting how you might go about revising your writing. While revision choices ultimately are yours, we like to explain some of the most important decisions you could make. It's up to you to decide whether to take this advice.*

In this example, Ann suggests that Paul work on the verb tenses that she has pointed out. She also suggests that he think about which sentence is his thesis and where he wants it to be placed. Finally, Ann tells Paul to proofread for errors, and she suggests that he proof the paper by slowly reading it aloud.

"Next"

(6) Video: [Advance to the next page that begins the text of the student's paper; show the opening paragraph only, making sure that the highlighted sentence is visible.]

I've always loved music, but it wasn't until I joined band in high school that I started thinking about becoming a music teacher. School in general was not easy for me and I struggled with academics, but band always made me feel successful. I joined as many musical activities as I could and found that I really enjoyed playing, but also enjoyed helping the other players around me to better understand music. When I transitioned to college, I found I enjoyed teaching music even more in the musical groups I had joined, and felt good about helping my peers. I gave music lessons to people in college who were struggling in their music classes and for those who didn't have time to take formal music classes. I aspire to become a music teacher in the hopes that I can reach students, like myself, who may struggle in school and to instill the love of learning and music.

Audio: *When you look at your tutored paper, the first thing you might notice is a use of various colored highlights, font styles, or character sizes to signal an important* *passage or sentence. In this case, colored highlighting signals a sentence that the tutor has questioned in the General Comments.*

"Next"

(7) Video: [Advance to the bottom of page 3 to the bolded text.]

> . . . In addition to the technical achievements they have on their instruments, children find a new confidence and courage to draw from within themselves to create musical ideas. I was once working with a child who thought they could not express themselves on the marimba, a keyboard-like instrument you hit with mallets. **[If the child is a boy, it is best to say: "…with a child who thought <u>he</u> could not express <u>himself</u>…" Use <u>she/herself</u> for a girl. This error from singular noun to plural pronoun is called a "number shift."]** I had him learn one note at a time while I played background music. After a while I would give him more notes, slowly, until he was free to express himself in confidence.

Audio: *The second thing that you're likely to find is what we call an embedded comment. These kinds of comments usually are very specific to your writing and they are embedded into the writing itself. Often, the embedded comments are where the tutor will note some of your word- and sentence-level issues. You might see an embedded comment in one of two ways.*

*The first way is shown here. The tutor's comments are written in **bold black font** and enclosed by brackets.*

"Next"

(8) Video: [Return to the first page of the tutorial where the first comment balloons are placed.]

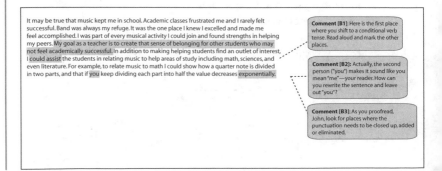

It may be true that music kept me in school. Academic classes frustrated me and I rarely felt successful. Band was always my refuge. It was the one place I knew I excelled and made me feel accomplished. I was part of every musical activity I could join and found strengths in helping my peers. My goal as a teacher is to create that sense of belonging for other students who may not feel academically successful. In addition to making helping students find an outlet of interest, I could assist the students in relating music to help areas of study including math, sciences, and even literature. For example, to relate music to math I could show how a quarter note is divided in two parts, and that if you keep dividing each part into half the value decreases exponentially.

Comment [B1]: Here is the first place where you shift to a conditional verb tense. Read aloud and mark the other places.

Comment [B2]: Actually, the second person ("you") makes it sound like you mean "me"—your reader. How can you rewrite the sentence and leave out "you"?

Comment [B3]: As you proofread, John, look for places where the punctuation needs to be closed up, added or eliminated.

Audio: *The second way that you may see embedded comments is in a "comment balloon" off to the side of the paper. This comment balloon is attached by a line to the place or places in the paper to which it applies.*

(9) Video: [This is an interruptive moment that the script/demonstration should take over the cursor. Demonstrate the three steps.]

Audio: *If the embedded comments are not in bold black font, and if you're using Microsoft Word but can't see the comment balloon, please try the following:*

- *Go to your toolbar,*
- *Find "Show" or "View," and in that pull-down menu,*
- *Click the "comments" feature to enable it.*

"Next"

(10) Video: [Advance to the fourth comment balloon about "introductory clauses."]

To relate music to science I could explain that pitch (music note) is a sound wave, and the faster the wave moves or vibrates, the higher the pitch. When a student understands how to relate things that they love to areas of academics that are uninteresting to them, then they may be able to give meaning and connections to those other academics.

Comment [B4]: This sentence begins with an introductory clause ("To relate music to science"). Typically, we separate the introductory clause from the main clause with a comma. For an example, look at what I did in this sentence and the prior sentence.

Audio: *How can you make the best use of this tutorial? Let's spend a minute looking at a specific example.*

In this example of an embedded comment, Ann points out a sentence that has an introductory clause, and she explains that introductory clauses are set apart by a comma. She provides Paul with two example sentences in her own explanation so that he can see what a properly placed comma looks like in an introductory clause. Then, she asks Paul where he would place the comma in his own sentence. Therefore, Paul can:

- *See a problem sentence,*
- *Understand what the problem is, and*
- *Learn how the sentence should look through*
  - *an explanation of the sentence rule and*
  - *two examples.*

It's Paul's job to figure out how to correct his error. After he learns about introductory clauses, Paul has the opportunity to apply that rule to other sentences in his essay.

"Next"

(11) Video: [Return to the beginning of the tutorial.]

> Hi, Paul. My name is Ann. I've read your essay today and I really learned a lot about your vision for yourself as a music teacher. Below there are *writer's strengths, general comments,* and *next steps*. Within your paper, I've embedded a few specific comments using a "comment balloon."
>
> Writer's Strengths:
> Your writing seems really strong in several ways:

Audio: *It's always your choice whether to implement a tutorial suggestion or guidance. In addition, it's important to remember that the online tutors are not going to point out every strength or weakness in your essay. Therefore, it's your job to look for patterns of errors and strengths—using the tutorial as a way to learn more about improving your writing overall.*

Finally, remember that every time you submit an essay to the Online Tutoring Center, you'll be asked for information about your assignment. To get the best tutorial possible, you should explain your assignment thoroughly or, if you have a digital copy of it, attach it at the beginning of your essay and submit it with the essay. You'll also have an opportunity to ask for specific kinds of help. Be as precise as you can with your questions for the online tutor, and the tutor will make every effort to answer your questions in the context of your writing and your assignment.

(12) Video: [Enable the students to scroll through the entire tutorial and essay. Signal that they may scroll while they listen.]

Audio: *Feel free to take some time reviewing the writing conference on these pages so that you can be familiar with the general format of an online tutorial. If you have any questions, remember to ask them when you submit your own essay to the Online Tutoring Center. We look forward to reading your essays in the Online Tutoring Center!*

Conferencing Action Plan for *orienting and preparing students for online conferences*

1. Using conference examples, develop and test methods for introducing students to the modalities and platforms they will be expected to navigate in online conferences.

2. Orient students to the practical experience of meeting and/or sharing writing in the online settings you will be using.

3. Prepare a lesson that engages student feedback about the look and feel of the types of online conferences in which they will participate.

4. Using Example 3.1 as a model, develop a streaming video or other type of digital orientation tool that students can use independently in your particular setting.

Setting Instructional Expectations

Creating the learning environment by orienting students to the look and feel of an online conference is part of the trust-building process. Students also learn to trust their instructors by knowing what teachers/tutors expect from them. The most obvious types of expectations involve opportunity, frequency, and requirements for conferences. Students need to know whether they can contact an instructor whenever the platform makes them aware of the instructor's presence in the online classroom or tutorial setting. If there are restrictions, like the need for an appointment or to honor certain office hours, students should be told when an instructor welcomes such contact. If students are expected to get tutorials to supplement their work with the course teacher, they need to know when and how often they can access the assistance, as well as whether accessing or applying such assistance is required or recommended. In an online or a traditional class where the instructor will review or grade essays asynchronously, students need to know how often they can receive their teacher/tutor's assistance before the essays are graded. And they need to know whether their grades are influenced by submitting their writing for online review or by meeting with the teacher or tutor.

Another kind of expectation that online instructors should address is more complex. Students need to know what they are expected to do as a result of the interaction after it has occurred, and they may need to have this expectation repeated or reinforced during the semester. For example, students probably can make the distinction that peer group review provides feedback that they may or may not use when revising. But when an instructional interaction occurs between a student and a teacher/tutor, the expectations for its use need to be set clearly. Online tutors, for example, might want to establish expectations at the beginning of an asynchronous interaction by saying something like:

Hi, George. My name is Beth and I'll be giving you feedback today. When you read my comments, feel free to decide which ones you want to apply to a revision. Your actual revision strategy is up to you. However, if I strongly believe that you need to do something specific to improve your writing, I'll tell you and I'll explain why I think it's important to address. I'll probably ask you to complete a short mini-lesson exercise that will help you learn how to address the issue. You can resubmit your revised writing or questions to me or to the online writing center, and you can check with me or your teacher for further advice.

Example 3.2 illustrates the kinds of conflict that students might experience when such expectations are not clearly set or reinforced.

Example 3.2
("Grant") Asynchronous Conference (Local Commentary)

Student Original: Soon I found my self taking notes and learning as much as the boy. It turned out the boy's grandfather was in World War I and was a doughboy. <u>After the father was done with the history lesson, he asks the statue (his dad) a series of personal questions I refuse to include.</u> Then he stood silently staring at the statue while the boy ran around splashing in puddles, it seemed like he was waiting for answer or maybe in fact getting his answers.

Online Tutor Local Commentary: Why won't you include the questions? I can understand if you feel that you need to protect his privacy—the sacredness of the moment. However, could you explain those reasons to us instead of just writing that you "refuse to include" the details? Think about how your words will affect your readers. Do you want to alienate your readers by refusing to tell us something, or do you want to explain to us why you are not telling us and what that not telling has to do with sacredness? Could you tell us how you felt as you listened to him? How did it feel for you to hear what he said? What felt sacred about that moment?

Student Revision: Soon I found my self taking notes and learning as much as the boy. It turned out the boy's grandfather was in World War I and was a doughboy. <u>After the father was done with the history lesson, he asked the statue (his dad) a series of personal questions, such as, how are you doing, do you think I am a good dad, etc? I will not quote the man because I do not feel it is important to the essay.</u> Then he stood silently staring at the statue while the boy ran around splashing in puddles, it seemed like he was waiting for answer or maybe in fact getting his answers.

In this example, my writing student, Grant, wrote about his town's World War I memorial depicting a soldier in a doughboy uniform. In a supplemental asynchronous tutorial, his online tutor asked him to reconsider a sentence that might puzzle readers. Unable to reply directly to the tutor, Grant brought both indignation and an angry response to the next class meeting, explaining his take on the tutorial and refusing to "change" the draft because he was "right." He stubbornly held onto his textual ownership, saying that he would ignore much of the conference because he had said what he wanted to say and gotten what he had wanted from writing the essay. The subtext of his words, particularly in the public forum of our classroom, seemed to be that he was not certain to what degree he could decide for himself what his writing could or should express—hence his heightened affect. In other words, I think that he was not sure of *my expectations* as his classroom teacher versus *his responsibilities* in responding to a tutorial. He seemed to be asking whether I insisted that he had to do what the tutor had recommended to him. I responded equally publicly that he should think about his message and what he was trying to communicate to readers, and then think about any feedback that he received from tutors, peers, or me; ultimately, I said, he should revise as he thought best. In revision, as Example 3.2 shows, Grant held his ground about his subject's privacy, but he did make a change that responded somewhat fiercely to the tutor's comment. Despite his apparent conflict over the decision he needed to make as a writer, Grant's view of his autonomy and responsibility to his subject's privacy were stronger than his responsibility to an online tutor's commentary.

I provide this example in detail because it suggests how difficult a student's decisions can be in terms of applying—in this case—tutorial advice. It also speaks to the challenges that I outline in Chapter 4 regarding what online instructors believe is their primary responsibility to students. Early in the semester with Grant's class, I had prepared students for using online tutorials by discussing their role in our class. However, Grant's dilemma and his strong feelings about his decisions reveal that *once they are set, expectations may need to be reinforced through repetition*. As his teacher, I needed to make clear my expectations for use of any feedback about his writing. The lesson is that instructors should proactively ease the kinds of conflicts that Grant's writing demonstrates by setting and repeating clear expectations, which increases students' trust in us and in themselves. In this case, such expectations could be illustrated by providing and discussing with students some example scenarios that highlight their authority in decision making relative to the online instruction and discuss how to make those decisions.

Conferencing Action Plan for *setting*
instructional expectations

1. Whether you are a classroom or online teacher who conferences with your students online or an online tutor who meets
with unknown students, decide whether you are providing
only critical feedback or also teaching ideas and skills. Determine what actions students should or might take in relation to
your comments. In other words, determine your role and expectations. Where necessary, make such a decision in conjunction with the departmental writing director or other members
of your writing instructional team.

2. Explain your expectations clearly to students, using digital
examples, multimedia, or face-to-face instruction as needed.
Reinforce those expectations in various online conferences as
issues arise.

3. In your online conferences, state as clearly as possible what
students *must* do and what they *might* do, while avoiding potentially confusing statements. Use problem-centered teaching
whenever possible to help students understand the kinds of
writer's choices that are most important to making their meaning clear.

Helping Students to Set Agendas and Make Choices

Online instructors also should assist their students in setting their own
agendas for conferences and in making informed choices about how
to apply the instruction. Students benefit from understanding how to
make and express their own agendas for an online conference. Not
only does such action empower them to guide their own writing and
revision processes, it also helps to ensure that their most significant
needs can be met in the conference. Indeed, in the online setting, it is
especially important to get students talking about why they are writing and what is happening in their writing processes. Without explicit statements, the online instructor has only his or her perceptions,
which should have some value to the student but may not be what the
student most needs to consider.

Agenda setting can be challenging in the asynchronous conference because once a draft is submitted, the agenda already will have
been set by the student; often, there are no "do-overs." Thus, students
need upfront preparation for their conferences. This preparation may
be accomplished by an in-class discussion (via online media or in the

traditional setting) about what students need and how to ask for it. The classroom teacher or online tutoring center also might provide students with a worksheet (located online or printed and distributed) that will help them to focus their needs. An especially effective strategy would be to build into an asynchronous platform the questions that students most need to answer, making them "required fields" that must be completed before the paper can be submitted. In tutorial settings, for example, prompts might include:

- Context: What is your assignment? When is it due? What is your course number (or level, grade, or year)? If a tutorial submission, then who is your teacher?
- Process: Where are you in your writing process? Topic identification? Idea development? Organization? Preliminary draft? Revised writing that already has received feedback?
- Needs: Ask three questions that you would most like to have addressed in this online conference.
- Preferences: What do you like best about your writing so far? What do you like least about it? Why?
- Revision: If you could change anything about this essay (and you can!), what would that be?

Alternatively, It would seem easy to get students in a synchronous session to express an agenda for it, but that is not always the case. When a student is not certain what to ask for or when the context is not clear, it may take a series of questions and answers for the online instructor to understand how to address the issue. Example 3.3 provides an illustration of a teacher for a distance-based course who is synchronously conferencing with his student and trying to establish an agenda.

Example 3.3
Synchronous Agenda Setting A

Student: Hi, Mr. Green. This is Donna. I'm writing my essay for class.

Online Instructor: Hi Donna. Tell me what you understand the assignment to be. done

Student: It's supposed to be 3-4 pages. Comparison contrast kind of paper. I need help with my transition.

Online Instructor: Tell me more, Donna. What is the question you're working with and where do you need a transition? done

Student: My question is: whether violence in the media leads to violence in youths who are exposed to it. I need a transition between the two sides of the issues. can you help

Online Instructor: I'll try to help you out here. First, give me a little more information about the assignment from your perspective. done

Student: Its an exposition. I have to take an issue and equally represent both sides of the issue without showing my own bias or opinion. I have to represent both sides by including "points" that differ on each side of it. Done

Online Instructor: I know this is a tricky paper to write. Do you have the two sides developed and the points you want to cover? Done

Student: I have a basic idea though I'm still trying to organize and define them more. I want to do the sides of media causes violence vs media doesn't. points would possibly be: media desensitizes kids to violence, media distorts their reality of death and punishment, media causes kids to copycat actions. Done

Online Instructor: Great start, Donna! Now, let's set up a chart with both sides so we can work on your transitional statement.

Notice how many questions the teacher asks to get full information from his student. He knows the assignment because he created it, but he needs the student's understanding of it for the conference. Mr. Green's goal is not only to get his student to clarify the context, however; it is also to get Donna to set the agenda clearly in her own mind. In this case, Donna is quite certain that she needs to work with her transitions, and her work indicates that her stated concern is probably appropriate. Contrast this example with that of Example 3.4 where Mr. Green does not get at the student's real concern, which seems to be whether the argument she is constructing is interesting enough to read.

Example 3.4
Synchronous Agenda Setting B

Student: Hi, Mr Green, its Shelly. I'm doing my essay about youth and violence.

Online Instructor: Hi Shelly. Tell me what you're writing about. done

Student: I'm doing the effects of hip hop culture on youth violence today. Do you think my subject is interesting?

Online Instructor: That sounds interesting. Have you developed a thesis yet? Or are you just outlining your ideas for yourself? done

Student: My thesis states that the rise in hip hop culture may be responsible for the violent actions committed by youths today. How does that sound to you?

Online Instructor: I don't know a lot about hip hop culture, but I'm not sure you'll be able to develop a leak-proof argument out of that. Aren't there several different kinds of groups of people in hip hop culture? done

Student: I'm relating a big deal of my paper on the violent lyrics and music videos listened to by teens.

Online Instructor: So maybe you'll just need to qualify your statements a bit to say you're just looking at the violent aspects of the trend. Okay. Do you have any other questions? Done

Student: No, no thanks. I'll just keep working on this for now. Can I meet with you again if I need to?

Online Instructor: Sure. Bye, Shelly

Shelly's question about whether her topic is "interesting" represents a fairly vague notion; the question seems to be a prompt that the student uses to get herself online and into the conference. Mr. Green is a bit off his game, though. As her online teacher, he chats with Shelly, but he fails to engage her in a profitable conference that can help her develop her writing. In fact, by asking whether Shelly has "any other questions" when there is much more to explore, Mr. Green abdicates any responsibility for helping his student set an agenda with which they can work together. Shelly might even sense that she is being hurried out of the conference. A more effective strategy would be for Mr. Green to work like he did with Donna, asking specific questions that would get the student talking more about her subject and leading her to indicate more specifically what she needs to know beyond the "interesting" nature of her topic. For example, he might say something like:

I think the relationship between hip hop culture and violence is interesting, and I'm looking forward to reading your paper. Tell me more about why you chose this subject, though. What interests <u>you</u> about it? What do you think will interest your readers? What kinds of evidence do you think you'll find for your thesis? I'm all yours for the next 20 minutes, Shelly! Done

Students also need help with making choices about their writing. We expect that they will use the conference at least minimally for feedback— for a sense of their own progress and our thoughts about it—but I suspect that most of us rightly, hope, for change in the writing as an outcome. But how do students make their decisions? For instance, in Grant's case (Example 3.2), his revision shows that he might benefit from instruction in ways to address his subject's privacy and thoughts, as well as in how to express his thinking *as thoughts* in writing. At the point where he presented me with a revision based on his work and the online conference, it became my responsibility to help him sort out those issues. However, beyond the writing instructor's overall work, which is detailed in numerous fine books about pedagogy, there is the specialized work of helping students to read and interpret instruction that is presented *textually*.

As Chapter 5 indicates, it may help both students and their in-structors to discuss the subject of instructional language—instructional intention and students' inference—in the classroom setting. The point is to challenge both our own and our students' assumptions regarding online commentary. Chapter 5 provides numerous examples of online instructional commentary that may be good starting points for asking students pertinent questions:

- What do you think the online instructor is telling the student by saying _____?
- What is the action that the online instructor recommends? How do you know that?
- If the online instructor writes either "couldn't you make this long paragraph into two paragraphs?" or "break this longer paragraph into two paragraphs at the point where you change subjects," which one is clearer to you? Are there any differences in what you think you should do to the writing? What would you do in this case?

Discussion that emerges from such questions can help instructors demonstrate to students the depth and breadth of their choice-making capability as a writer in general or in a particular instructional setting.

Finally, Example 3.5 illustrates an issue about which students would need to make revision choices: that of content and organization of the comments.

Example 3.5
Online Commentary (Local and Global)

Student: The debate of whether television causes a child to become more aggressive and act out violently toward others has been in the public eye for years. On one side, the view is that the child imitates what he sees on television because of how it appears "cool" or "sexy". However, others feel that the use of violence in entertainment does not cause a child to become aggressive because the child can tell the difference between the reality of life and the fiction on the show he watches. This essay will examine the role of television in a child's life and whether it causes violent actions in his life. **[You have a strong opening paragraph. The sentences contain effective language, and your thoughts are expressed clearly and economically. Nice work!]**

Online Instructor (Global): One final thought: The last sentence of the first paragraph claims that the essay will "examine the role of television in a child's life." Does your essay do that? What is the role of television in a child's life? If you agree with me that the essay does not address that issue directly, you may want to alter the wording of the original sentence or add a section that addresses the topic.

In this case, the local, embedded comments appear to contradict the global, overarching comments, which seem to have been written last. Specifically, the instructor praises the opening paragraph in terms of its language and expression. Whether the word *strong* applies only to language issues or also to the content of the introduction could be addressed in discussion with students who are learning how to interpret instructional comments. Perhaps the global comment is more challenging for student interpretation; here, the online instructor questions the writer's thesis—whether it is actually addressed directly in the essay draft. Instructors will readily see that there are two issues in these comments: (1) the quality of the introductory paragraph's expression and (2) whether the student actually addressed the thesis in the essay's body. Students, however, are likely to mistake the *praise* about the introduction—where this thesis resides—for a statement that the thesis does not need any revision. It follows that they may misunderstand the global comment about the thesis—believing that the online instructor has contradicted herself or that the global comment does not need their attention. This example, therefore, provides an opportunity to challenge students to read closely and deeply before making revision choices. It offers instructors, too, an opportunity to practice their own strategies for addressing an issue where one part of a paragraph works well, while other parts of the same paragraph do not.

Conferencing Action Plan for *helping students*
to set agendas and make choices

1. Talk with students about why they're using online conferences and what they can expect from the conferences: What's the purpose of an interaction? Who'll be talking with and/or responding to the student? Using this context, help them to practice setting an agenda for their writing before beginning the conference.

2. Practice how to get students to set and stick with an agenda in a synchronous writing conference. Then, practice how to help them reset the agenda when it's not clear or may not lead them to fruitful writing and revision.

3. Teach students how to use the set instructional expectations and their own agendas to make choices among the feedback and lessons they receive in their conferences.

4. Work directly with students in a group-based online or traditional class setting by offering example choices and discussing with them the benefits and challenges of making them.

Connecting with Students

Part of developing trust involves mutual connection and interest in conference communications. While it is always helpful to check in with students to make sure they are engaged with their learning, in online settings, doing so is especially important. Checking in can be accomplished via email but may be most effective in synchronous chat. As many have observed, a significant difference between traditional and online settings is that generally we cannot watch students' body language and facial cues nor hear the oral phatic language that signals understanding, confusion, interest, and disinterest. Instead, we must rely on typographical cues to convey the same information. Many students currently use IM to communicate online with their friends, for example; they have developed IM-ular writing—a series of abbreviations and phatic-like informative cues to keep lengthy and often complex conversations going and comprehensible. They may say, for example, "brb" ("be right back") to indicate that they are leaving the computer or the chat for a moment; or they might say "sec" to indicate that they need a few seconds (or even minutes) before responding. "Thinking," "um," or a series of dashes or ellipses convey a sense of presence while sorting through sometimes complicated message threads. "Finished," "period," or "done" might indicate the completion of a thought, signaling that the other party can speak. "Hmmm" or "????" might indicate puzzlement or confusion, while "ok" or "k" indicates that the reader has "heard" and the chat can continue. Such textual cues are important to online conversation, and some of these, while most important for synchronous conferences, also can be used in asynchronous ones.

In talking about connecting with students, it is especially helpful to understand some of the textual cues that students are apt to use in synchronous conversations. However, it is also useful to understand how to prompt these kinds of cues when there's a lengthy silence on the other end of the chat—regardless of the platform being used. When a student initiates a conference, the online instructor usually can assume that the student has a reasonable level of interest in the meeting. The same is true for a planned or required conference related to a particular assignment or stage of the course. However, once the initial question is answered, a student may be less interested in continuing the discussion—particularly if the instructor has additional questions that might put the student on the spot. In addition, it is important to remember that when it comes to engagement, both parties need assurance of ongoing attention and interest. Examples of interest-conveying prompts include:

- Using a student's name and speaking directly to him or her, which can encourage the student to speak as directly to the online instructor in response. Self-introduction in the greeting is helpful, too, even though many students will remain aware of authority and hierarchy and may be less inclined to talk to the instructor by the given name no matter how prompted.

- Signaling one's own attentiveness by frequent reference to the writing, the assignment, or something that's been shared as part of the writing or writing process. Such a tactic not only keeps the conference on point but also reminds students that their instructors are focused on their writing or writing processes.

- Asking students open-ended and genuine questions (not yes/no, rhetorical, or leading questions, as discussed in Chapter 6 and Appendix 2) that require more information in the response. Such questions also serve to model the kinds of questions that students should be asking in order to get the contextually full and helpful responses that they need.

- Asking students whether they have their own questions. Students might be hesitant to take more time or to pose their own questions, even to the point of responding that they understand a point that is unclear to them. They might worry about showing what they perceive as ignorance, making it necessary to go one step further by offering some question cues: *Do you have any questions about how your content is developing—or about your thesis or timeline or anything else?*

- Requiring students to commit their ideas to writing—to write something, anything—to change their drafts, or to try out new skills in response to the conference, whether asynchronous or synchronous.

- Checking in frequently regarding the student's understanding of what is being said. Synchronously, one might say, *"Does this make sense?"* or *"Please tell me what I just said using your own words."* Asynchronously, one might say *"In other words,"* and then rephrase or otherwise redefine the potentially confusing (thus disengaging) statement.

- Offering clear, honest, critical reader response to the writing. Such a tactic includes giving the student a personal response and phrasing it as such: *"I'm awed by your strength in this situation"* or *"When I see your detailed writing, I become really interested."* Such reader response, much discussed in composition pedagogy literature, also helps when providing less positive feedback: *"I'm confused by this entire paragraph. What did you want readers to understand?"*

- Being personable, genuine, specific, clear, thoughtful, and self-engaged in the conference and the student's writing. Although we cannot always choose our work schedules, it seems best whenever possible to avoid online conferences when overtired or grumpy with students or otherwise less than interested in their writing. In some ways, the almost null emotional conveyance of the online setting can protect students from an online instructor's bad mood, but it cannot protect against bad advice or poor reading or less-than-attentive diagnostic skills that can be part and parcel of such a mood.

- Believing that the student is interested, which is a valuable attitude in both traditional and online educational settings. Such interest should be anticipated whenever the student initiates a conference or attends a required or scheduled meeting with the instructor. In other words, trust the student to be a participant. Even unwilling students can come around when they sense that someone believes in them.

These strategies can be especially helpful in keeping a synchronous conference on track. However, due to the nature of synchronous conversations, it is also realistic to acknowledge that a student's apparent disinterest may be caused by circumstances outside of the instructor's control. In other words, the instructor may be misinterpreting the student behavior as disinterest when actually it is being caused by other conditions. The student may have only a short time to talk, may be multitasking, may not be comfortable with learning in the online setting, or may have poor typing and spelling skills. In such cases, the instructor's intervention via the conference might not work, making it necessary to change the approach. Sometimes it is useful to ask the student straightforwardly what is happening regarding the conference. Other times it is best to schedule another online conference or to move to other media, like email, telephone, or—where possible—to meet in person at a mutually agreeable time.

Conferencing Action Plan for *connecting with students*

1. Learn firsthand about issues of attention and disinterest in synchronous conferences by conducting casual IM conversations with students and colleagues. Consider how a teaching interaction necessarily differs in terms of affect, focus, and strategies for reading, writing, and comprehension.

2. Read professional literature that discusses the nuances of real-time online talk in various platforms: chat, whiteboard, mixed.

3. Practice your synchronous teaching skills with expert feedback from colleagues before trying them on live students. For example, role-play with a colleague by acting first as an attentive, helpful student and then as a recalcitrant one.

4. Consider how these strategies may be usefully applied to asynchronous conferences as well; try them out in simulated essay responses or problem-solving communications.

5. Understand that working with different modalities to get past a "stuck" or otherwise unhelpful conference doesn't represent a failure of the original modality. People often need to make contact in different ways depending on a variety of circumstances.

Caring for Students

Most writing teachers/tutors are passionate about conveying to students the pleasures of writing well and their own love of teaching. Because writing is such a personal experience regardless of the genre or subject matter, writing instructors frequently go the extra mile: helping students discover topics, showing them how to locate research sources, helping them reach out to their readers. Thus, it can be especially frustrating when instructors begin teaching online where they cannot see or hear their students as they work through the writing process. Because of this, many of the online instructors in Ehmann Powers' report wonder whether the instructional process is deficient when the instruction occurs online—particularly when it is asynchronous. This discussion of trust, therefore, would not be complete without considering what it means in practical terms to care for students in online settings.

Anderson writes in *How's It Going?*: "To teach writing well—to confer with student writers well—we must be affected by our students and the details of their lives. That is, we need to fall in love with our students for the first time" (2000, 189). Many of the writing teachers I know hold dear that very willingness to fall in love—or at least in "like"—with each student. It is a matter of being engaged with and by the student. This characterization would not sound silly or "touchy-feely" to composition instructors. But how does one enact such pedagogy in practical ways when teaching online? The point, I believe, must be to keep the computer-based conference from becoming merely a technical and mechanical process.

This book is grounded in the premise that both semantic integrity at the levels of word and intention and problem-based teaching are integral factors in strong online conferences. Additionally, it proposes a consciously eclectic theory/practice relationship in order to meet students at their points of need rather than to adhere rigidly to a specific ideology. I believe these are the most basic ways to demonstrate care for online students, but we can also do more.

For one thing, online instructors can form associations, or groups, with other educators internally in the same institutional setting or even externally; such external associations already exist in listservs like OWI-L, TechRhet, WPA, and WCenter. Interactions with educators in similar situations are a form of self-care; without it, one may feel isolated, making it difficult to sustain a caring stance with students. Hewett and Ehmann talk about association as a training principle that "attends to the human nature of online training participants by addressing affective, interactive, and collaborative needs that promote and assist the participants' *development as online instructors*" (2004, 18). In practice, it involves having methods (for example, listservs, IM or "cyber-watercooler" chat, and asynchronously shared reflective opportunities) for digitally communicating with others to create a sense of "team," or joint goals in the online instruction (2004, 17–20). Although topics for discussion generally arise from practice-based experiences, one potential discussion point regards how online instruction may differently represent one's teaching efforts. Some sample questions might be:

- Does it take longer to teach synchronously or asynchronously online? Is time spent with students measured differently using different media? If so, how?
- Are instructors more or less invested in online instruction than in traditional settings? Why or why not?
- Do online instructors worry about appropriation and/or "plagiarism" regarding online instruction?
  - In what ways, if at all, do such concerns reflect one's own epistemological beliefs? How do those beliefs play out in individual educators' practices?
  - How do such concerns affect students' needs and/or writing performances?

Another potential discussion regards the online instructors' perspectives of the students' roles in the conference:

- Are students a sharing partner in the conference process even when the online instruction is delivered asynchronously?
- How are students potentially disconnected from the conference process? Alternatively, how are students potentially connected to it?

- How do students make decisions about what advice to apply (or not) to their revisions and future writing?
- How do online instructors feel about students who do not use or appear to address all of the comments that are provided in a conference? (For example, is there a sense of students as "lazy"? If so, what would be a sufficient response to the lesson?)

Such discussions enable online instructors to form an association or working community while sharing ideas about important pedagogical and affective concerns, which will strengthen and support their innate capabilities to care about students in online settings.

Another way to enact one's caring for the online student is to accept the limitations of the medium and platform being used. Undoubtedly, the online forum is different from traditional educational settings. It is important to acknowledge those differences, as the discussion points above illustrate, while recognizing that difference does not necessarily mean deficiency. For example, as previously mentioned, many educators worry about the loss of body language, facial expressions, and verbal cues—their own as well as students'—in online settings. Yet, practical ways exist to enact caring and to present a human face in online settings:

- When necessary or useful, change media. For example, if the conference takes place synchronously and the online instructor senses that something is missing from the connection or that the student is less attentive than usual, a change of media might include an asynchronous communication like a private email or journal entry follow-up that recaps the session and asks for student feedback. If the textual lesson seems ineffective, then a telephone call or face-to-face meeting with the student might be appropriate. If more than one student's individual conference references the same kind of problem, then a synchronous group conference or an all-students lesson might help.
- Use student names frequently. While using student names helps to get and keep a student's attention in an online conference, it is also an effective way to demonstrate caring for the student. People like to hear their names used and, as we know, reading is hearing in online settings. Similarly, as appropriate, use details that students have revealed about their lives to maintain interpersonal connections—like talking about their animals or their jobs. Posting a photograph, biography, or video also adds to the human intimacy that can be created in online settings. Such visual and textual acts are phatic-like in that they backchannel the fact of the online instructor's presence in the conference.

- Remember that some students work best with a sense of anonymity, which the online setting nicely affords. In such cases, the intimacy level that is created through using names, life details, and photos may be more than sufficient to keep them engaged. For others, much less intimacy is desired. One student told me that having an asynchronous conference was like hiring someone to mow the lawn: It was a satisfactory transaction because he and the one who mowed the lawn did not need to meet in real time to ensure that each party completed the job right. Other students may never find enough intimacy in a completely online setting, preferring a hybrid setting where they know their instructors face-to-face as well as digitally. There is no "one size fits all" in the online conferencing environment, just as it does not exist in the traditional one. Likewise, the online setting accommodates a wide range of teaching and learning styles—sometimes perfectly and often imperfectly—just as any other setting would do.

Nothing can substitute for genuine caring in a writing conference, and to enable such caring, sometimes it is necessary to release other concerns. For example, if conferencing online is an educational activity that appears to be deficient when compared to traditional methods, it seems helpful to let go of that judgment while working with students and their writing. When the instructor is open to it, students will become the primary focus, irrespective of the medium. If a feeling of professional inadequacy emerges every time there is an online conference—asynchronous or synchronous—such instructors might need to stick with traditional instructional venues. Not everyone is predisposed to online teaching. Before walking away from online conferencing, however, please remember that doing so cuts off fruitful digital instructional forums that students increasingly will come to understand and expect in their education.

If conferencing online produces anxiety because of the inability to "fix," "correct," or teach everything that the student needs at once, the instructor likely needs a reality check. At all grades and levels, writing teachers must learn to accept flawed writing because all the problems can (maybe should) never be addressed. Anderson reminds us that any piece of writing is "bound to have several flaws. We have to make our peace with that inevitability" (2000, 166). Thus, it is a sign of caring for the instructor (and the student) to accept that not every detail can, or should be, addressed within a conference or even series of conferences. North, as noted in Chapter 1, has often been cited as saying that it is the writer, not the writing, that we teach (1984). Especially when teaching online, we need to remember that the writer learns through writing.

Before leaving the subject of caring, I want to discuss what it means to invoke a "conference voice." Anderson says:

> As I'm sitting next to students, I speak in my "conference voice." That is, I make sure that I don't talk louder that the student with whom I'm conferring, or than any of the other students in the nearby vicinity who are talking with each other about their writing. And I work hard to make sure that the tone of my conference voice is a respectful one, and expresses an interest in the content of a student's writing, as well as the work he's doing as a writer. (2000, 157)

What is a conference voice or tone in an online setting? How does one avoid talking louder than the student, who often speaks only through the writing in review? I suggest in this book that a conferencing tone is one of educational authority, whereby the online instructor owns expertise but allows for the student to develop his or her voice and message individually. It is respectful: The conference voice enables teaching in a straightforward, problem-centered way. It is a voice of semantic integrity. But this conference voice is bound to look and sound different to every online instructor, and so I leave this section with these questions: What is your online conference voice? How does it enact your care for students in online settings?

Conferencing Action Plan for *caring for students*

1. Become part of an association of online instructors, talking with them frequently as a way to explore the pedagogical and affective issues that arise in online conference settings.

2. Explore and understand the strengths and limitations of the online setting in order to find your own best methods of demonstrating your care for students.

3. Practice being personable, intimate, and friendly even while considering where and when it might be necessary to conference more formally or with a more authoritative stance.

4. Make phatic-like contact with students through such means as emoticons or backchannel cues that designate interest. Consider what a smile looks like in words or images such as smiley faces, <grins>, or other textual means.

5. Learn what your conference voice sounds like and use it with confidence. Your care for students will shine through.

Letting Students Care for Us

A very important way of caring for students is to allow them to see their online instructors as individuals, as people for whom they, too, can care. As Anderson says, "students need to fall in love with us, too" (2000, 190). Thus, some of the same strategies that enable on-line instructors to demonstrate their caring for students—calling them by name, using details of their lives, accepting flawed writing—also enable students to find their instructors to be interesting, worthwhile human beings. Students need to know what name to call online instructors, something about them, and that they, too, are writers who have strong and weak writing. Students especially need to know their online instructors *as writers* who make writing decisions and who want to convey a message through their writing. To this end, I recommend Robert Zoellner's wisdom, articulated in 1969 before computer conferencing was even a dream.

In his monograph arguing for a behaviorist pedagogy of composition, Zoellner writes about the scribal act and offers, among other strategies, the possibility of a chalkboard that would wrap around the classroom and on which the students could write their ideas while talking about them. In such a way, they would enact his "talk-write" theory of first uttering what one wants to say and then inscribing it. Indeed, until the 1990s, many people drafted their ideas by handwriting and some even handwrote their assignments, making the chalkboard scribally appropriate for such in-class writing activities. However, now that many people draft their ideas using a computer, that chalkboard, which provided an effective but technologically clunky tool, has been all but replaced by the computer, enabling vast amounts of shared writing space for common viewing. In such space, writers can share more sophisticated versions of their ideas whether or not they talk out those ideas first. Because much of Zoellner's theories should be of interest to educators who now have the tools to enact and test some of them, I will not argue their merits or limitations here. Instead, I will focus on one of the most practical strategies that he recommends—indeed, in daring fashion—to teachers who want to teach their students to write:

> It's even more important to see the enormous implications of modeling and vicarious reinforcement techniques for both present and future compositional pedagogies. Permit me to make my point in personal terms. During my own K–12 years, during my undergraduate years, and during the fifteen years that I myself have taught English composition, I have seen English instructors deliver lectures on rhetorical principles such as unity, coherence, and emphasis; I have seen them comment on the textbooks which develop such principles; I have seen them analyze textbook readings and student themes in terms of such principles; I have seen them hand out mimeographed materials of their own composing which illus-

trated such principles—but I have *never*, repeat *never*, seen a composition instructor, whether full professor or graduate student, walk into a composition classroom cold-turkey, with *no* preparation, ask the class for a specific theme-topic perhaps derived from a previous day's discussion and then—off the top of his head—actually *compose* a paragraph which illustrates the rhetorical principles that are the current concern of the class. The skiing instructor actually skis for his students; the pianist actually plays for his; the teacher of dance can occasionally be caught dancing. We English teachers, generally speaking, are different: as far as the students in our composition classes can see, we are very good at talking *about* writing, *but we never write.* (1969, 310–11)

"In short," Zoellner continues, "we never model the scribal act" (1969, 311). In all fairness, perhaps in 1969 this statement was correct, but since then, teachers have routinely modeled the scribal act in terms of writing and journaling with their students, blogging with them, and generally sharing writing more fully and freely in workshop settings. In one sense, then, contemporary teachers do model composing more frequently than in Zoellner's time. However, when it comes to students having the opportunity to view the actual unrehearsed act of writing at the basic, early draft stage, I suspect that it is rare for instructors to do much sharing. Zoellner says:

> Moreover, the entire class ought to have many opportunities to observe the talk-write instructor modeling the scribal act, which is a very complex behavior, involving such motoric elements as phrasing, rephrasing, hesitating, vocalizing, erasing, striking out, recasting, and even actually *failing* on first venture into the writing situation so that an entirely fresh start has to be made. (1969, 311)

Viewing these "motoric elements" common to any writer is extremely valuable to novice writers, who tend to think they should write perfectly the first time or that they are the only ones with such writing behaviors.

Long ago, much impressed by Zoellner's dare, I began writing for my students at least once each semester. Until computers and "smart cart" projectors, I wrote by hand on the chalkboard, always asking them for several topics from which to choose. Usually, we settled on a somewhat personal subject, which enabled students to see me as a human instructor who wanted to connect with them. Several times, however, I wrote about more general topics that they suggested; once it was about the qualities of the common types of drinking straw. Students inevitably remarked on my own tendencies to hesitate, return to previous sentences, and scratch out or add text. These tendencies remained even when I began typing my paragraphs using a computer and projector. Example 3.6A shows one of these typed paragraphs composed for students in its original form.

Example 3.6A
Sample Paragraph (Original)

My first year of teaching college English followed far too closely after actually graduating from college. I left college in Maryland in May and started teaching as a graduate assistant at Kansas State University in August. I was only three months older as a new graduate student than I was as a graduate! I was anxious about my knowledge, my students, and my ability to be a good teacher. The first thing I realized upon beginning to teach was that I didn't always know *why* what I said was "right" was actually right. It was like I had only an intuition about writing and not a really good sense of why things are good writing and why some things are weaker writing. Actually, that's true. I didn't know; I didn't have that vocabularie or depth of understanding that an experienced teacher would have about writing. The second thing I realized was that I was only four years older than my students. I could have been their big sister, but because I had just gotten married and was a grad student, I was Mrs. Hewett. What a change! In addition, I was scared by them: I didn't want them to find out that I was a fraud, that I really didn't know everything I should have known. And how could I even think to give them grades? I thought any bright student would find me out and report me to the dean—who was I to be teachihng them? If my worried attitude about the students wasn't enough to make me fearful everytime I walked into the classroom, then the fact that I was a student myself and learning from other professors how to teach was a third thing that really kept me anxious. I was getting helop from them, yes. But I also was being judged and evaluated by them, just as I was by my students. Sometimes, I had to fight the urge to walk out (or run out) of the classroom. Being a student helped me to remain aware of what it is like to be a student and that helped. But it also gave me a lesser place in the academic food chain. Students automaticxally would dismiss some of what I said merely because of my own student status. Somehow, I survived that first year and kept teaching; but even after 22 years in the classroom, I still have to remember that being a teacher is being a student, too.

After I completed the writing, which often took twenty to thirty minutes, we revisited the piece first to list some of my own scribal behaviors and then to both praise strengths and suggest improvements, taking the piece into more than one revision either on the board, via photocopied handouts, or later on screen. We highlighted the paragraph's topic sentence (see bold underline in Example 3.6B) and its key points (see bold phrases in Example 3.6B). From the revisions that I needed to make, we talked about how common those kinds of issues are in original pieces of writing—their own as well as mine. At some point, whether that day or the next class meeting, students saw my revision process via additions and deletions, as minimum revision operations. Example 3.6B illustrates my beginning revision of 3.6A.

Example 3.6B
Sample Paragraph (Revision Process)

I started ~~M~~my first year of teaching college English ~~followed far too closely~~ *far too soon* after actually graduating from college. I left college ~~in Maryland~~ in May and started teaching as a graduate assistant at ~~Kansas State~~ *a* ~~U~~university in August. I was only three months older as a new graduate student than I was as a graduate! **I was anxious about my knowledge, my students, and my ability to be a good teacher** *own status as a graduate student.* **The first thing I realized upon beginning to teach was that I didn't always know** *why* **what I said was "right" was actually right.** It was like I had only an intuition about writing and not a really good sense of why *some writing is strong* ~~things are good writing~~ and why some ~~things are~~ *writing is* weak~~er writing~~. Actually, ~~that's true.~~ I didn't know; I didn't have that ~~vocabularie~~ *vocabulary* or depth of understanding that an experienced teacher would have about writing. **The second thing I realized was that I was only four years older than my students.** I could have been their big sister, but because I had just gotten married and was a grad student, I was *"Mrs. Hewett" to them.* What a change *from just being "Deth"!* In addition, ~~I was scared by them~~ *they scared me:* I didn't want them to find out that I was a fraud, *and* that I really didn't know everything I should have known. And how could I even think to give them grades? I thought any bright student would find me out and report me to the dean—who was I to be ~~teachihng~~ *teaching* them? If my worried attitude about the students wasn't ~~enough to make me fearful~~ ~~everytime~~ *every time* I walked into the classroom, then **the fact that I was a student myself and learning from other professors how to teach was a third thing that really kept me anxious.** I was getting ~~helop~~ *help* from them, yes. But I also was being judged and evaluated by them, just as I was by my students. Sometimes, I had to fight the urge to walk ~~out~~ (or run) out} of the classroom. *On the positive side,* ~~B~~being a student helped me to remain aware of what it is like to be a student ~~and that helped.~~ But, it also gave me a lesser place in the academic food chain. Students ~~automaticxally~~ *automatically* would dismiss some of what I said merely because of my own student status. Somehow, I survived that first year and kept teaching; but even after 22 years in the classroom, *each time I begin a class,* I still ~~have to~~ remember that being a teacher is being a student, too.

Finally, we reviewed the piece in a more final form after I had worked on it at home, away from the classroom, just as the students would be doing with their own writing.

I presented them with my best shot at the topic, which—by the way—sometimes was not very good, and I would explain to students what satisfied me about the piece and what I would have liked to change if I had all the time in the world. The students then could begin to see me both as a person and as a writer, which allowed them to care

Example 3.6C
Sample Paragraph (Completed)

When I started my first year of college teaching, it seemed to be too soon after actually graduating from college. I left college in May and started teaching composition as a university graduate assistant in August. Only three months before, I was a student and now I was a teacher! I felt worried about whether I knew enough, whether my students would respect me, and how being a graduate student would affect my teaching authority. The first thing I realized when I began to teach writing was that I didn't always know *why* what I said was "right" was actually right. It was because I only had an intuition about writing and not a really good sense of why some writing is strong and why some writing is weak. I didn't have that vocabulary or depth of understanding that an experienced teacher would have about writing. The second thing I realized was that I was only four years older than my students. I could have been their friend or older sister, but because I had just gotten married and was a graduate student, I was "Mrs. Hewett" to them. What a change from just being "Beth" to everyone I knew! In addition, they made me nervous: I didn't want them to find out that I didn't know everything I thought I should know. My students actually were nice—helpful and generally willing to give me the benefit of the doubt. But still, I wondered how I could even think to give them grades when I didn't believe I knew much more than they did. If my worried attitude about the students wasn't enough to make me fearful every time I walked into the classroom, then the fact that I was a student myself and learning how to teach from other professors was a third thing that really kept me anxious. I was getting help from my teachers, but I also was being judged and evaluated by them, just as I was judging and evaluating my students. Sometimes, I had to fight the urge to walk (or run) out of the classroom. On the positive side, being a student helped me to remain aware of what it is like to be a student (and how much I wanted to get away from classes and homework sometimes). But, it also gave me a lesser place in the academic food chain. I thought that students automatically would dismiss some of what I said simply because I was a student myself. Somehow, I survived that first year and kept teaching; but the lesson I took from that year was an important one for me. Even after 22 years teaching, each time I begin a new class, I still remember that being a teacher is being a student, too. There's always room for me to learn more.

about me and encouraged them to let me care about and teach them. Example 3.6C illustrates a completed piece.

Typically, in their final evaluative remarks about our class, some students commented positively about this writing experience and what it taught them about their own writing processes. Professionally speaking, I always learned something from their comments and silently thanked Zoellner for daring me to stretch and reveal myself.

My point with these examples, of course, is that with computers, educators have much more flexible tools for conducting such writing demonstrations. In conferences, these writing demonstrations can occur in a variety of ways:

- Asynchronously, the instructor can prepare some of his or her own writing to share, much in the same way as the earlier mimeographed pages. In such a case, where spontaneity is limited, online instructors should ask students first for a series of topics from which to choose, which provides immediacy to the writing.

- Synchronously, the potential for using this kind of writing opportunity grows.

  □ For example, in chat, the online instructor might ask the student to offer a topic about which to write and then the instructor can write a short piece—limited only by textbox size and/or time for the conference. Mistakes and typos can remain and the discussion can be about the kinds of strengths and weaknesses that the completed piece shows. Then, it seems fair to ask the student to do something similar. A student's courage to risk mistakes can be bolstered by the online instructor's demonstrated writing.

  □ In a whiteboard or document-sharing setting, the online instructor could show the students the writing as it occurs, if the whiteboard is real time in nature or has a familiar document appearance (some whiteboards only show the text after "enter" is clicked, like IM chat). Since some boards afford group viewing, the conference can include multiple student viewers and their comments can better represent what happens in a traditional classroom.

  □ Moreover, in a whiteboard setting, it is often possible to import an asynchronously produced piece of writing, inviting student comment on it, and then revising for students in real time. This activity, again, shows students both the writing process and something of the online instructor's self that lets the students practice their caring about their teacher.

There are nearly endless ways to incorporate self-writing for students in online conferences. Over time, such technological tools as flash video will become more simple and common, enabling additional modalities to the interaction. However, the lesson remains the same. As Anderson states, "And when students see us not only as people, but as people who write about their lives, they know we have something in common to talk about—the work we do to make pieces of writing about our experiences" (2000, 191). Enabling students to care for us through our writing means taking risks, but such risks can make us memorable in students' eyes.

Conferencing Action Plan for *letting students care for us*

1. Feel free to tell students by what name you prefer to be called and sign yourself on and off a conference that way.

2. Consider it fair play to give students some way to care about you as a human and as a writer, always keeping in mind your own comfort level and not becoming uncomfortably or inappropriately personal.

3. Take Zoellner up on his dare: Write for your online students and make lessons from your own writing processes and products. You'll learn as much about yourself as a writer as they will about themselves.

4. Especially for those who teach entirely online or who are tutors in a supplemental or learning assistance setting, talk within your association of peers about other ways to let students care for you.

Chapter Four

Theories for Writing Response in Online Settings

Responding to Writing

One of the reasons conferencing online can be difficult is that whatever is written will be read as the message. If one writes hastily or unclearly, the potential for misunderstanding increases. For example, in a recent online course, I wrote the following directions for an online class discussion: *Write original responses to at least two subconferences and respond generously to at least three peers' posts.* A student emailed asking what I meant by "original responses to at least two subconferences." In rereading, I agreed that the directions were unclear—a by-product of writing them just before midnight. I rewrote: *Choose two ideas/questions to which you want to respond. Then, write original responses to those "subconferences." Finally, respond generously to at least three peers' posts.* If the student had not alerted me, the entire class might have been baffled by the assignment.

Like writing directions, online conferencing about student writing has much in common with responding in traditional settings. Clarity is essential, for example. When essay response is an instructor's primary contribution to either an ongoing or one-time conversation about writing *and* when that conversation and its attendant teaching occurs entirely online, message clarity seems more crucial, particularly in pedagogies that value dialogue:

> If students are having difficulty understanding the teacher's written communication in a face-to-face course, they can simply ask the teacher to clarify; in an online course, that option is not available. These problems are not only frustrations, opponents argued; they are also blocks to learning. (Peterson 2008, 381)

Such potential blocks to learning online emerge not only from burning the midnight oil, as my poorly written directions show, but also from failure to write explicit and directive comments—comments that are typically more interventionist than in face-to-face teaching and tutorial sessions. I understand that some teachers and tutors resist making such comments on student writing, but this reluctance can create confusion and negatively affect student learning especially in online settings. I think this reluctance to be forthright in teaching students can be traced to three conceptual theories: (1) expressivism, (2) social construction, and (3) postprocess. Important as these theories are, I believe they have had unfortunate consequences for one-to-one online teaching and tutoring.

Expressivism and OWI

In the 1960s and 1970s, expressivist theory reversed the instructor's presumed authority over student writing that had been so prevalent in current traditional theory and pedagogy, causing many teachers to be both less directive—or "dictatorial"—and less authoritative about qualities they sought in "good" writing. As Christopher Burnham explains: "Expressivism places the writer in the center, articulates its theory, and develops its pedagogical system by assigning highest value to the writer and her imaginative, psychological, social, and spiritual development and how that development influences individual consciousness and social behavior" (2001, 19). A number of instructors employ expressivist approaches to help students become self-aware, reflective, and self-expressive, and to "heal" in terms of "fostering personal development, in the great Socratean tradition of 'knowing thyself'" (Fulkerson 2005, 667–68).

Pedagogically, the expressivist approach is reflected in an acceptance of the student's vision as found in his or her writing. Rebecca Moore Howard says that expressivist rhetoric is facilitative:

> One of the values of expressivist peer-response pedagogy is that it not only removes the teacher from directive instruction, but it also prevents students from assuming that role in their responses. Instead of offering each other untrained and often incorrect instruction, peer respondents assume the role of reader and give the writer a heightened sense of audience. (2001, 60)

Peer work, therefore, often is seen as an ideal corrective to a teacher's supposed tendency toward directive instruction; it is a key approach for online peer instruction as well.

Writing center pedagogy is indebted significantly to expressivist thinking. Muriel Harris, for example, promotes writing center tutorials as expressivist, indicating that tutorials are designed to get writers to discover their own writing issues and ideas, whereas, she suggests, peer groups provide information to the writer in a more directive way (1992, 376–77). The issue becomes the autonomy of the writer versus the ways that peers might express themselves directively (for example, *"change this verb"* or *"proofread your writing"*).

For OWI, as in traditional classes, an expressivist approach has often meant that student writing primarily should receive nondirective and affirming responses from instructors. One typical view is offered by Leigh Ryan and Lisa Zimmerelli, in *The Bedford Guide for Writing Tutors*, who state that "written comments [as opposed to oral ones] can also be perceived as being more authoritative, permanent, and directive than intended" (2006, 76); similarly, Andrea Ascuena and Julia Kiernan believe that it is important to "teach consultants how to resist what technology encourages: short directive statements and, thus, positions of authority." Perhaps, but I agree with Howard, who says in relation to writing center interactions: "the policy of noninterventionism is, however, 'ethically suspect,' for it constrains the potential learning experience" (2001, 58). Noninterventionism leads to strained instructional practices whereby much of writing instruction can seem impossible. Particularly in online settings, expressivist instructors often hesitate to inform writers about how best to express themselves. Sometimes they simply offer a recital of nonspecific "truisms" about the writing process that may or may not hold true (for example, *"Most people expect to see a thesis sentence at the end of an introductory paragraph"* or *"Focusing on your content means not digressing"*). Although they can talk generally about the writer's content, they will not say how to resolve what appears to be a problem or what next steps to take, since doing so might "co-opt" the writer's authority to choose the writing's content and form.

Because of the primarily hands-off attitude about directive instruction, many instructors—and especially tutors trained in contemporary writing center theory—attest that their job is to guide or facilitate the student *indirectly* to become a better writer, leaving the content and form of the text to the student and enabling the instructor to avoid the risk of "appropriation" (Sommers 1982; Greenhalgh 1992; Howard 2001).[1] *Appropriation* is a word that teachers/tutors often use to represent a negative act; such use may have originated with Nancy Sommers' 1982 seminal essay, "Responding to Student Writing," where she states that *"teachers' comments can take students' attention away from their*

---

[1] Ann Moser's study of OWL tutors provided an interesting example of this practice: Participant 1 wrote primarily reflective feedback to her students, while Participant 3 adhered fairly strictly to an expressivist questioning pedagogy designed in part to broaden idea development while adding no specific revision guidance.

own purposes in writing a particular text and focus that attention on the teach-ers' purpose in commenting; the teacher appropriates the text from the student by confusing the student's purpose in writing the text with her own purpose in commenting" (1982, 149, italics in original). In other words, instructors appropriate student text "particularly when teachers identify errors in usage, diction, and style in a first draft and ask students to correct these errors when they revise," which gives a disproportionate importance to surface errors at the wrong part of the writing process (1982, 150). Stephen North echoes these concerns in his canonical article, "Training Tutors to Talk About Writing." He states that the "greatest bugbear" of novice tutors is the need to "master in tutoring an appropriate sense of control, an ability to identify and pro-mote direction without taking over from the writer" (1982, 437–38).[2] Contemporary theory and practice often define appropriation as taking away student autonomy while dictating control. Unfortunately, this definition leads instructors to be ineffective when teaching students online (see, for example, Straub 2000; Greenhalgh 1992). Even when students indicate that they prefer directive commentary because it helps them learn how to strengthen their writing, instructors often ig-nore these preferences on the grounds that *any* directivity or potential appropriation is a negative pedagogical act. Ernest Smith's research, for example, demonstrated that students preferred his directive commen-tary on their writing if they could not get into a one-to-one conference with him; yet, despite the students' preferences for occasional direc-tive instruction, he assumes that prescription and direction are never an acceptable approach (1989, 258–59). My experience is that OWI instructors need to intervene more directly to be effective. Without careful but explicit direct instruction, online instructors essentially are handicapped in the ways they can respond that will prove helpful.

Social Construction and OWI

Social theory, a product of the 1970s and 1980s, takes the view that knowledge is socially bounded and constructed—relative to the com-munity that engages it.[3] While social construction also espouses non-directivity and nonappropriation of student text, it focuses particular attention on a renegotiation of authority from the individual to the group. Further, it promotes writing as a form of inquiry among co-learners (see, for example, Onore 1989, 248.).

---

[2]North's use of the adjective *appropriate*, a verb for Sommers and many since her, is meant to address "control of a dictatorial kind" that "is fairly easy to exert" (North 1982, 438).

[3]See, for example, Bruffee 1984, 1993; Straub 1996, 1997, 2000; Onore 1989; Smith 1989.

Howard explains that in the 1970s, "[i]ndividualistic teaching methods proved ineffective for the new population of nontraditional university students, whereas collaborative pedagogies such as peer tutoring answered their needs" (2001, 54). Writing center administrators and tutors are major proponents of social constructionism. While many pride themselves on being eclectic pedagogically (Hobson 2001, 175, 178), they ground their work primarily in the social constructionist epistemology:

> Peer tutoring is the means through which collaborative learning has played its most prominent role in shaping writing center theory and practice. Peer tutoring as a form of collaborative learning assumes that helping other writers to learn to handle concepts and skills more effectively creates an education system built around a community of learners instead of single authority figures. (2001, 171; see also Hewett and Ehmann 2004, 31–53)

Beyond peer tutoring, the social constructionist approach values the pedagogy of educational collaboration through peer response groups, classroom discussion, and collaborative writing projects. Thus, in part it offers itself as a corrective to expressivism, which some social rhetoricians critiqued—seeing "expressivism's primary flaw as a false and otherworldly epistemology of the self that privileges individualism and rejects the material world," consequently directing "students away from the social and political problems in the material world" (Burnham 2001, 28).

According to Hewett and Ehmann, social constructionism has been an important grounding theory for OWI (2004, 38):

> Philosophically, OWI and its attendant instructional methods are a natural outgrowth of, and commitment to, the social constructivist epistemology, which anticipates that writing development can emerge from frequent sharing of student texts and discussions about those texts. The innovative factor is that OWI instructional settings engage the social element textually (and, increasingly, graphically), rather than orally. (2004, 41)

They suggest that "over time, as many people have posited a productive connection between social theory and OWI, this perception may have developed into a perceived cornerstone of OWI" (2004, 45). Indeed, technologies for OWI especially support online discussions, text sharing, and peer response, as well as access to online writing centers.

Interestingly, some educators who might otherwise favor social constructionism worry that it can lead to plagiarism. Howard says: "so firm a grip does the solitary author have on modern representations of writing that collaboration is sometimes perceived as plagiarism—as cheating"; this perception actually reinforces "the long-accepted model of the individual author" (2001, 55, 61). She explains that although such resistance is less frequent than it once was, "it continues as a palpable counterforce to collaborative pedagogy" (2001, 55). Further-more: "Teachers throughout the university, while wanting their students to become better writers, are also concerned that their students not have others 'do' their writing for them; they may regard collaboration as plagiarism"—or as a misappropriation of others' ideas or words (2001, 58). Outside of obvious cases of duplicated essays, inadequate citation, or outright theft discovered by plagiarism-detection software, classroom writing teachers who encourage collaboration may be reluctant to address such appropriation because if it is noticed at all, it occurs in a gray area where it is not always possible to know from whom or where the ideas or words originated. Regarding writing centers, according to Irene Clark and David Healy, the "response to such suspicions has been to embrace a pedagogy of noninterventionism that precludes both the appropriation of student texts and any challenge to teachers' authority occasioned by questioning their judgment of a writer's work" (1996, 32). In either case, a problem emerges for OWI because textual sharing of both individual and socially constructed ideas among students and instructors would seem to favor such appropriation as a desirable use of the collaboration.

A different sense of appropriation is one found in linguistic (Mortensen 1992) and some composition studies (Spiegelman 1998; Hewett 1998, 2000; Hewett and Ehmann 2004). In this different sense of the word, writers who collaborate—as they are expected to do in peer writing groups and tutorials, for example—may "read their essays aloud, and often they appropriate sections of each others' texts and re-figure them in their own papers" (Spiegelman 1998, 250). Hewett empirically classifies such appropriations as direct, intertextual (imitative and indirect), or self-generated (1998, 164), and finds through textual analysis that the students in her study actually appropriated others' texts *less* frequently when they conducted their peer work online than when they collaborated orally. Furthermore, given their collaborative tasks, they did so naturally and without expressing any conscious sense of having misappropriated others' ideas or words. Hewett's findings suggest that we should reconceive the notion of appropriation as a suitable or even desirable action when writing is shared between online instructor and student, as well as among peers—particularly when developing pedagogy specific to OWI.

Postprocess and OWI

In both the expressivist and social constructionist epistemologies, writing can be interpreted as somewhat unteachable because it is considered unique to the writer, relative to the group, and unpredictable in nature. Ideas about teachability, individuality, relativity, and predictability can lead to worries about what is possible to do for and with students in online as well as traditional settings. In this context, being noninterventionist seems safe. Concerns about teachability also abound in postprocess theory as first articulated by Thomas Kent. He argues that "no codifiable or generalizable writing process exists or could exist," which translates to many as a suggestion that writing cannot be taught (1999, 1; see also Flower 1994).

For many compositionists, postprocess theory means that writing cannot be taught because this theory opposes the notion of "mastery" of writing and supposes that "process" presents itself as "content" to be mastered; but, if process is not a "content," then it does not lend itself to teaching. Hence, there is no particular pedagogy of postprocess theory although a focus on dialogue often emerges (Kastman Breuch 2003, 105, 120). The result is a theoretical movement that eschews the process-based approach to writing while promoting different types of content as the subject of writing. Therefore, other subject matter is introduced into the writing classroom, through, for example, cultural studies (George and Trimbur 2001, 82–85) and "critical" or liberatory pedagogy (George 2001, 92); such subject matter creates a distinctly noninterventionist writing instructional setting.

Not surprisingly, Richard Fulkerson, among others, holds that: "composition studies is a less unified field than it was a decade ago. We differ about what our courses are supposed to achieve, about how effective writing is best produced, about what an effective classroom looks like, and about what it means to make knowledge" (2005, 680–81). Diana George and John Trimbur similarly perceive lack of agreement as to what precisely comprises postprocess approaches to composition. They describe a broad range of disciplinary interests and ideologies as falling under cultural studies such as: "encoding/decoding studies, ideological critiques, microethnographies, literacy narratives, networked classrooms, contact zone pedagogy. Its interests, moreover, overlap with other significant currents in composition studies, especially feminism, race and ethnic studies, and queer theory" (2001, 86). The result of such disagreement, according to Nancy Welch in *Getting Restless*, is that the teaching of writing itself receives short shrift:

> [Alice] Jardine (1989) reminds me that these declarations and charges, the creation of yet more boundaries between compositionists, don't arise from a gaze that is cool and detached. They are very much enmeshed in networks and transference—of investments and projections, of desires and fears, of attachments and displacements, all played out according to age-old cultural scripts of alliances and enemies. (1997, 5)

Welch worries that writing instruction, especially revision, is ignored (1997, 24), a particular problem in OWI if instructors fail to respond to student writing in ways that are instructive.

Eclectic Approaches and OWI

With expressivism, the student's personal growth, which is valued through language and written words, can lead instructors to wonder what they can say to writers that honors one's singular vision. Educators are warned not to appropriate student writing for their own purposes of providing a different vision for the piece, which includes their view of what a corrected piece would be. A social constructionist pedagogy read narrowly can be interpreted as "collaborate, but do not appropriate." This injunction seems all the more powerful in an online setting whereby the sharing is accomplished textually and students may fear both being accused of plagiarism and of being plagiarized themselves. Additionally, there is an attempted leveling of instructional hierarchy that is intended to strip from teachers any pretense at authority, yet that authority is always obvious in their duty to evaluate and grade student writing. For online tutors, a different authority—that of having specialized knowledge about writing—is difficult to hide, but some attempt to do so anyway in order to link contemporary practice with theory. The apparent loss of teacher authority that results from postprocess approaches to the teaching of writing also can have significant consequences in the online setting. Indeed, current discussions in scholarly literature and research studies focus less on the nuts and bolts of writing, while interactions with students tend to be discussion-based and various "methods" or "processes" for teaching writing one-to-one fall by the wayside. These three theories leave students teacherless when the instructor abandons teaching authority and becomes invisible to ongoing self-development, collaboration, or critical thinking. Yet, as this book argues, an instructor's authority need not be disowned. Drawing on Paulo Freire's ethos as a well-known proponent of liberatory pedagogy, Ann George tackles questions about the nature of authority and what authority a teacher does or should have:

> A teacher, by definition, has authority; for a teacher to deny that authority, Freire claims, results in license, not liberty. For Freire, it's important to distinguish between authority, which teachers must have, and authoritariansm, which is the abuse of power—a distinction that's easy enough to understand if not always to apply. Sometimes, however, radical educators work so hard to explain away teacher' obvious authority that their language could set off a doublespeak alarm. (2001, 105)

Despite all of the good that expressivism, social construction, and postprocess have accomplished, they have left many online instructors operating in a vacuum that offers them few strategies for conferencing with students about the essence of their writing. Content can be discussed and even disputed, of course, but how can students be assisted in their writing and rewriting without learning to deeply rethink and revise their own texts? And how can online instructors be comfortable in their pedagogy when they are denied the power of their own voices, of their own earned (and necessary, according to Freire) authority? How can they authentically conduct their work when forced to speak in highly guarded words that tiptoe around writing concerns?

My research and experience lead me to conclude that online writing instructors need to be eclectic: They need to use any and all effective strategies from any and all epistemologies. Welch, for example, finds value in various pedagogics, from Ann Berthoff's double-entry notebooks to Peter Elbow and Pat Belanoff's log writing and Sondra Perl's open-ended composing process:

> These theorists tell me we need to remain at the intersection between "process" and "post-process" conceptions of composing, not quickly push past that intersection, not call one side the "past" and the other the "present." We need more border talk between the classroom practices and detailed case studies of the 1970s and 1980s, and current calls for institution-wide revisions of community, genre, academic discourse, and academic authority. (1997, 163–64)

Online instructors can find the same values in examining the approaches to which they are most drawn and then adding strategies that complement them. Doing so can enable them to use their voices to their students' best interests as developing writers.

Rhetorical approaches, for example, can help teachers/tutors teach about audience, purpose, argument, genre, and discourse communities (Fulkerson 2005). Classical approaches can address issues of ethos, pathos, and logos. Process approaches can focus on drafting and revision, and so on. Even those who consider themselves radical educators can adapt some rhetorical or cognitive approaches purposefully to teaching writing and apply them in online settings.[4] These approaches are complementary to various tenets of contemporary theories that lead to such practices as de-centering classrooms, setting up collaborative student interactions, and using critical subject matter. And, all of these approaches can be adapted for one-to-one online conferences.

Regardless of the approaches taken, however, responding to writing online is particularly challenging primarily because what one writes does not merely represent the instructional voice; it *becomes* that voice. It is unfortunate that the act of teaching itself—of intervening into a student's writing—may be interpreted as a negative, unkind, or appropriative act rather than a natural part of the conference process. I call

---

[4]Cognitive theory tends to view students more systematically by describing the writing process through the similarities and differences between novice and expert writers (see, for example, Flower and Hayes 1980, 1981; Flower 1979; Flower et al., 1986).

instead for an epistemological approach that embraces accuracy, brevity, and instructional ethos, and that recognizes the potential for fidelity between words and meaning in an online interaction. For teachers/tutors in text-based settings, one *must* be able to say what one means and, similarly, one *must* be able to mean what one says. Equally, students *must* be able to trust what they are reading. When applied inappropriately to online settings, contemporary composition and response approaches developed in traditional settings can choke the instructor as speaker. As a remedy, I think an eclectic approach can free the instructional voice and empower it to do the work that students want and need.

In the online setting, to deny one's teacherly voice—whether as teacher or tutor—is to be rendered mute, leaving students without the instruction that they want. Using one's voice, in contrast, does not mean usurping student authority or co-opting their writing, giving them the answers, or neglecting potentially critical issues. Such a voice has, as this book argues, characteristics of semantic integrity:

First, strategic online commentary is systematic and problem-centered, focusing on identifying a few select writing issues rather than identifying many issues in a scattershot manner. Problem-centered interactions intervene by: (1) being focused; (2) tying together the major writing issues by addressing, identifying, and teaching to them; (3) showing how certain problems affect the text as a whole; (4) modeling good writing; and (5) teaching a lesson that requires some responsive activity on the student's part. In addition, such interactions address the skills that students need to improve more generally as writers rather than all the various revision changes that would benefit a single piece of writing. In a problem-centered approach, online instructors are consciously aware of the theoretical constructs that ground their practices and adjust them to students' needs rather than adjusting students (or their writing) to the theories.

Second, online instructors have the responsibility to share their thinking straightforwardly and respectfully with students, providing next steps and possible new directions for the content and context of the writing, all the while encouraging thoughtful student choices and accepting fair use of collaborative interactions in written products. Generally, students need to be taught about—and not given answers for—form-based, surface considerations in order to provide corrective strategies for addressing stylistic and mechanistic infelicities; they also need to be taught about content development relative to genre, organizational strategies, and other concerns necessary for expressing ideas both within and outside of academic genres. Focused attention to writing process and product can work together in an online instructional interaction to help students with particular pieces of writing and to provide permanent learning aids applicable to their future writing.

Finally, online instructors who are experienced in various ways of addressing writing development may have the easiest transition into OWI because there is a significant learning curve associated both with learning to teach writing and learning to teach writing online. Since even instructors who are experienced in traditional settings can feel challenged when adapting to online instruction, less experienced instructors may need additional guidance and practice. Particularly helpful are asynchronous and synchronous simulations with other online instructors who can provide feedback.

Chapter Five

First Steps for Writing Response in Online Settings

Know What You Are Talking About

High-quality online instruction is systematic and problem-centered in nature. For example, one reliable system for focusing the instruction on both strengths and weaknesses is to first think about higher-order concerns like ideas (fluency) and organization (form), and then look at lower-order concerns like surface issues (correctness). These criteria are not particular to the online setting in that good writing instruction always involves focusing on what students most need as writers, and it always requires instructional skill, precise vocabulary, selective teaching, and so on. Yet, such criteria, especially in light of the asynchronous modality's relatively low interactivity between instructor and student, are critical in online settings. Furthermore, while archived or "saved" interactions can benefit both online instructors and students, they make a less-than-perfect instructional interaction endlessly available to a student who uses it for revision. Thus, it is important to have command of the subject.

Example 5.1A features the writing of a student that I studied to learn more about one-to-one conferences. In this example, an online tutor responded to Michael's writing; other examples in this chapter and the rest of the book represent either a tutorial or classroom teacher-to-student conference. Unless otherwise noted, my thoughts apply whether the instructor was a teacher or a tutor.

The tutor offers embedded commentary about a "paragraph." Forgetting for a moment that the student has, in fact, represented one "sentence" as a paragraph, let's consider both the problem and the advice offered. Taken out of context of other paragraphs, it does seem odd

Example 5.1A
Student Michael (Paragraph and Embedded Commentary)

It will assess the current status of animal cloning, including outcomes of previous trials whether knowledge of assisted reproductive technologies can be applied to cloning a human criteria that should be used to evaluate the safety of human cloning and public policy issues, including responsible conduct of research. **[1] A paragraph should never be one sentence long. [2] Consider splitting this sentence.**

that this sentence is presented as one paragraph. Generally, student writers are encouraged to provide supportive detail that develops each paragraph's topic, which in turn develops a main idea or thesis. The tutor does not teach any of those concerns here, however. Instead, in comment 1, he states that paragraphs "should never be one sentence long" and in comment 2 that the student should "consider splitting this sentence." The first piece of advice is teaching lore that prohibits the novice writer from doing what experienced writers frequently do. Usually there is a good reason hidden in such lore; for example, Michael needs to learn how to write fully developed paragraphs that support his thesis before departing from the norm. To a degree, then, talking about a one-sentence paragraph is a responsible action—if the instruction is correct in substance. The second piece of advice is even less helpful than the first, however. What does it mean to "split" the sentence? Is this set of clauses, in fact, a sentence by common definition and boundaries? Where would Michael split it? And, if the sentence were split, would the paragraph then be okay?

In this case, the student has not received adequate instruction. Bringing broader context to this isolated example, one can see with Example 5.1B that the tutor has missed more than one opportunity to address Michael's paragraphing and sentence structure.

The tutor has pointed to Michael's second sentence as one that is missing a word. Yet, he either has ignored or failed to notice the "run-on" of Michael's first sentence, and he has pointed to the fourth sentence, which many would recognize as a comma splice, as a "run-on." He has provided no in-depth instruction about a run-on here or in the general comments, where he said, *"You have quite a few run-on sentences that need to be addressed and revised for clarity. Check the following links [to the online handbook]."* Although he has guided the student to a writing handbook, he has made no distinctions among the sentence he noted as a run-on and those sentences he overlooked. Finally, a cursory glance shows that Michael's second paragraph also is only one sentence long. In fact, a comparison of the two single-sentence paragraphs

Example 5.1B
Student Michael (Three Paragraphs and Embedded Commentary)

So because people don't know about cloning does it make it okay? Is cloning not bad as it seems? **[1] Missing word.** Is it just another experiment that needs to be done for glory? To me cloning is definitely wrong, trying to duplicate an image or person is wrong. **[2] Run-on sentence. [3] Also, it seems to me that duplicating an image is much different then duplicating a person. [4] What do you mean by image?** Only the man upstairs is allowed to make or create people, by giving Adam, and Eve and all other humans and animals privates to reproduce. **[5] Consider using a different word than "privates." [6] It seems a bit informal and slangy for an article.**

But because of confusion outside the scientific community concerning the differences between human cloning and embryonic stem-cell research, the study also will explain the distinctions between these two endeavors. **[7] Are you referring back to the previous study here? [8] Consider making that clearer. [9] Also, consider mentioning the difference between these two things so your reader has some idea what you're talking about.**

It will assess the current status of animal cloning, including outcomes of previous trials whether knowledge of assisted reproductive technologies can be applied to cloning a human criteria that should be used to evaluate the safety of human cloning and public policy issues, including responsible conduct of research. **[10] A paragraph should never be one sentence long. [11] Consider splitting this sentence.**

with the first paragraph in Example 5.1B suggests an even bigger issue: The second two paragraphs do not seem to have the same author as the first one, suggesting that Michael has not learned how to paraphrase or cite sources yet, which leaves him open to charges of plagiarism. We will consider this issue later in Chapter 7, but for now, let's look at some of the major writing issues that Michael's online instructor could have chosen to address from these three paragraphs alone:

- Idea development
- Paragraphing (how they look and paragraph-writing techniques)
- Source integration, quotation, paraphrase, and citation
- Sentence structure
- Proofreading strategies

Of these choices, what is an appropriate or helpful response will differ in various instructional settings and contexts. The student's assignment, for example, likely will suggest what the teacher finds important at this stage in the semester or in the student's development. Any previous interactions with this student also will provide a clue as to

Example 5.1C
Student Michael (Original Sentence and Revision)

Original: *"So because people don't know about cloning does it make it okay?"*

Revision: *"To me cloning is definitely wrong to duplicate an image or person is wrong. Only the man upstairs is allowed to make or create people, by giving Adam and Eve, it seems as, if people don't know a lot about cloning it make it okay?"*

what the student most needs to address next. For our purposes, it is most important to acknowledge that while instructional responses may vary, they must be adequately instructive and provide correct information.

Not surprisingly, out of Michael's twelve revision changes to this essay draft after the conference, only four responded to the conference's instruction. Michael had not changed any of the above-outlined issues in his submitted revision. Instead, he responded only to comments 3 and 5. Unfortunately, the revision was even less comprehensible than the original.

Examples 5.1A and 5.1B demonstrate an online instructor's failure to address some basic issues in a student's essay; Example 5.1C reveals that the student, too, failed to address revision substantively and carefully. Although the instructional interaction attempted to intervene, it did not create positive change, most likely because the online instructor did not show that he knew what he was talking about. Just as important, he was not teaching in a systematic, problem-centered manner, but rather in a scattershot attempt to catch errors, a strategy that interfered with presenting a coherent lesson to the student.

Conferencing Action Plan for *knowing what you are talking about*

1. Get experience in face-to-face conferencing. Then, decide how those skills need adjustment for a text-based online conference.

2. Practice online conferencing in both asynchronous and synchronous modalities with other online instructors.

3. Learn how to instruct in systematic and problem-centered ways (for example, addressing fluency, form, and correctness, or higher- or lower-order concerns).

4. Learn enough about writing to be able to recognize and teach basic idea development and surface writing issues.

5. Look for patterns of error or stylistic, structural patterns that, when revised, can improve the piece of writing significantly.

6. Then, become familiar with more challenging writing issues and learn how to teach about them.

7. Keep a handbook, either a hard copy or online version, at your fingertips when teaching online. Use it both for your own edification and for teaching lessons.

Use Vocabulary Specific to Writing Instruction

When conferencing online, it is essential to use vocabulary that clearly conveys writing conventions, instructional expectations, and how to achieve them. Usually, when I use written language to talk to a student—or to colleagues—about writing instruction, I reread my messages closely for precision, accuracy, and clarity. The example that began this chapter shows that I am not always successful; often, I need to revise several times to get my expression right. Sometimes my writing, including my commenting, may seem overly formal, but I prefer formality to lack of clarity. I imagine that other online instructors have had similar experiences. Regardless of our knowledge, we must always guard against writing relatively unhelpful comments to students. In such cases, we fail to help them to revise in part because we fail to specify through our vocabulary what is in need of revision, how to revise it, and—at times—the expectation that a meaningful revision must address particular issues. Examples 5.2A and 5.2B demonstrate the need for specific vocabulary.

Example 5.2A
Student Robin (Partial Paragraph and Embedded Commentary)

This excitement occurred only to the youngest. The most innocent of hearts, a connection that was embraced only if you couldn't tie your own shoes, knew nothing about multiplication facts, and spent your Saturdays watching Big Bird on Sesame Street. **[1] This sentence is a little unclear to me, [2] can you revise?** A feeling I find hard to describe, a rare association with a fantasy, a dream equipped with all the belongings of a childhood, one that holds all the wants, all the desires I could fantasize about as a girl of eight. **[3] Good description, but this is a run-on. [4] Might break it into more than one sentence, or add some conjunction (i.e., "and") to help link all the clauses.**

In Example 5.2A, Robin has written a series of fragmentary claus-es that are almost poetic in their description of childhood innocence. Her words evoke memories of a childhood only recently past, which the online instructor rightly calls "good." With this one vague and qualified statement of praise, these embedded comments reveal their primary weakness. The online tutor did not specify what is "good" about Robin's description. More important, she did not use any rea-soning or support for her comments. For example, in comments 1 and 2, the online tutor did not specify why the earlier sentence is "a little unclear to me" or why and how Robin should attend to her rhe-torical question, "can you revise?" In comments 3 and 4, she failed to specify why the sentence is a "run-on" and how or why Robin might "break it into more than one sentence" or why adding "some conjunction" (and *precisely* what that is) would help.

In this case, Robin's revision reflected an unclear understanding of what was expected from her. Example 5.2B shows her revised sen-tences; like Michael's revision, it is no clearer than the original version.

In response to comments 1 and 2, Robin deleted the phrase *"A feeling I find hard to describe, a rare association with a fantasy, a dream."* In a permutation, where she both rearranged and substituted words, she wrote, *"A girl of eight could fantasize about"* to *"I as a girl of eight."* Robin was remarkably devoted to revising her essay; she made an amazing ninety-seven revision changes to her draft. Only sixteen of the total changes were connected to the conference, however, and of these some were incorrect or rhetorically insignificant. The online tutor missed an opportunity to help Robin with deep revisions in large part because of imprecise vocabulary and failure to specify what Robin could do to improve. At the very least, the online tutor needed to say why the sentences were "unclear" and that Robin had written fragmentary clauses linked by commas. What makes them so poetic, so descriptively "good," is their use of adjectives combined with a lack of verbs that would characterize them as standard sentences in the first place.

Example 5.2B
Student Robin (Partial Revised Paragraph)

This excitement occurred only to the youngest. The most innocent of hearts, a feeling that was embraced if you couldn't tie your own shoes, knew noth-ing about multiplication facts, and spent your Saturdays watching Big Bird on Sesame Street. A dream equipped with all the belongings of a childhood, one that holds all the wants, all the desires a girl of eight could fantasize about.

Whether it was a momentary error or a genuine deficiency of instructional skill, as Examples 5.1A and 5.1B indicate, calling the second
series of clauses a run-on was imprecise. Had Robin included verbs in
her clauses, she would have had a series of comma splices, which in an
English course likely would have proved problematic. Thus, even had
the online tutor addressed the core issue, it is unlikely that her mis-
labeled advice *could have helped* Robin. Certainly, the advice to "break
into more than one sentence" (which, along with "splitting," seems
to be a standard piece of advice when instructors are unsure of why a
"sentence" is not working) or to add a "conjunction" *did not* help her.
Robin did not receive completely bad instruction because some of it
was on-target and led to some correct and rhetorically helpful revision.
However, had the tutor used specific, precise, and accurate vocabulary,
Robin would have been better able to improve her writing. Without
that use of language, even the most willing student like Robin cannot develop consistently strong revisions that demonstrate evolving
writing skills. For novice writers especially, commentary that uses and
defines specific, precise, and accurate vocabulary is critical to online
instructional success.

> **Conferencing Action Plan for *using vocabulary
> specific to writing instruction***
>
> 1. Learn how *to write about writing*, using vocabulary that
>   conveys:
>   a. Writing conventions,
>   b. Instructional expectations, and
>   c. Help on how to achieve both.
>
> 2. Practice these skills with expert feedback from colleagues
>   before trying them on live students.
>
> 3. Be specific, precise, accurate, and consistent with your
>   feedback.

Write at the Student's Level

It is important to use language that is not too "academic" or otherwise
beyond the student's comprehension level. Some online instructors
worry that they may have only this one chance to help a student on
a particular piece of writing. This concern, although often unfounded,
should be sufficient reason to address students at a level they can understand. My analysis of student revisions compared to their conferences

Example 5.3A
Student Sam (Introduction Paragraph)

Imagine this, you are driving home one evening after work. You are tired and hungry and you just want to get home. Suddenly, out of nowhere five deer come crashing down the hill and into your car. The car totaled and you hit your head off of the window. Two out of five of the deer are dead and the other three are injured and probably will not survive. Why do you think this happened?

Example 5.3B
Online Instructor General Comments about Sam's Introduction

[Introduction/Conclusion] **[1]** The case scenario you present in the first paragraph to catch the reader's attention is certainly compelling. **[2]** However, I am not sure your audience will automatically be able to understand what connection it has back to your discussion on hunting. **[3]** If you want to use this material, I would suggest referring back to it and why it pertains to your topic.

[Organization] **[4]** Also, it seems the overpopulation problem might be a place where you could refer back to the case scenario and explain why this highway scene you open the essay with is affected by hunting or the lack of it. **[5]**

strongly suggests that they respond best to short sentences, repetition, and familiar vocabulary (or, at the least, contextually defined vocabulary) in the commentary. Example 5.3A shows Sam's introductory paragraph to an essay. Example 5.3B shows two places where the online instructor provides global, general commentary about it. Although apparently well-considered advice, in this case it seems to have been written beyond what the student could understand.

In the comments connected to the Sam's introduction and conclusion (Example 5.3B), the online instructor used three phrasings that might be challenging for a less-prepared student. Comment 1 used the phrase *case scenario* and the word *compelling*, while comment 3 used the word *pertains*. Even though comment 4 referred again to a case scenario and even though such repetition generally is helpful, it is likely that Sam was unable to connect the idea of a case scenario to the story, or vignette, that he provided as an introductory paragraph. Sam was in a developmental writing class. While it is important not to assume that novice writers have certain vocabulary abilities just because of their course levels, the potential for lack of clarity in textual settings suggests that it is best to define the terms in context or to use noncomplex vocabulary. For example, to further define *case scenario*, the online instructor could say, "*In your opening paragraph, you use a 'case scenario,' or example, to introduce your readers to why people hunt and to get them interested in what you're going to say next."* Similarly, the online instructor could use *convincing* or *gripping* as substitutes for *compelling*; she could use another synonym or in-context definition for *pertains*.

Further, because the major point of the instructional interaction is to provide commentary that teaches and responds to the writing, it is vital to use language that students can understand; indeed, online instructors often can take their cues from the student's writing. This paragraph alone reveals that Sam did not have sufficient control of punctuation and verb tenses. If we can improve students' vocabularies without interfering with the conference's major purpose as instruction, then it is a bonus.[1]

In this case, the online instructor's main point was to encourage the student to make internal connections within the essay to the opening example. While Sam did not do that in his revision, it really is not important that the student made a different choice in revising; that is what authorial ownership is about and our instructional advice is, in the long run, just that—advice. And, although it is possible that Sam may not have valued the online instructor's commentary, it is more likely that he did not understand it or that he did not agree with it. He made thirty-three revision changes in this draft, but only four of them were connected to the conference. Interestingly, three of these four changes altered the meaning of the essay in significant ways, which indicates that Sam was willing to listen and revise beyond surface-level changes. Thus, particularly in asynchronous conferences, when students typically do not provide feedback as they might in a face-to-face setting, online instructors should examine the revisions against the conferences, looking deeply into the unapplied commentary for clues to the student's thinking. Then, when possible, instructors should check directly with their students to confirm their understanding.

---

[1]Sometimes, a vocabulary lesson actually stems from an attempt to obfuscate one's own authority and to deny one's ability to read student writing as it was intended. Ascuena and Kiernan (2008) provide this advice for tutors in acknowledging a writer's "agency":

> Take for example the two following statements: 1) *You need the word "granted" here rather than "granite"* and 2) *I'm a little confused here. Do you mean granite (like the type of rock) or granted (like it is assumed by most people)?* In the first statement, a consultant is an editor who assumes authority over intention whereas in the second statement, the speaker is a reader who asks for clarification from the authority of the intended meaning.

Undoubtedly well intended and typical of the expressivist agenda found in many writing centers, the recommended version is regrettable in that the writer's context surely enabled the instructor to discriminate between granite and granted. In essence, this vocabulary lesson wastes both the instructor's and student's time for the limited benefit of correcting a single misspelling. Chapter 7 and Appendix 2 further explore this phenomenon.

Conferencing Action Plan for *writing at the student's level*

1. Use short sentences, repetition, and familiar vocabulary.

2. Especially when tutoring, learn to recognize the student's level from contextual clues like the course number, as well as the strengths and weaknesses of the writing.

3. Define complex terms and writing-based terminology in the sentence.

4. If you learn that the student has not used your feedback or lesson in revision, review your advice to see how you might have written it more simply, clearly, or precisely.

5. When possible, talk to the student to learn more about why the student chose not to use that particular feedback or lesson for revision.

Choose Desired Outcomes

Perhaps the most important strategy regarding online instructional content is that of making conscious choices about what to address according to the outcomes we hope to achieve—picking our battles, so to speak. Even though the conference is occurring online, whether asynchronously or synchronously, it is the student—a human on the other end of the interaction—who is being taught and not the piece of writing. It is equally important, of course, to make the distinction that the student is being taught *through* the piece of writing. An online instructor needs to realize that even if this is the only opportunity to provide help, the student can only absorb so much feedback at one sitting, which is why I recommend limiting any conference to a thirty-minute average (see Chapter 7). Further, if the issues that the online instructor has chosen to address follow a reasonable system of priorities (such as considering first fluency of thought or content, then form, and then correctness), a few idea-based revisions might eliminate the student's need to address other form-based concerns. And if correctness is a major issue, as often seems to be the case, then the online instructor may be able to help the student more by addressing and teaching only one major concern—in a problem-centered manner—than by identifying numerous errors for the student. As Anderson says about conferences: "Once we've given students feedback, we teach. We teach students *one* technique or *one* strategy or *one* concept" because to teach more can be overwhelming despite their needs as writers and because there are always other students who need our attention, too (2000, 60).

Indeed, it can be helpful to think about conferences in terms of parts with goals for each part. In an asynchronous conference, for example, one might consider the following parts:

- Student:
  - □ Providing context about the assignment and other background information;
  - □ Asking for particular kinds of help; and
  - □ Submitting the writing.

- Online instructor:
  - □ Reading the writing for strengths and weaknesses and
  - □ Responding to the student by:
    - Greeting the student,
    - Writing specific details about one to three genuine strengths that warrant praise;
    - Providing a targeted amount of specific feedback about how the writing needs to develop from the higher-order and/or lower-order concern perspectives;
    - Teaching a mini-lesson about one specific issue that, if addressed, would help the student to strengthen the writing;
    - Including a series of specific and doable actions or next steps that the student can undertake in revision;
    - Arranging or asking for future conferences if needed; and
    - Closing by signing off the conference.

Particularly in an asynchronous interaction, the onus is on the student to retrieve the conference and to apply it to his or her writing.

On the other hand, a synchronous conference might have the following parts:

- Greeting each other;
- Determining the focus of the conference;
- Asking the student to write an example of the concern, such as a thesis, brief outline, sentence, or phrase;
- Providing appropriate feedback, including praise where warranted;
- Teaching a mini-lesson that addresses the problem;
- Giving the student opportunity and space to try out the skill or issue being taught—in other words, getting the student to enact the lesson in writing;
- Including a series of specific and doable actions or next steps that the student can undertake in revision;

- Arranging another meeting if needed; and
- Mutually signing off.

Finally, a word about praise is useful here. My observation, supported by research into numerous conferences and revisions, has been that students do not revise where there is praise. They may read even qualified praise (that which has an overt or implied "but" or "however" statement directly following) as a signal that nothing further needs to be done. Therefore, it is critical to offer clear, specific, and unqualified praise only where it is warranted. Further, it is helpful to explain to students why that writing is praiseworthy so they might use it as a model for future writing. When praise is thus contextualized, critical feedback that reveals a need for revision can be read without the potentially confusing addition of qualified praise.

Having considered these parts to the conferences, let's focus on the specific strategy of choosing desired outcomes for the session. Such outcomes will be expressed both in specific critical feedback and a mini-lesson that teaches one issue pertinent to the student's writing and/or writing process. Examples 5.4A and 5.4B address the strategy of choosing the desired outcomes for the session.

Example 5.4A
Student Francis (Paragraph and Embedded Commentary)

I really did not know what to do after I got off the phone, I tired to calm down so, that I could actually talk to my friends that were there. **[1] Check comma use. [2] Also, you've used the wrong word here.** Finally, my sister came and got me from my friend's house. After, I had called almost everyone in the family to find out what is going on? **[3] Check punctuation.** All, my sister could say was mom is at the hospital cause Joel had a heart attack this morning. All I wanted to know at the time was he ok, and is he going to be ok? The reason why I was so up set is because this guy was so special to me. I never really had a dad and he had been a part of my life for almost three years. He was the only did that I had in my life. **[4] Wrong word use.** He really and still does mean allot to me. **[5] Misspelled word.** Finally, My sister and I got to the hospital, and we found my mom and the rest of the family. I ran up to my mom and gave her a bug hug. **[6] Misspelled word.** I could not believe what was happening it was like a dream. **[7] Comma use.** All I wanted was Joel to be ok, and the family to be happy again. **[8] You start a lot of sentences with "All." [9] Consider varying your sentence structure and starting sentences in different ways so your writing isn't repetitive.** We waited in the waiting room forever it seemed like. That was because we were all worried and wanted everything to be ok.

There are a lot of surface errors in Francis' paragraph, many of which the online instructor addresses. In Chapter 6, where I discuss expression, I talk about such comments and return our attention to this example. For now, I simply want to indicate that the instructional language using imperative and declarative statements about formal issues and other problems appears to have been helpful, particularly in the context of the whole interaction. In his general comments, the online instructor connected these formal issues and explained them further, as Example 5.4B shows.

In this case, the online instructor was clear about what the problems were (sentence-level mechanical and grammatical errors), what Francis needed to do (check the embedded comments), and why she should do that (to clarify the writing for readers). He signaled to the student that he knows what he is talking about, used adequate vocabulary, and spoke to the student at her level. In revision, Francis addressed all of the formal issues that the online instructor noted in embedded comments. However, she missed every single surface error that he did not notate. This result suggests that the instructor needed to go a step further by teaching a mini-lesson about the most persistent of the surface errors with which Francis had trouble, such as comma usage. In such an approach, the online instructor would have chosen the desired outcomes for his formal instruction rather than using a scattershot method that caught some annoying formal errors and not others.

By choosing the desired outcome, the instructional interaction would be focused on some of the sentence-level issues and not others. Additionally, by picking *core* issues, others likely would have been cleared up in revision. For example, comments 8 and 9 in Example 5.4A refer to Francis' repetitive uses of the word *all* to begin sentences. This is a good call as far as it goes: Using *all* to begin sentences three times in one paragraph is redundant and not helpful rhetorically. That the online instructor noted the repetition signals a certain level of competence on his part. However, he missed another important teaching opportunity with the statement, "*Consider varying your sentence structure and starting sentences in different ways so your writing isn't repetitive.*" Sentence variety

Example 5.4B
Online Instructor General Comments re Francis' Formal Errors

Grammar & Mechanics: You have a lot of mechanical and grammatical errors in your paper—particularly on the sentence level. Please go through and check my comments. My primary concerns were your use of commas, misused words, and awkward wording. These are concerns because at times these issues made it difficult to follow what you're trying to say, and so it's hard for the reader to follow your paper.

would help, as would eliminating the redundancy of *all*, but a student like Francis who misspells common words and has difficulty with run-on sentences and coordination most likely will not know how to vary sentence structure. In fact, even though repetition in this case was more a stylistic problem than a rhetorical strength, the online instructor would have done well to guide Francis in overhauling each of these sentences, which probably would reduce the use of *all* anyway.

Among other issues in this paragraph, Francis was writing excitedly, possibly recalling the drama and anxiety of the moments she described. She did not seem to understand how to use dialogue, and so she inserted dialogue into the sentence without any punctuation to distinguish it. Similarly, she did not seem to know when she had stated the idea of a question or whether she actually had asked a question, which resulted in faulty uses of the question mark. Further, she seemed confused both about internal sentence boundary markers—which led to comma splices—and about how to use commas after introductory phrases and clauses. To be effective, the online instructor could have selected this one paragraph as his focal point for both idea-based and formal outcomes, analyzed the core issues, and written a mini-lesson. This mini-lesson could have used one of the student's sentences in an example, explained why it is problematic for readers, shown different ways to revise it, and then asked her to revise other similar sentences. Example 5.5 demonstrates such a mini-lesson.

Example 5.5
Problem-Centered Mini-lesson on Sentence Construction

Francis, let's look at paragraph 2 together. There is a lot going on in this paragraph. I can almost hear the upset and excitement in your sentences. For example, you wrote: "*All, my sister could say was mom is at the hospital cause Joel had a heart attack this morning.*" In a way, the sentence sounds just like what your sister might have said; for example, you use "mom" and "cause" (instead of "because") to show your sister's speech. Do you want this sentence to be dialogue (i.e., your sister's actual words) <u>or</u> to represent what was happening less directly? Here is a <u>revised example</u> of both:

- *Dialogue: All my sister could say was: "Mom is at the hospital! Joel had a heart attack this morning."*
- *Sentence: All my sister could say was that our mom was at the hospital because Joel had had a heart attack that morning.*

Can you see the difference in the <u>phrasing</u> and <u>punctuation</u> when you express what happened in dialogue and in a sentence that represents what happened? Notice that in the beginning of the dialogue example you would be narrating and then showing with <u>quotation marks</u> what your sister said. When you write that same information in a sentence, however, the <u>verb tense</u> about Joel's heart attack changes and there are <u>no quotation marks</u>.

Let's try another sentence from this paragraph: *"All I wanted to know at the time was he ok, and is he going to be ok?"* In this case, you are mixing up two <u>questions</u> with <u>sentences</u> that represent questions you thought to yourself. If these are actual questions that you want to show with <u>question marks</u>, they need to begin with <u>question words</u>: *"Is he okay? Is he going to get better?"* You could write another sentence before these questions to indicate that these were your concerns: *I wondered: "Is he okay? Is he going to get better?"*

Francis, to improve the sentences in this entire paragraph, <u>try these steps</u>:

- *Reread each sentence and ask yourself whether it conveys, or shows, <u>one main idea</u>.*
- *Also <u>ask yourself</u>: Does it make a statement? Does it ask a question? Does it indicate dialogue?*
- *<u>Mark each sentence</u> that might not be as clear as it can be.*
- *Then, <u>revise</u> it using <u>precise words</u> and <u>punctuation</u> appropriate to your message.*
- *You can send your original and revised paragraphs together in one document for <u>another online review</u>. Be sure to explain what questions you have.*
- *Then, when you have made this paragraph as clear as you can, <u>work on the rest of your essay</u> in a similar way. You may have to add or delete some ideas to make other ones more clear, but that's ok. It's part of the writing process.*

I look forward to seeing another draft of this paper soon, Francis!

The student's task, in other words, should be both clear and doable. The problem-centered approach should give the student practice in a skill that she could use throughout this draft and in future writing. By choosing the desired outcome(s), the online instructor eliminates focus on a broad variety of concerns and may, of course, risk the student making new errors, but that is a risk worth taking if the instruction is written to develop the student's understanding about writing overall.

> ### Conferencing Action Plan for *choosing desired outcomes*
>
> **1.** Don't try to address every problem in the writing in one interaction; instead, consciously pick your battles knowing that the students cannot address every issue in a revision either.

2. Remember that you're conferencing with a student, not the writing. There's a human on the other end of the computer.

3. Also remember, however, that you're conferencing with a student *through* the submitted writing and *through* your own writing. The student has to understand what seems obvious to you, and he or she has to do it through text, with which the student may not be especially comfortable or fluent.

4. Provide unqualified praise where it's deserved, as well as specific critical feedback in each conference.

5. Teach one problem-centered mini-lesson in each instructional interaction about the most significant, or core, writing concern.

6. Give the student a revision task (or series of next steps) that is both clear and doable. Checklists can be especially helpful.

Writing Mini-lessons and Next Steps

Although I have tried to demonstrate what I mean by mini-lessons, a few things remain to be said. There can be no doubt that using mini-lessons and writing a series of doable next steps in online instruction are key strategies for choosing outcomes in the conference; these strategies apply some of the best practices in response to student writing. Richard Haswell states that the purpose of response is not "the mere grading or evaluating of a piece of writing but further the recommending of ways to improve it" (2006, 1). So, too, Sommers reiterates an old position in a twenty-five-year retrospective of her seminal "Responding to Student Writing": "Criticism is not enough; like praise, it has to be paired with instruction" (2006, 252). She continues: "By giving students a generalized sense of the expectations of academic writing, teaching *one* lesson at a time, and not overwhelming them by asking them to improve all aspects of their writing at once, instructors show their students how to do something differently the next time" (2006, 253, italics in original). These educators leave no doubt that instruction through explicit teaching is a primary goal of teacher response.[2]

Example 5.6 takes the mini-lesson approach and applies it to a higher-order concern about writing an argument intended to convince.

---

[2]See also Richard Straub (2000) and Erika Lindemann (2001, 235).

This student's essay draft contextually follows two previous essay assignments that practiced summarizing and using secondary sources in support of a thesis. The student has had lessons in assertion, or thesis, writing. Now the preliminary draft reveals that he is having difficulty writing a thesis in an argument setting. The mini-lesson is intended to help him see the difference between what he has written and what he needs to write. The next steps are intended to guide his revision, which might seem insurmountable to him because he has to begin again with a focus on researching the problem. Although the instructor could have written much more, it is up to Dylan to take the lesson and run with it. The invitation to another conference and to use resources like his classmates' feedback and the online writing center offers him ways out of a potential morass and into a productive writing process.

Example 5.6
Problem-Centered Mini-lesson on Academic Argumentation

Dylan, I admire your passion about the topic you've chosen. Clearly you've thought about it a lot and you have a good idea of what you want to argue. Your topic is an important one.

There's a fundamental difference between having passion and making a good academic argument, however. This essay assignment is intended to teach you how to write an academic argument, which isn't an opinion piece. As the assignment explains, you are to have **earned your opinion** by virtue of researching the issue. Unfortunately, I don't see any evidence (except one possible place that I marked) that indicates you've researched. It might be helpful to think about this draft as a way to have gotten your "opinion" out of your system. Your next job is to substantiate your thinking with evidence from other sources. Remember how you had to provide evidence from the texts for Essays 1 & 2? That requirement hasn't changed except to become more important!

For example, instead of writing the following: *Everyone is worried about how early our under age children are sexually active and how easily they dismiss questions of morality and sexual health. But actually, we have done this to ourselves and we have created these problems ourselves.*

Support your statements: *According to XYZ (Date), parents are* "worried" [use a quote that makes sense from your source] *by how early our underage children are sexually active and how easily they dismiss questions of morality and sexual health. (p.X). These concerns lead them to blame others for the problem, However, parents themselves are responsible for XYZ.* [XYZ becomes your assertion, Dylan. Make sure it's supportable with evidence from your sources.]

Next steps:

1. Return to the examples I provided you as model essays for this assignment and also to the essay I wrote for you in the beginning of the course. Notice how each statement is supported by some kind of evidence from outside sources. You must do the same.

2. Determine which sources would be best for your argument. I discuss how to do this in your assignment sheet, and your textbooks also discuss this task.

3. Look in your current draft for your possible assertion and for potential topic sentences that you'd need to support in a revision. I've highlighted some possible ones for you in your draft. The mini-lesson above also provides an idea.

4. Pay attention to what your peers are telling you, too.

5. Revise to develop an essay that has a clear assertion/thesis in the end of the first paragraph, clear topic sentences that are supported not just by your beliefs but by evidence, an organization of the arguments that makes sense logically, and a conclusion.

6. Follow the assignment's directions about using APA style for your internal citations and bibliography and having a separate page for the title page and the bibliography.

7. Work on the sentence level for the entire revised essay. (For example, "adolescent" needs to be pluralized with an "s" wherever you mean more than one and it only needs capitalization when it's in the beginning of a sentence or in your title).

If you need special help, let me know and we'll arrange a conference chat. Your classmates Susan and Rick would be really good sources for help, too; you could email them or chat with them. You also could use a tutor's help from the Online Writing Center.

Enjoy revising, Dylan! It's how we all get to be better writers.

Another conference strategy necessary to developing strong mini-lessons is to provide a series of next steps at the end of the commentary, as evidenced in Example 5.6. Giving students next steps makes especially good use of problem-centered teaching. Providing specific, doable next steps is an effective method for teaching revision and for creating conceptually and qualitatively strong conferences—perhaps because the instructors who write them are comfortable with their role as teachers and tutors in online settings. In fact, next steps lists can help develop clarity for *both* the online instructor and the student especially when involved in complicated interactions. The very act of writing the next steps forces the instructor to conceptualize the student's job in concrete terms, which often is what students most need for beginning to revise.

Students tend to pick and choose among the next steps lists, electing to perform some steps and not others, an act that speaks to their ownership of their writing. While revision choices ultimately are up to the student, the instructor should explain some of the most important decisions that the student could make. It is always up to the student to decide whether to take this advice, and, if the instructor has been clear and straightforward, it generally is not a reflection on the conference if the student decides not to follow the advice. Indeed, as research into revision practices demonstrates, the student also generates his or her own ideas and is influenced by his or her peers and other readers outside the online or on-campus instructor or tutor, so the online instructor's guidance may be only one of several kinds of support that a student receives on any one piece of writing.

In Example 5.7, the online instructor advises the student about revision strategies and gives the student a potential plan in a general order of importance to follow. They are not generic statements of advice; instead, they are targeted specifically to the individual student's needs and they are phrased in clear, straightforward language, an issue that Chapter 6 and Appendix 2 address in detail.

Example 5.7
Next Steps

Next Steps:

For your revision, I suggest the following steps:

- Review each paragraph carefully. Does its message convey what you want readers to understand about you as a writer? How does it address the writing process over the assignment—or vice versa? Consider making some deep changes in the writing to clarify your message.

- Get an honest opinion from your favorite peer readers about what you're trying to do here. Do they think you succeed? Why or why not?

- Pay attention to verb tenses and choose which tense makes most sense here. I mention this in embedded comments below.

- I know part of the point of the essay is that you write until you are finished. And you indicate that you purposefully edit the beginning of the paper but not the end. But the intent of the essay would come out more clearly without the errors I see (for example, "other" for "mother"). Proofread and edit carefully throughout so that annoying typos, misspellings, and incorrect punctuation won't detract from your main point about loving to write (or are you actually saying that you hate assignments?). Try reading very slowly out loud to catch these errors.

I look forward to reading the next draft of this essay!

When combined with a targeted mini-lesson, a series of doable next steps like these offers students a powerful opportunity to learn productive revision strategies for their writing.

Conferencing Action Plan for *writing mini-lessons and next steps*

1. In addition to critical feedback, write mini-lessons about one core issue in the student's writing.

2. Be sure to explain the problem and teach one or more ways to fix the problem.

3. Give students a series of doable tasks as follow-up revision steps. Decide on three to four specific tasks from which the student's writing would most benefit.

   a. Write each task as a direct speech act, not just saying *what* to do but also *how* to do it.

   b. Make sure that each task is clearly explained and doable in the next revision draft.

   c. Close the next steps with a positive statement that welcomes or encourages a next meeting or draft submission.

Chapter Six

The Orneriness of Language

What Students Say They Need in Conference-based Commentary

To develop an epistemological language along with accuracy, brevity, and instructional ethos, we need to address how and why our written conferences do not always meet that mark. Language can be an ornery beast, but ultimately, its use is connected to what we think about those on the receiving end. If we see students as people who need to retain their authority at all costs, then our language will reflect that belief. If we are uncertain about how to balance our own authority as teachers/tutors with students' authority as writers, the language of our conferences will reflect that belief, too.

Greg Ahrenhoerster and Jon Brammer question whether educators have the right to "maintain our obsessions with pet theories or our advocacy of process/dialogue approaches when only select students are benefiting from that experience" (2002, 4). In other words, the theory might sound good, but how well does it work in practice? I think that noninterventionism, appropriation without collaboration, and a belief that process is not teachable have become such pet theories and that they have engendered damaging, noninterventionist pedagogies, often without sufficient study of their actual effects on students and their writing. Thus, in order to understand just how selective these benefits of "pet theories" and "approaches" are, we must consider student views.

A questionnaire is one way of asking online students "How's it going?" as Anderson urges teachers to do in conferences. The following selected student responses come from an informal questionnaire that sought open-ended feedback about the commentary they had received from online tutors and whether and how they used it in their revisions.

All of the tutors also were college-level teachers in other traditional and online settings. The patterns in the student responses offer compelling evidence of both successful online instruction and problematic language related—I think—not to tutorial roles but rather to epistemological concerns.

Students' General Writing Concerns

Many of the students point to formal issues as one of their major writing "problems." They name such issues as grammar, organization, sentence structure, word ordering, citing references, addressing awkward wording, and correcting grammar and spelling. For example, some students say they sought the online instruction:

- *"To get help with grammar, organization, etc";*
- *"Tense shifts and clarity of my writing because without clarity there would be confusion";*
- *"Grammar and commas";* and
- *"I used the advice on sentence structure problems and problems with grammar and spelling."*

That students value help with formal issues like grammar and mechanics is not surprising; Hewett's study of their general revision practices related to asynchronous conferences confirms that the students she studied most frequently applied feedback regarding formal issues to their revisions (2004–2005).

However, it is important not to overemphasize students' stated needs about formal issues. Students also request and apply advice regarding the content of their writing and writing processes. They often want help with idea-, context-, and organization-based concerns. One student sums up: *"I needed the extra help. It was very resourceful. I believe it offered my writings more depth in the arguments."* Other responses include:

- *"The tutors helped me in the interior text of my essays. Many of my thesis statements needed work. The tutors helped with my assertion and direction of my text block according to the thesis";*
- *"I used a lot of the brainstorming and counter-argument advice they gave me";*
- *"I used the help with essay-development ideas I ask for help about, i.e., content development, introduction, and conclusion";* and
- *"They helped me with outlines to develop supporting details."*

When asked whether they used the conference advice in their re-visions, some students assert that they felt empowered to retain their authorial ownership and make choices:

- *"I mostly used the advice that we agreed on"*;
- *"[I used] Some. Just the advice that I considered helpful"*;
- *"B/c I saw the mistakes that I made that I didn't see beforehand"*; and
- *"I looked at there [sic] comments and if it made sense and I agreed that it need working [sic] that area then I used their suggestions."*

Of course, some students are less self-confident, and although their writing does not show evidence of relinquishing ownership to the on-line tutors, the less experienced writers in particular express a ten-dency to make decisions based on an instructors' authority:

- *"Because I needed the opinion of another experienced writer in order to correct my mistakes"*;
- *"Mainly where they show [sic] where I had errors in my paper, I use their advice because I know that I am not able to get rid of all my errors by myself"*;
- *"Everything that was suggested I tried to use because they know what they are talking about"*; and
- *"I changes [sic] what they said was wrong and rewrite some sentences. I also was instructed to break some paragraphs apart and I did."*

Students' Criticisms of Instructional Language

As the example conferences in Chapter 2 show, online conference-based instructional commentary has many of the same characteristics as other essay response aimed at writing formation. The goals of critical feedback and a mini-lesson are to give the student a personal response and to specifically address and teach about their most pressing needs as writers. The major difference is that for some educators—like most dis-tance online teachers, digital graders/evaluators, and online tutors—the context is completely textual. Thus, the semantic choices of the online commentary can make or break the interaction. An online instructor who might have an impressive knowledge of composition pedagogy or exceptional academic writing skills still can have an unsuccessful online conference. *How* one expresses the commentary online (which includes the subtext of *why* the instructor has chosen certain commu-nicative strategies) can be as important as *what* one says.

Especially intriguing are student responses to a question about how their online instructional experiences could have been improved.

Nearly a quarter of the surveyed students indicate dissatisfaction or puzzlement related to language choices that the online instructors used in their teaching interactions. These critical remarks point to at least three separate issues. First, they reveal concern about online instructors responding to their writing with "questions" instead of "answers." Second, they express a need to be given information and writing advice in a more "clear" manner. Third, they express a desire for more complete "help" that addresses "solving" or "fixing" a problem.

The first type of comment reveals potential problems with online instructors' questioning strategies:

- *"I feel that there were times that they never really answered my questions; instead they asked me questions in return";*
- *"Some of the tutors didn't just say what was wrong but instead asked me questions and that didn't always help me";*
- *"It could have been more helpful if the tutor would have specifically helped me instead of asking too many questions. . . .";*
- *"If they would have taken more time to answer specific questions I asked."*

The second type of remark indicates that instructional comments sometimes are not clear:

- *"It could have been more helpful if more advice was given and worded in a clearer way";*
- *"Sometimes I thought they would ramble a little or try to teach me an English lesson";*
- *"Sometimes it wasn't clear enough, like I didn't know what they meant at certain times";*
- *"The advice could have been more clear in how they said things";*
- *"It could have been more explanatory";*
- *"If they would tell me more clearly."*

The third type of remark indicates that students sometimes receive inadequate help:

- *"She could have told me a little more on what I should have in my paper."*
- *"More specifically what needed to be changed";*
- *"If they would have highlighted more problems and told me how to fix them";*
- *"Give examples in the essay that show to be problematic";*
- *"Suggesting words in place of others";*
- *"Instead of just pointing the problem, they could've helped solve it";*
- *"Maybe giving me more examples."*

Are these students' comments very different from what many students say about their tutors' or teachers' classroom instruction or written feedback provided in traditional instructional settings? I don't think so. The online setting, however, is more sensitive in that many times what has been written to students is the only instructional contact they receive. In that sense, it is important to understand that even those online instructors who feel relatively comfortable with their online roles may express concern about whether students can understand their intended meanings. Ehmann Powers, in her study, says: "one respondent reported that OWI was viewed to a degree as an exercise based on 'assumptions' about how students would understand his written instructional cues" (2003). Thomas Batt agrees with this concern. He says of any written commentary:

> . . . any response must recognize the possibilities, even probability, of miscommunication between student and teacher. The teacher may misread the student text, the student may not have communicated his intention, and the student may misread the teacher comment, which itself may not perfectly communicate the teacher's intention. And neither may be paying full attention to their own text as they write them. (2005, 214)

Similarly, we should pay particular attention to these students' criticisms because they respond to totally *textual* comments. If online instructors are writing commentary that puzzles students or that otherwise might be construed as ambiguous, and especially if there appears to be a pattern to such responses, then it is critical to consider such ambiguity as a *text*-based phenomenon. Indeed, whenever teaching occurs through text, if the text puzzles students, then teaching and learning are blocked.

Do such criticisms from students indicate that they want online instructors to do their work for them? If so, then such student desire would justify using the "hands-off" and "don't give the student the answer" instructional approaches that I argue against in this book. Certainly it is possible that some students are lazy about their own learning. But frankly, that has not been my experience in teaching writing students; when I see, hear, or read puzzlement, I sense more that there is a genuine desire to learn. When I have followed up with the puzzled students in an online chat or a phone call, they have shown themselves as eager to talk about the problem. I think, therefore, that we need to read such critique with open minds and a goal of generating solutions for the problems that these student comments reveal.

Direct and Indirect Speech

In this next section, I show what potentially troublesome comments look like and offer my thoughts about why educators would write them. When I examined over 200 asynchronous and synchronous teaching interactions, searching for potentially problematic utterances and analyzing their language structures, I found that some instructional comments really are ambiguous in terms of what the writing issue is or how the student should address it. The least clear comments are what the study of pragmatics calls *indirect speech acts* that I understand to function as *suggestions*. *Direct speech acts*, which generally function as assertions and commands, tend to be clearer to students.

Direct speech acts are relatively simple to discern in written commentary. For example, the declarative statement usually consists of a *subject + verb phrase* and offers information like *essay titles are capitalized*. The form of a declarative matches its function, which is to offer information. Exceptions exist, such as *"I don't know how to read this?"* where the question mark does not indicate a question so much as an intentional emphasis on the information offered—that is, that the writer is unsure of something. With imperatives, the subject ("you") usually is suppressed and the verb takes precedence, revealing an *unstated second person subject + a verb phrase* (for example, *"Use a dictionary."* Or *"See your professor about documentation."* Or *"Please contact me after class."*). Again, the imperative form matches its function to command. The interrogative usually reverses the word order to *verb + noun phrase + punctuation (question mark)* (for example, *How do I write a new thesis? Is the grammar correct?*). The expected word order also matches its function to ask a question. Exceptions exist here, as well; an example exception is one that tends to be stated orally, but that also might appear in a synchronous forum like IM: *"The grammar is correct, yes?"*

Indirect speech acts are harder to identify because they depend on context and intention to promote purposeful communication. Their form can be that of a declarative, imperative, or interrogative, but their function tends to be to offer information or to command with rare genuine elicitation. Such mixtures of form and function lead to a lack of clarity in what tend to be read as suggestions. Indirect statements can be subjunctive mood or conditional (if/then) statements, and they may include an auxiliary modal verb with or without a modal verb or intensifiers like *really* and *actually* (for example, *Do you* really *want to say that?*). Indirect speech often communicates through indirection, which—particularly in written instructional text—may lead to mixed messages and communicative misfires because the intended meaning often is not what the recipient infers it to be. Appendix 2 provides more information for recognizing and understanding the reasons for indirect speech acts.

For instance, for each of the eight suggestions that follow, I have provided one possible intended meaning (italicized in brackets) that an instructor wants to convey. Students, however, may take the statements literally, inferring that they do not need to revise or do anything further:

1. You might consider adding some concrete examples or personal stories about getting caught speeding. [*Add some concrete examples or personal stories about getting caught speeding.*]

2. You might try reading the draft out loud, slowly, so you can hear things you may miss by just looking at the paper or screen. [*Slowly proofread the draft out loud.*]

3. Perhaps you could base your essay on ideas found here. [*Here are some ideas for your essay.*]

4. Could you reword the information in the previous sentence to make it more readable? For example: *At John Frederick's funeral, I observed many people, including family members, who came to mourn his death.* [*Here is a way to reword your sentence.*]

5. Don't you list more than one "aspect" or "question" here? [*You list more than one "aspect" or "question" here.*]

6. Would it be more logical to put all the description together . . . ? [*It is more logical to put all the description together.*]

7. Can you tell your reader some more about the article? [*Tell your reader more about the article.*]

8. Can you avoid ending your sentence with "is"? [*Avoid ending your sentence with "is."*]

These comments were intended as directives, but because they communicated their "commands" indirectly, students considered them to be suggestions at best and felt free to disregard them. Why would experienced instructors use indirection when direct speech acts are, by definition, clearer? I think there are two motivations: (1) politeness, which includes face-saving strategies, and (2) reluctance to "give" a specific answer, which we know is eschewed by the expressivist, social constructivist, and postprocess epistemologies. Politeness and the desire not to overly appropriate student texts are important considerations, but online instructors need to incorporate more direct, explicit, interventionist strategies if they are truly to help their online students.

Intention and Inference

In considering student comments about their online instructors' questioning strategies, lack of clarity, and inadequate help, I wondered to what degree instructor indirection, the unwillingness of instructors to state in explicit ways what they want students to do, poses problems for online student writers. In a short questionnaire, I asked seventy-two

Example 6.1
Six Instructional Comments

1. I wonder if you couldn't capture attention even more strongly immediately by dropping some hints about your possible solution toward the beginning, rather than leaving it all until the end?
2. so I wonder if you could develop a stronger bridge [transition] between the two [paragraphs]?
3. Or it may be you could just reword that sentence a bit.
4. How can you make this sentence shorter?
5. What if you put "Queen Elizabeth" in the next sentence?
6. Perhaps you can elaborate on the other company's results.

first-year English and developmental English students to review six actual instructional comments. I also asked the study's online instructors and, through an Internet-based listerv,[1] fellow writing teachers/tutors from a broad geographical area to do the same; fifty-six responded.

The students were asked:

> If you were to read a comment like one of these, how would you *interpret* it? Docs it (A) *provide information* about the writing, (B) *tell or direct* the student about what to do, (C) *ask a question* of the student or the writing, or (D) *make a suggestion* about the writing or revision?

Using the same sentences and choices, the writing instructors were asked: If you were to write a comment like one of these, what would your *intention* be? The results reveal a distance between students and instructors, strongly suggesting that the degree of disagreement among students and instructors about the meaning of instructional comments is a potential barrier to student writing development when the instruction occurs online.

Of the instructional comments shown in Example 6.1, five of the six are indirect speech acts, or suggestions, because their form and functions do not match. Only comment 4 is a genuine question, where the form and function match that of an interrogative and create a direct speech act. However, because the respondents were not trained in this coding rubric, *how* they classified these comments is much less important than the *range* of differing opinions about them among students and instructors.

---

[1]W-Center, previously located at <http://lyris.acs.ttu.edu/cgi-bin/lyris.pl?enter=wcenter &text_mode=0&lang=english>. See http://writingcenters.org.

Students disagreed fairly broadly about how they would interpret these comments, which suggests that they saw different functions within individual comments. Comment 4, a straightforward question, is the comment on which students most agreed. Forty-seven students interpreted this comment as a question, a function that is consistent with its form. However, students were sufficiently unclear as to the form and function of a question that twenty-five coded it variably as a comment that informs (2), commands (12), and suggests (11). Student disagreement was more widespread regarding the other comments, where the form and function do not match. For example, even though half of the students interpreted comment 1 (36 of 72) as a suggestion and the majority interpreted comment 3 (39 of 72) as a suggestion, there was far less agreement for comments 2, 5, and 6. Such disagreement among the students reflects the potential for misinterpretation among participants in an online interaction.

Fifty-six writing instructors also responded to this survey. Like the students, they had some consensus concerning comment 4; thirty-one out of fifty-two instructors agreed that their intention for this comment would be to ask a question. However, even for an apparently clearly worded, form/function-matching question, two respondents marked the intention as providing information, sixteen believed that this comment was intended to command, and seven believed its intention was to suggest. Like the students, many of the respondents saw comment 1 as a suggestion (37 of 56). However, unlike the students, instructors were more divided about how they would have intended comment 5; one saw this as informing, twenty-two as commanding, seven as questioning, and twenty-three as suggesting a revision. Instructors were in the greatest agreement for comment 6, which forty-one of fifty-six indicated they would have intended as a suggestion. What seems striking is the degree to which the instructors actually disagreed among themselves. It is sobering to realize that teachers/tutors tend to write such comments in response to student writing both off- and online, and yet they do not necessarily agree as to their intentions.

When compared, not surprisingly student and instructor responses revealed that they also did not agree about the classification of these comments. A simple comparison of responses to comment 3 provides a succinct picture of how differently students interpreted and instructors would have intended these comments (Figure 6.1). While one responding online instructor wrote that the survey was "interesting in revealing how clear it must be to our students that our questions are usually just polite ways of directing or suggesting changes," these survey results indicate that many students *do not* clearly interpret suggestions as they are intended.

Figure 6.1
Student—Instructor Survey: Comment 3

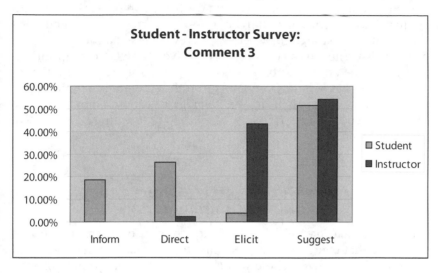

Implications of Indirection in Instructional Language

For online instructors, the context underlying an indirect speech act may be a belief that it can help to reduce student discomfort with a teacher's apparent "power" and "authority." I understand and sympathize with that motivation, but my experience has shown me that online instructors must reconsider their language choices when responding to students—using language straightforwardly to meet students at their levels and as a way to achieve semantic integrity as defined in this book. Because it is straightforward, problem-based teaching can seem more directive in nature than considered appropriate to contemporary pedagogy. Yet, it is an approach that can truly help students with their concerns. Problem-based teaching purposefully harnesses the declarative, imperative, and interrogative linguistic functions in online teaching.

Thus, a major point of this chapter is to urge online instructors to reconsider their language choices with regard to form and function when they respond to students in online settings. Among other goals, they should make their instructional intentions clear first to themselves and second to their students. Especially because teaching through text means using writing to meet students—whose interpretative reading skills may be weak—at their potential points of understanding, online instructors need to be hyperaware that students may not interpret written comments as they are intended. Further, instructors should consider how to adjust their commenting styles to produce unambiguous statements that enable students to interpret the instructional intentions as accurately as possible. The onus is on us to convey intention clearly and, when possible, to prepare students with strategies for interpreting that intention accurately. In the end, textual clarity and straightforwardness as revealed semantically may be a crucial issue linked to concerns of perceived "power" or "authority," and it may be addressed by overtly accepting a more eclectic theory and practice that emerge from a focus on the student, assignment, and actual writing rather than on the ideology of contemporary theories. The next section offers practical strategies for cultivating a language of precision, accuracy, and clarity.

"I've Got a Secret" (Direct and Indirect Commentary)

We turn now to practical strategies for the use of direct speech acts like those that overtly *inform* (declarative), *command* (imperative), and *question* (interrogative). These speech acts lead to more straightforward conferences than do indirect speech acts like those that covertly *suggest*. Examples of each of these types of speech acts illustrate how instructors can benefit from thinking specifically about how they *intend* and *use* direct and indirect speech acts.

Examples 6.2A–F illustrate how difficult it can be for students to interpret a suggestion's intention.

The written comments in Examples 6.2A–F have several qualities in common. First, all of them are suggestions, or indirect speech acts where the form and function do not match. Second, for reasons of politeness, indirection, or perhaps even the belief that such commentary will not "give the answer," each of them seeks to disguise the comment's intent; they are, in effect, evasive. Third—and perhaps most important—regarding student revision, only three of the six comments (D, E, and F) produced the intended response, which was a spelling change. Comment A seemed designed to avoid issues of appropriation though instructional commentary. It plays a game I call, "I've got a secret and I'll give you a hint" regarding word choice. In response to comment A, the student did not supply another word for *has*, and, frankly, I have no idea what the instructor was looking for in a word substitution. Comment B did not elicit a new paragraph, and comment C, comprised of two rhetorical questions, did not result in a different or deeper explanation of what the writer learned from his father. The three spelling corrections resulting from these six suggestions do not represent a big win regarding student learning or writing development.

Example 6.2A
Suggestion 1

Writer: If I would ask five people what they thought that the "perfect" mother would be, I would find that everyone feels that the perfect mother has different qualities.

Online Instructor: Can you think of a different word for "has?"

Example 6.2B
Suggestion 2

Online Instructor: Have you thought about starting a new paragraph here?

Example 6.2C
Suggestion 3

Online Instructor: Might you better explain "learned the violence involved with them"? I'm not sure of what you mean; can you explain what your dad communicated to you that day?

Example 6.2D
Suggestion 4

Writer: If they were to get a job, they would lode all of the brush and logs on the truck and haul it away.

Online Instructor: There's a spelling mistake here that a spell-checker won't catch. There's "load" and then there's "lode." Which one do you think you should use?

Example 6.2E
Suggestion 5

Writer: He never sewed the man who pulled out in front of him because he did not believe in sewing a person because of an accident.

Online Instructor: You've got "sewing" here, as in making clothes out of needle and thread. I don't think that's what you mean. Is it?

Example 6.2F
Suggestion 6

Writer: He sees that the actions of his favorite character are rewarded which causes him to act in the same violent manor.

Online Instructor: Should you look up the word "manor"? I think that you will want to spell the word differently.

Example 6.3
Instructional Commentary and Revision Samples

Writer: …is <u>this</u>. And during all of <u>this</u>, researchers are saying that the easiest way for people to find the problem is to do one simple thing: look in the mirror.

Online Instructor: Can you avoid repeating *this*? Perhaps *meanwhile* would work?

Commentary Revision Choices:

  (1) *How can you avoid repeating the word* this?

  (2) <u>And during all of this</u> *is a transition. What other transitions could replace this phrase to eliminate repeating the word* this?

  (3) *After the pronoun* this, **name the noun** *to which it refers. For example,* cat *in "this cat" is the noun to which* this *refers.*

A more helpful expression strategy is to use straightforward language that conveys intent unambiguously. Such comments can take the form of information, directions, questions, or a combination, as Example 6.3 shows.

The first revised comment uses a straightforward question. The second revised comment uses both a declarative statement and a question. The third revised comment uses both an imperative command and a declarative statement. Notice that each of these choices shows that the repeated word *this* is a problem and offers the student a doable revision step. The benefit of using direct speech acts is that instructors can teach the student how to revise without giving an answer, however vague, via a suggestion. In fact, I have become so sensitized to the potential of certain kinds of questions, for example, to be read as suggestions that I sometimes qualify my commentary to show that I am asking a genuine question rather than hinting about "the" answer that the student should guess: *"This sentence doesn't belong in this paragraph. Where does it go? As your reader, I just don't know."*

There are others ways of being vague that in context might confuse any level student writer. For example, in a recent 300-level online course, I used the word processor's highlighting function to indicate a place in the sentence where the student needed to edit. A nonnative writer, she had written: "An scientific article . . ." and I highlighted "an scientific." I thought she immediately would see what I saw in the mischosen article *an*. She did not, and she revised by deleting "an scientific" to begin her sentence nonsensically with the word *Article*. My use of the highlighter was a hint and not instruction. Because highlighting even "obvious" small errors can elicit no revision or incorrect choices, students benefit from whole-class instruction on what to look for when words or phrases are highlighted. For another example, using my experience as a dissertation coach, one of my mentees wrote the following sentence:

> The third issue, expressed by the question *"If analysis of the whole human genome is justifiable, how should it be conducted?"* grew out of the belief that the undertaking was worthwhile and, therefore, various methods could be debated.

As her online reader, I wanted to know for what purpose the methods could be debated, so I wrote a "fill in the blank" suggestive comment that I thought would be quite clear: ". . . various methods for doing XYZ could be debated." Despite my belief that she would immediately see *XYZ* as a placeholder for the word she eventually came up with ("analysis"), instead she asked in our next phone conference what three items *XYZ* were representing to me because she read my place-holder cue as *X, Y, and Z.* After we cleared up the problem, our working context allowed me to make XYZ-type of suggestions without undue confusion, but I learned a valuable lesson about assuming that any online conference can be sustained with stand-alone suggestions.

Happily, sometimes there is no confusion about a comment that could be read as vague in certain contexts. One student wrote this sentence in his technical writing paper about astronaut rescue plans: "At some point, it should be possible to achieve mid-flight poop rescue of astronauts " The online instructor used a bubble comment to say simply, "poop?" No other comment was necessary; the student, who laughingly admitted he sometimes just types nonsense words to get over temporary writing block, corrected the text for that and other mistyped words.

With these ideas in mind, useful guidelines emerge for using direct and explicit comments when writing conferences:

- Use comments that inform often and freely.
- Write straightforward directions, and include examples and/or choices from which the student can learn.
- Write open-ended questions that use *how* and *wh-* words.
- Avoid suggestions except those that are straightforwardly presented (for example, *"I suggest that you do* _____ *in the next draft because* _____*"*).

These guidelines focus on writing "head-on" or overt commentary, resulting in a problem-centered conference that makes good use of direct speech acts. The following two examples of problem-centered mini-lessons illustrate the usefulness of such written commentary. In Examples 6.4A–B and 6.5A–C, I describe the form and function problems in the instructional sentences before demonstrating a problem-

Example 6.4A
Instructional Comment 1 Revised

Online Instructor: I wonder if you couldn't capture attention even more strongly immediately by dropping some hints about your possible solution toward the beginning, rather than leaving it all until the end? *[Suggest]*

Example 6.4B
Instructional Comment 1

Online Instructor:

An *introduction* to an argument like yours should "hook" or "grab" the reader's attention right from the start. *[Inform]*

One way to get the reader's attention is to provide hints, or ideas, about possible solutions to the problem <u>in the introduction paragraph</u>. *[Inform]* These ideas also help to orient, or guide, your reader through your argument. *[Inform]* Then, the rest of the essay discusses, supports, and justifies these ideas. *[Inform]*

The *conclusion* repeats or rephrases those solutions for the reader. *[Inform]*

Your <u>key job,</u> though, is <u>to figure out what those "solutions" to the problems are</u>. *[Inform]* Very often, you won't know what you think those solutions are until after the first or second draft! *[Inform]*

<u>Next steps:</u> *[Inform]*

- *After you write the first draft, review the essay to see whether you've come up with "solutions" or possible "actions" for the problem.* [Direct] *Use a colored marker to highlight those solutions or actions.* [Direct]

- *Then, revise your introduction to include one or two of these highlighted solutions.* [Direct] *At the very least, write a statement that indicates solutions do exist.* [Direct]

Your essay will become more interesting to your reader. *[Inform]*

centered approach to each. For the purposes of our discussion and the clarity of examples, in this case, I have labeled each comment by its linguistic function.

Instructional comment 1, which responds to a student's argument about a position, is an especially tangled suggestion that we encountered earlier in this chapter.

The conditional language (*I wonder if you couldn't*), confusing use of adverbs and adjectives as intensifiers (*even more strongly immediately*), and punctuation (question mark with a declaratively phrased sentence) all point to a form where the function does not match. Certainly the intent, if not the sentence itself, could be unclear to many students, leading them to misinterpret or ignore it altogether. Students might wonder whether they are to:

- provide "hints" to the essay's solution in the essay introduction,
- delete "hints" in the conclusion,
- provide and repeat "hints" in both the introduction and conclusion, or
- provide some "hints" in the introduction and others in the conclusion

—any choice of which avoids *"leaving it all until the end."* Students might also wonder just what "hints" are. How could an online instructor reword this sentence to clarify intention? A problem-centered approach to the student's writing (Example 6.4B) would consider whether the student understands how an introduction and conclusion function in an argument.

This problem-centered mini-lesson on introductions and conclusions is written primarily using declarative statements. The lesson also contains several imperative statements intended to focus and guide the student's next steps. While it does not "take over" the student's writing by telling the student what content to write, it does provide focused direction by addressing critical reader/writer orientation issues and potential next steps. The revised comment does not use any indirect comments that in themselves can confuse students. The lesson itself obviously is longer than the suggestion that it replaces. However, as a mini-lesson it teaches much more and enables the student to make deeper revision changes. Additionally, where time is an issue (see Chapter 7), online instructors can adopt this problem-centered approach as a way to concentrate on and limit their advice to one primary and two to three minor writing issues in a session.[2]

Similarly, instructional comment 2 in Example 6.5A creates a conundrum for student writers. For the purposes of contextualizing the sentence, I added the words *transition* and *paragraphs* in brackets. In the original conference, the comment's placement in the essay indicates that

---

[2]In terms of an instructional practice scenario where teachers/tutors might practice revising poorly worded or confusing commentary, program directors and online instructors immediately will see many different ways to rephrase this mini-lesson, especially ways that involve the context of the student's actual topic and writing. Nonetheless, in a practice or training setting, unless instructors are practicing with writing instruction that is simply wrong, I recommend allowing the form and function to take precedence in practice commentary revision sessions.

the online instructor assumed that the meaning of "two paragraphs" was contextually clear. The word *bridge*, however, is unfamiliar vocabulary that was left for the student to figure out. Like comment 1 in Example 6.4A, the online instructor used conditional language (*wonder if you could*) to suggest the student's appropriate action, as well as punctuation (a question mark) to create an indirect statement.

A problem-centered approach to teaching transitions online, and one that would clarify intention for students, first needs to match up the comment's form and function, as in Example 6.5B.

These revised comments match in form and function through two sentences that provide information and an open-ended question. They easily can be supplemented by a focused mini-lesson about transitions, as shown in Example 6.5C.

Example 6.5A
Instructional Comment 2

Online Instructor: ... so I wonder if you could develop a stronger bridge [transition] between the two [paragraphs]? *[Suggest]*

Example 6.5B
Instructional Comment 2 Revised A

Online Instructor: These two paragraphs need a stronger transition. *[Inform]* What transition words would create that "bridge" between the two paragraphs? *[Elicit]*

Example 6.5C
Instructional Comment 2 Revised B

Online Instructor:

These two paragraphs need a *stronger transition*. *[Inform]* What transition words would create that "bridge," or connection, between the two paragraphs? *[Elicit]*

Transition words link ideas from one paragraph to another. *[Inform]* They can:
- *show results (for this reason, consequently, therefore),*
- *offer alternatives (alternatively, instead, otherwise),*
- and *organize the reader through words that demonstrate order of time or ideas (first, second, finally, then, now). [Inform]*

There are many ways to create a transition. *[Inform]*

Your online English handbook at the college website (www.XYZ.edu) or your class textbook will have more information under the keyword "transitions."

[Inform] Using your handbook as a guide, *[Direct]* what kind of connection do these two paragraphs need? *[Elicit]*

<u>Next step:</u> In your next draft, use this lesson to be sure that all of your paragraphs have the most accurate transitions for your message. *[Direct]*

In this mini-lesson, once again the student maintains autonomy because the final writing choices are his or hers alone; the only directions from the online instructor are to use a handbook as guidance (after having provided appropriate ways to find that information) and to apply this lesson to the entire essay. The language reflects primarily information-based direct speech acts.

Examples 6.4 and 6.5 demonstrate that the online instructor does not need to do all the work for the student, as some might worry. Neither does providing a more complete problem-based lesson necessarily "give the answer." However, the written comments should name and reflect the student's core problem, which most experienced instructors can see fairly quickly. Problem-centered teaching using mini-lessons is one way to help online instructors to focus their comments using direct, rather than indirect, speech acts—all the while avoiding "doing the work" for the student.

Conferencing Action Plan for *avoiding secrets and hints*

1. Think through the lesson you believe the student needs to learn before you begin commenting.

2. Learn to recognize direct and indirect speech acts in your comments, whether in a face-to-face or online instructional setting.

3. Practice using direct speech acts in all of your teaching.

4. If you want to make a suggestion, do so in a straightforward manner. Say, "I think you should . . ." or "I suggest that you . . ." which tells the student clearly that this is a choice you are recommending.

5. Practice coding commentary and essays for direct and indirect messages; even the experience with coding one to three conferences will help you to understand your own online commentary tendencies.

6. Seek guided practice in revising your written teaching commentaries to practice a mix of direct commenting types. Take opportunities to critique each other in nonthreatening but specific ways that support your online writing program's goals.

Chapter Seven

Using What Works

Engagement

Getting and keeping students' attention is never easy. Even in traditional classroom settings, teachers have to compete with the first snow of the winter, clanking radiators, and lunch-induced sleepiness. Now, however, cell phones, laptop computers, text messaging, and electronic games also distract students. I recently read about a law school that banned the Internet in its classrooms because too many students surfed the web, checked email, or got lost in inner space. If it is so hard to keep student attention in law school, where students presumably are mature pre-professionals, then how much harder can it be to hold student attention in a writing course? Many students do not want to be in writing courses to begin with—add the diversions of computers and the Internet, and we must wonder what can be done to keep them on track.

Life with my son and his digital-native friends has taught me that educators can reduce a lot of stress by acknowledging that contemporary students often use computers to multitask in both private and classroom settings. And although some may argue that to multitask is to do many things poorly, it is an inescapable phenomenon of twenty-first-century life. Computer software is designed with "windows" for the purpose of multitasking, and many of us, like our students, keep more than one window open. As I drafted this chapter, for example, I jotted notes in another document, checked my email, talked with my son via IM, and read the news online; I also answered the phone many times and ate lunch at my desk.

When teaching in a computer-based setting, I typically multitask. I am always aware, however, that I cannot do a great job of attending simultaneously to the students, their writing, the course material, and the technology; I usually have to subordinate at least one of them. I am even less able—and less inclined—to multitask in traditional classroom settings. Students who are digital natives, however, may not perceive such difficulty or almost unthinkingly multitask when in any classroom. And, although teachers likely see it as rude or irresponsible behavior, students often would not agree, seeing their activities as natural and normal ways to inhabit the classroom.

In a networked classroom setting, we can address such problems by temporarily locking keyboards, answering students' cell phones, speaking from the back of the classroom, or walking around the room in detective mode. In potentially more satisfying actions, we can ask the students to achieve consensus about appropriate classroom behavior in order to exert peer pressure and find value-based ways to address interruptions.

Such classroom solutions, however, simply are not practical in an online conference. The nature of the one-to-one conference, whether asynchronous or synchronous, is that both parties are communicating through the computer and when, where, and how that happens typically is not apparent to the instructor. An online instructor might not have many clues that the student is playing a video game while talking synchronously or that she is talking on the phone while typing a request for help with a paper. These variables have consequences, however, and we need to think about them in light of the one-to-one conference.

While we always should check in with students to make sure they are engaged with their learning, doing so is especially important online. As we have observed, a significant difference between traditional and online settings is that instructors cannot watch students' body language and facial cues, and they cannot hear the oral phatic language that signals understanding, confusion, interest, or disinterest. Instead, they must rely on typographic and semantic cues to convey the same information. In talking about engaging students, it is especially helpful to understand some of the textual cues that students are apt to use— particularly in synchronous conversations where we expect two parties to be present (mentally, if virtually) and interactive. For example, as discussed in Chapter 3, many students use IM to communicate. While their IM-ular writing provides informative, phatic-like cues for sustaining the chat, it also reveals a sense of engagement in terms of needing time to think, completing a thought, or signaling understanding. Such textual cues also may occur in some asynchronous conferences, as one party might actively imagine the other as an audience who is "listening" attentively and ready to respond. In brief, these cues indicate engagement with the conference, and their presence is a good thing.

Sometimes, though, we might experience a lengthy silence that makes us think we are communicating to cyberspace rather than to a person. The silence might involve many hours or days between interactions in an asynchronous conference or the real-time silence of minutes in a synchronous chat. How can we prompt these phatic cues when there is silence from students?

It is important to consider the purpose of the conference—such as asking a question, providing an answer, offering formative essay response, commenting about that response, or seeking to resolve course-based problems. It is also important to recognize that whoever initiates the conference probably will be the more active party. When students initiate a conference, we can assume that they have a reasonable level of interest in the meeting and will be attentive. The same can be supposed for a planned or required conference related to a particular assignment. If the online instructor initiates the conference or if the initial question already has been addressed, some students may become less interested—particularly if it is the instructor who has additional questions that might put them on the spot. Regardless of active interest levels, however, when it comes to engagement, both parties need the other's assurance of ongoing attention and interest.

To convey interest in either an asynchronous or synchronous conference, online instructors can employ various techniques.

- We can use students' names and speak directly to them, encouraging them to speak directly to us. We should introduce ourselves using whatever combination of preferred title, first, and/or last name in the conference greeting (for example, *"Hi, Jim. It's Dr. H. here."* or *"Welcome to our chat, Lily—Ms. Pahl."*), but we should not take offense if some students do not address us back by name. For example, despite my signature as "Dr. Hewett" or "Dr. H" in some instances, I have been called "Hey, Professor" and told "I don't know what to call you." Additionally, possibly because they remain aware of our authority and their place in the instructional hierarchy, some students seem disinclined to address an instructor by his or her name no matter how they are prompted. As I have already discussed, I think it is neither possible nor entirely wise to completely level the interaction between instructor and students in online settings, and so the students' awareness of hierarchy seems quite natural.

- We can signal our own attentiveness with context cues like frequent reference to the writing, the assignment, or to something that has been shared as part of the writing or writing process. Specifically referencing some area of content or linking a pertinent personal detail also can be helpful. Such cues not only keep the conference on point but also remind students that their instructor is focused on their individual writing content and processes.

- We can ask students open-ended and contextually genuine questions rather than closed, yes/no, rhetorical, or leading questions, as discussed in Chapter 6. Such questions usually begin with *how* or *wh* words that require information and encourage a contextualized, more engaged response. They also serve to model the kinds of questions that students should be asking of us in order to get the contextually full and helpful responses that they need.

- We can ask students whether they have their own questions. Students might be hesitant to take more time or to pose their own questions. I have even seen students say that they understand a point that they later admit is still unclear. As in any educational setting, some students worry about showing their confusion, uncertainty, or ignorance. Therefore, it can be useful to jump-start the conference with question cues: *"Do you have any questions about how your content is developing? Or about your thesis or timeline or anything else?"* and *"What else can I tell you about what I see in your writing?"*

- We can require students to commit their ideas to writing—to explain their main ideas, change their drafts, or try out new skills in response to the conference. As we have seen with problem-centered mini-lessons, it is important to prompt student writing development with clear explanation and follow-up steps. It is impossible for students to respond to such prompts without some level of engagement in the conference—and in their own learning. While such prompting is a bit easier in a synchronous conference, instructors can prompt a response in an asynchronous conference by asking for a follow-up email (preferably within a designated time frame) or to be shown the actions taken in the next class session.

- We can check in frequently regarding students' understanding of what's being said. To reinforce learning, students can be asked to explain the points made in their own words, which gives them a chance to clarify their understanding for themselves and for us. Synchronously, we might say, *"Does this make sense?"* or *"Please tell me what I just said using your own words."* Asynchronously, we might say, *"In other words,"* and then rephrase or otherwise redefine the potentially confusing (thus disengaging) statement. Again, it seems important to give the student a method (such as email, IM chat, or telephone) or location (for example, next class or office hours) to provide such a response.

- We can offer clear, honest, critical responses to the writing. This strategy includes phrasing such as: *"I'm awed by your strength in this situation"* or *"When I see detailed writing like you've done here, I become really interested in the topic."* Attentive reader response, much discussed in composition pedagogy literature, also helps when providing less positive feedback: *"I'm confused by this entire paragraph.*

What did you want readers to understand?" or *"I think I've missed a connection between X and Y. How can you help me?"*

- We can be personable by being genuine, specific, thoughtful, and self-engaged in the conference and the student's writing. Although we cannot always choose our work schedules, it is best to avoid online conferences when fatigued, grumpy, or uninterested in the students' writing. In some ways, the online setting's absence of obvious emotional cues (for example, an exasperated tone of voice, angry gestures, and frustrated facial expressions) can protect students from an instructor's bad mood, but it cannot protect against bad advice or poor reading or less-than-attentive diagnostic skills that can be part and parcel of such a mood.

- We can believe that the student is interested, which is a valuable attitude in both the traditional and online educational settings. To be sure, we should anticipate such interest whenever students initiate a conference or attend a required or scheduled meeting with the instructor. In other words, we need to trust and encourage students to be full participants in their learning processes. Even reluctant students come around when they are thoughtfully engaged by an instructor who shows willingness to believe in their desire to learn.

Synchronous conferences may require a few additional strategies to keep students engaged and on track. In this setting, students might show disinterest by extended silence, lack of detailed or thoughtful response, or unwillingness to move beyond what they perceive to be the instructor's agenda. Due to the nature of synchronous conversations, however, it is realistic to acknowledge that students' apparent disinterest may be caused by circumstances outside of our control. For example, students may have only a short time to talk, may be interested in the conference but not giving it full attention because they are multitasking, may not be comfortable with learning in the online setting, or may have poor typing and spelling skills. In such cases, intervention via the conference may not work, making it necessary to change the approach. Before changing venues, though, ask students directly what is happening regarding the conference and describe to them what seems disengaged about it. Very often, students will show surprise that an online instructor assumes disengagement when they are actually absorbed in the problem at hand. Therefore, as much as possible, we need to keep communication lines open—especially in completely digital settings where face-to-face interactions are rare or nonexistent. Ultimately, in either modality, it may be best to schedule another online conference as a follow-up or to move to other media, such as email, telephone, video conferencing, or—where possible—to meet in person at a mutually agreeable time. A conference that begins digitally does not have to stay digital if it is not in the student's best interest.

Conferencing Action Plan for *engagement*

1. Learn firsthand about issues of attention and disinterest in synchronous conferences by conducting both casual and focused IM conversations with students and colleagues. Consider how a teaching interaction necessarily differs in terms of affect, focus, and strategy for different issues like reading, writing, and comprehension.
2. Read professional literature that discusses the nuances of real-time online talk in various platforms: IM chat, whiteboard, document sharing, or mixed settings.
3. Practice your synchronous teaching skills with expert feedback from colleagues before trying them on live students. For example, practice role play with a colleague acting first as an attentive, helpful student and then as a recalcitrant one.
4. Consider how these strategies may be usefully applied to asynchronous conferences as well; try them out in simulated essay responses.
5. Understand that working with different modalities to get past a "stuck" or otherwise unhelpful conference doesn't represent a failure of the original modality. People often need to change contact strategies depending on a variety of circumstances.

Where to Comment

Using primarily email and the telephone, I recently coached Amy, a nursing master's degree student, as she completed a literature review that was to stand as her final exam; she had failed the exam on her first try and had one more chance to prove herself. All of her work had been completed for an online university, which is remarkable given that she'd had a stroke two years earlier. In her rehabilitation, she amazed her doctors and therapists by learning to speak, read, and write again. But the stroke left Amy with permanent cognitive disabilities, which is why she was allowed to use my assistance. In particular, her short-term memory and organizational/spatial skills were damaged, which made it very difficult for her to understand and apply the readers' commentary she received on her first attempt at the literature review.

A mature student well past her first-year writing courses, Amy expressed the helplessness and frustration often heard from novice student writers. Her already significant challenges were increased by the primarily textual nature of the online medium through which she interacted with her readers, whose feedback proved incomprehensible to her. So, she also sent her draft to the institution's online writing center;

as such, the conference was intended to be instructional in nature. When she called me expressing a sense of despair, she sent me a copy of that conference (see Example 7.1).

Although the conference provided some very useful feedback, Amy could not read it because the feedback was insufficiently distinguished from her text both visually and spatially. The online instructor used asterisks to indicate her feedback and broke into the middle of Amy's sentences. Despite the yellow highlight that indicated a keyword (shown here in bold, italicized text), Amy could not distinguish her text from the instructor's feedback even with me coaching her by phone; for her, asterisks did not provide enough of a signal that she needed to switch reader modes from that of author to that of student writer. Furthermore, the mid-sentence breaks confused Amy and left her unsure of what to do. She had difficulty seeing her own sentences as complete without the instructional interruption. In our conferencing, we found that a change in where and in what form the online instructor commented would have helped Amy to understand certain problems and decide on revision strategies.

Amy's challenges, while exacerbated by the ravages of a stroke, illustrate the importance of attending to what the commentary looks like—where it is placed and how it is formatted. Just as the text becomes the instructional voice in the online setting, placement and formatting provide a sense of vocal tone and emphasis.

Example 7.1
Amy's Text and Feedback

In addition to the literature searches done, Linehan and Associates
*** is this a name of a business? I am just wondering if it should be with a small "a" for "associates" as in the previous mention. There's a difference between referring to people as associates (whose names may change) and to the name of a permanent business or clinic which will be capitalized.
***was** contacted at the Behavioral Research and Therapy Clinic in Seattle to determine if unpublished works existed in the use of DBT as a treatment modality for BPD. Linehan is credited for authoring twenty-five chapters in books addressing DBT; eight books, some of which were translated into German and or Dutch; forty-three articles and two research monographs.
*****Were these works actually reviewed in this literature review? Why do you bring them up here? These totals about Linehan's output are interesting but are they pertinent to the focus of this section (i.e., the organization of <u>your</u> review)? In fact have you really discussed the <u>organization</u> of your review? Which material will you discuss first, for instance? Why and how have you broken up the non-research section into various topics? What follows the non-research section?

Example 7.2
Comment Balloon

Local comments, which are embedded into the student's text by [**bracketing in bold, black font**] or by using comment balloons, tend to point or link to three to five specific sentence-level issues (strengths and weaknesses) to which the student writer could attend in revision.

Comment [B1]: This is a comment balloon, created by blocking the text under consideration and "inserting" a "comment."

For example, synchronous conferences can benefit from the focused and conscious placement of commentary. In a chat form, synchronous conferences more or less organize themselves by the subjects that each party raises in the give-and-take of talk. However, with whiteboard interactions, the board can be planned in the online instructor's mind for both efficiency and efficacy as an archival study aid—just like one would plan a chalkboard lesson (see Example 2.3).

Specific to asynchronous conferences—the major focus of this section—it is doubly true that where online instructors actually place commentary can be almost as important as what they say to students about their writing. There are two basic types of asynchronous commentary: local or embedded comments, and global comments. Their names indicate their scope but not necessarily their placement or format.

Local comments, which are embedded into the student's text by methods such as **[bracketing in bold, black font]** or by using comment balloons, tend to point or link to specific sentence-level issues (strengths and weaknesses) for student writers to address in revision. In Example 7.2, we see a comment "balloon" or "call-out," which typically is developed by blocking the key text, and then inserting a comment via the word-processing program's tools. There are other ways to locate local comments such as digital footnotes that can be seen by mousing over the text, but I suspect that the closer the feedback resides to the student's actual text—without interrupting or overwhelming it—the more helpful the feedback is for students.

Indeed, my own study of student revision suggests that embedding local commentary in the text encourages revision. By counting the number of revisions related directly to local comments versus global ones, I saw that students used the local comments slightly more frequently. While these findings are provisional, strategically formatted local commentary like that in Example 7.3A can draw students' eyes to the area and resonate concretely in terms of instructional feedback. Although there is a danger that drawing the eye in this way can lead students to think that local comments "fix" the essay, embedding

Example 7.3 A
Online Instructor Embedded Response

Many tend to blame media violence, such as television programming, for the violent behavior today's youth are portraying; however, many also have an opposing view. **[By "opposing," do you mean that many think that media violence should not be blamed? Precise wording helps readers understand your meaning. Because "opposing" is confusing, you need another word.]** All cartoons, sitcoms, and movies viewed by children contain some type of violence. **[Be careful when using the word "all," which is a generalization. "All" means every cartoon/sitcom/movie ever produced in every country. How can you qualify the statement?]** In fact each of these shows includes at least 20 violent acts. **[As it's worded, this statement is difficult to defend or support. Is it based on research? Your readers need to know.]** Also, the glamorization of violence in these programs is another issue. The violent acts children see are depicted as *heroic* which causes them to imitate the character they admire most. Nevertheless, many believe that violent behavior is *learned* from the child's parents. Exposure to "real-life violence" seems to have a longer lasting and stronger effect on a child's behavioral patterns. <u>This essay will address violent programming and youth violence.</u> **[Please read my comments at the beginning of the essay, Tina.]**

comments makes sense. When I receive feedback on my own writing, I take global responses into account, but I am most immediately influenced by local comments. On an affective level, I think that's because local comments confirm whether I am on target; if I am not, I think to myself, why would the responder bother to consider particular sentences or sections in isolation? Even when I am wrong and the respondent's main message is that the writing needs significant overhaul, local comments often provide very specific guidance that can help me get unstuck or improve my syntax and coherence. In other words, local comments often do give me the answers I need to make some incremental steps forward. While a natural correlation, however, the perception of embedded commentary as a "quick fix" is correctable. As Chapter 3 indicates, setting appropriate expectations for local comments in the beginning of the course or conference would include letting students know that these comments indicate specific areas where particular strategies can improve the writing and that the entire essay likely will require similar revision using those strategies.

Example 7.3A illustrates strategically placed embedded commentary specific to Tina's introductory paragraph. Formative feedback is provided in bold text set off by brackets, and there are no mid-sentence interruptions. In this case, while the online instructor wisely did not address every possible issue in this paragraph, she did comment on three substantive ones that the student needed to consider when revising her draft, especially clarity and research.

The final comment, where the instructor had underlined the student's proposed thesis, points to coordination between the local and the global commentary, which can help students see the local commentary as more than fix-it advice. As Example 7.3B shows, the online instructor addressed similar issues—avoiding adding many more to the lesson—in the global commentary, which presented Tina with a focused conference.

A third way to indicate local comments is to teach more directly through a tool that tracks changes automatically, revealing additions, deletions, substitutions, and permutations. This interventionist tool might be used in addition to other local commenting approaches to teach students editing processes and strategies. Because it shows writers the depth (or narrowness) of their revisions, it can help them conceive of revision as more than simply "fixing errors." I have found that many students do not know how to track their own changes and appreciate seeing what revision looks like both locally and globally when changes are shown. Example 3.6B uses tracked changes to demonstrate instructor writing for students.

As opposed to the specificity of local comments, global comments tend to summarize some specific strengths and weaknesses of the writing and may be more general in nature. The summary nature of global comments provides excellent opportunities for teaching through mini-lessons. Typically, overarching or general comments are placed either at the beginning or ending of a student's essay, where they can address overarching concerns and they can either preview or summarize the embedded commentary. Global comments include things such as (1) a greeting, (2) essay strengths, (3) critical feedback, (4) a mini-lesson, (5) next steps, and (6) some kind of closing statement.

Example 7.3B illustrates problem-centered teaching that is explicitly connected to the local comments shown in Example 7.3A. After having underlined Tina's apparent thesis in the essay, the online instructor wrote a mini-lesson about thesis sentences in the global commentary. This mini-lesson probably used a pre-developed lesson about thesis sentences that was then tailored to the student's writing. The global lesson included various elements of strong instruction in a one-to-one conference, as discussed earlier. The online instructor:

1. included a statement of specific, unqualified praise;
2. connected the embedded comments to this comment;
3. pasted in the student's own thesis so that both participants could be on the same page;
4. provided common definitions or guidelines about thesis statements;

5. asked an open-ended question;
6. explained the problem with the student's thesis;
7. pasted in the student's final sentence to consider whether would be a more accurate thesis; and
8. gave the student a specific task for the next draft.

Such problem-centered general comments complement and extend the useful embedded commentary shown in Example 7.3A, which is the single most addressed paragraph in the conference. To talk about more issues as they occurred throughout the essay most likely would overwhelm Tina and would not necessarily prompt stronger revision.

Example 7.3B
Online Instructor Global Response to Thesis

Tina, your assignment asks you to present two opposing views on a topic and to avoid taking a personal stand on that topic. You have followed that instruction very well. Good work!

In terms of your *thesis sentence* itself, I think that you can create a stronger <u>statement of what your research showed</u>, however. In your essay, I <u>underlined</u> what I thought was your thesis.

You wrote: "*This essay will address violent programming and youth violence.*"

This sentence tells the reader <u>what the essay will address</u>, but not very specifically. The thesis helps readers more when you <u>make a claim about the subject.</u>

Here is a brief review of *four functions of a thesis:*

1. It identifies and narrows the subject.
2. It makes a claim or an assertion about the subject.
3. It sets the tone of the writing.
4. It often indicates the order of main points.

Overall, a strong thesis gives the reader a specific idea of what to expect (or what evidence to look for) when reading an essay or article. Which of these functions best fits what your thesis says?

Tina, when drafting an essay, sometimes writers actually write a more accurate statement of the thesis at the *end* of the first or second draft. In other words, we "write" our way into what we actually want to say. In your case, the <u>final sentence</u> of your essay may be one you can revise into a more accurate thesis sentence.

You wrote: *"Although there is no single answer to the connection between violent programming and youth violence, evidence strongly supports that the cause for violent behavior is television violence."*

Next steps:

- Does this sentence represent your essay's thesis—what you found in your research?

  □ If so, in your next draft, try rewriting your thesis to include the information in this statement.

  □ If not, try writing a sentence that does represent your thesis. You can use the four functions of a thesis (above) to guide you.

- Next, as you revise your essay, make sure that each paragraph addresses the points that your new thesis indicates. Some parts of your essay may change in substance, but that's okay. Revision helps to sharpen your points all the way through the essay.

- Finally, you still can use your final sentence (or one like it) in your conclusion to help you to restate your main points.

The question of where to comment also should encourage us to consider how that commentary will look to students. Using formatting techniques for global comments and mini-lessons can make instructional comments more effective. Whenever possible, instructors should develop visually attractive and comprehensible commentary, provided that the student's platform or program shares the ability to "read" it. As Examples 5.5, 5.6, and 7.3B illustrate, strategic formatting does more than make a conference visually pleasing; it can make it easier for students to read and interpret the instruction. And, for students like Amy who have a cognitive disability that reveals itself in reading (or writing) text, such formatting may be crucial to communicating about writing in an online conference.

In either asynchronous or synchronous online conferences, some ways to format strategically are:

- Demonstrate revision through "track change" features of the word processing program to help students envision how one might develop, revise, or generally change a section of text. ~~Track changs~~ Track changes can be helpful in teaching students editing skills, too.

- Experiment with font sizes and sans serif fonts like "Arial" and "Verdana," which are used to distinguish the examples provided in this book's text boxes.

- Create text boxes—like those in this book—for commentary that should stand out or operate more permanently in a student's mind.

- Use **bold**, <u>underline</u>, *italic*, highlight, and color to create a perma-nent teaching aid that students can transfer to future writing. It's a good idea, however, to use only one to two variant colors in a single instructional interaction and to explain to the student what the colors indicate.

- When possible, create lists with bullets or numbers. Such lists pro-vide order; opportunity to rank ideas, tasks, or strategies; and the visual relief of white space.

- Generate a set of formatting templates and/or mini-lessons to copy and paste into student work. Even though they should be person-alized to particular students, they can both save time and enhance the conferences through carefully designed clarity and focus.

As online instructors, we should experiment, add to this list, and talk to each other about the possibilities that formatting, color, and graphics provide. Finally, we need to remember that the "bells and whistles" of fancy formatting can never replace the strength of solid content and clearly expressed commentary. The quality of our teaching itself will most help our students in one-to-one conferencing.

Conferencing Action Plan for *where to comment*

1. As you read an essay the first time, jot down a few issues that you might want to discuss as global commentary and those that seem the most helpful in terms of local commentary. If you're reading in preparation for a synchronous conference, this list will serve as your agenda for the meeting.

2. Decide on the general comments and the mini-lesson that you want to conduct. Know what strengths you want to identify and why.

3. For asynchronous conferences, try writing a greeting, then the strengths, the general comments (including mini-lesson, as needed), next steps, and a closing statement. Experiment with the order and emphasis of these elements. Then decide: Will these elements be most effective placed before the essay, after the text, on a separate page, or somehow split up?

4. Mark and briefly discuss any local comments by embedding short comments after the sentence or paragraph in question or using a comment balloon. Once you've decided on an effective placement for your commentary, stick with that organization so that students can become familiar with your response style.

5. Learn how to use your word processor's formatting tools and try saving them in different document file types. For example, find out whether the formatting you have created in a common program like Microsoft Word will save in rich text (.rtf), plain text (.txt), and WordPerfect (.wpd).

6. For synchronous conferences, consider how you would use these placement guidelines in developing a focused chat. Experiment with formatting in whiteboards particularly during down times to be prepared for trying new approaches in live conferences.

7. Ask students whether certain presentation styles are more helpful than others and why.

Too Much and Too Little Commenting

It's 9:20 P.M., and I have already read and responded to fourteen of nineteen drafts and had two IM chats. I've been working on student writing off and on since 2:00 P.M. I want to send my comments back to students tonight so that we have time this week to talk about steps for the next draft in our online discussion. I can devote only another hour or so to the final pieces before I turn into the proverbial pumpkin. But I am not very comfortable measuring my responses by time. Sometimes I feel guilty because I know that some students need more and others less from me and that I should be flexible.

Nonetheless, I have found that I must measure my online work by some unit or I become fatigued and write unhelpful comments. And, when those formative responses are the primary means of teaching, as they are in some networked classes and most online courses and online tutorial settings, the quality of the response is critical. Effective conferencing online does not mean exhausting and sacrificing myself to students; nor does it mean giving an hour to each student who seems to need it (don't they all need it at some point?). Rather it means measuring my responses by reasonable time limits and commentary lengths—and doing so without undue guilt. I have learned that efficiency can benefit both online instructors and students by focusing the interactions and establishing a reasonable framework within which the work can be done.

Since we are not robots and have different conferencing styles, I can speak only generally here about time limits. Certainly, individual institutions and educators will have different views—at one online university, it is common for their online writing center to provide conference sessions between one to two hours long, and they are proud of their dedication. But not everyone has that kind of time and resources to offer, and experience suggests that there is a point beyond which the conference is less efficacious because of instructor mental fatigue and student information overload.

Generally speaking, an asynchronous conference that responds to a student's emailed question may take two to ten minutes depending on the question and the response's language precision and tone. On the other hand, a conference intended to provide formative response to an essay may take about thirty to forty minutes if it is the first or second time reading a draft and if we are focusing on the most important issues for revision. In terms of content, that would comprise three to five strategically placed embedded comments and a global response with a mini-lesson and next steps. Rubrics are tools that can help both online instructors and their students in visualizing an essay's progress, which of course demonstrates the writer's development. Rubrics can have an effect both on time and conference efficacy, so I talk more about these in Chapter 8. With practice and knowledge about individual students, we can become efficient at locating the essay's greatest strengths and those weaknesses that need most immediate attention in the next draft. But unless the draft was promised only a cursory reading, even with practice, a focused reading and response may absorb thirty minutes or more.

In contrast, a useful text-based synchronous conference can last between fifteen and forty-five minutes, again depending on its purpose. Certainly it can take more time, but we must measure the benefits of that time against the potential for too much breadth and the mental fatigue that can come with typing and reading a lengthy, threaded digital conference. Recalling that a synchronous conference is best used to talk about focused concerns that the student may raise or that a quick reading of the paper reveals, it naturally will be more narrowly focused than an asynchronous one. However, it usefully may address one or two varied issues such as thesis ideas, detail development, organization, argument styles, or grammar and usage. Even a digital whiteboard-based conference, where both students and instructors can simultaneously look at the draft and chat about it, needs a time limit. I recommend stating up front how long the conference will run. It may take a while to become comfortable with conferencing online using time limits, but anyone who has responded to a "quick question" with an hour-and-a-half online chat—losing the lunch hour while remaining unsure that the student has resolved all confusions— will soon want to use chat time efficiently and effectively.

Time is one measure of helpful conferences. Length of commentary is another. Strategically limiting the conference's length can help students to revise more completely. In fact, when it comes to commentary, less may be more. In my research, students disregarded approximately

40 percent of the asynchronous commentary intended to encourage particular kinds of revisions and about 30 percent of the synchronous commentary. For a variety of reasons—like what other readers might have told them or their own preferences—they picked and chose deliberately the guidance they used for revision. Students are not likely to use all the commentary provided to them (even when they think or say they do!), which means that a targeted, consciously developed length is valuable to both online students and instructors alike.

When I say that less may be more, I do not mean that students necessarily benefit from a few words sprinkled here and there—the proverbial "awkward" or "develop detail" or "spelling" that we still see in so many essay responses. Too little commentary, like the hints discussed in Chapter 6, only points to problems; it does not teach or explain and often leaves students frustrated. In both the asynchronous and synchronous modalities, however, I have seen some online instructors write much more than students initially write, occasionally twice as much as the essay draft itself; such response often attempts to address multiple problem areas as opposed to the also long but very focused mini-lesson. This practice is unhelpful because it is overwhelming and highlights too many issues, some of which are far less important than others. The tendency to overwrite is not surprising given how much easier it is to type a lengthy, detailed message than to handwrite it. One online instructor told me that a lengthy response was one method of showing her students how much she cares about their writing. But just as measuring time spent in conferences does not mean lack of caring, using reasonable comment lengths does not equate to a lack of caring. Keys to success include writing shorter, more succinct comments, as well as drafting a response and then reading and revising it to clarify the message.

In this book, I have used examples that demonstrate both shorter and longer asynchronous global comments. For example, the mini-lessons in Examples 5.5, 5.6, 6.4B, 6.5C, and 8.1 address substantial revision concerns. As I have demonstrated, one way to strategize response is to provide one solid mini-lesson per asynchronous or synchronous conference, perhaps in a global comment, and then to respond more minimally to other issues in strategically placed embedded or additional comments. Another strategy is to respond routinely to students with less rather than more commentary; that way, if an occasional issue requires a more lengthy response, it may stand out to students both visually and cognitively and get their full attention. The best strategy, however, may be to combine instruction with a set of concrete next steps, as recommended in Chapter 5.

Additionally, it is critical to remember that we cannot and should not try to respond to everything. Experienced writers would feel overwhelmed and even offended by such thorough critique; it is equally unnecessary and unwise to try to teach students through excessively detailed commentary. Moreover, especially asynchronously, while it is tempting to comment on every error (like the instructor in Example 5.2), such frequent and scattershot commentary can do more than frustrate the student—it also can misrepresent the core issues that need to be taught. We need to remember whether we want to address global or local concerns. Synchronously, it is wise to encourage students to write (talk) as much as possible, which enables them to practice and strengthen the skills they need to learn.

Finally, teachers often express concern at how many students they have in their online classes and how many of these classes they might be expected to teach. Tutors, too, rightly worry about how they can meet student needs when their numbers exceed that of available tutors. These are administrative issues for which, at this time, there is no clear set of best practices. To address such issues systematically and empirically, I think that online instructors need to learn their online pedagogies, consider how many students they reasonably can work with in group activities *and* one-to-one conferences, and then determine the number of students they can teach responsibly in a given time period. Thoughtful accounting for online instructional time that includes one-to-one conferencing will help in discerning OWI best practices that meet both instructors' and students' needs.

Conferencing Action Plan for *too much and too little commenting*

1. Think about the mini-lesson the student most needs, moving from the core needs of content (fluency), organization (form), and surface issues (correctness).

2. Asynchronously, adjust the length of embedded comments to make them (a) complete and clear and (b) short and succinct.

3. Asynchronously, remember that less can be more when it comes to a conference. Students don't need to (and probably won't) read comments that are as long as or longer than their own writing. It's also unlikely that students will act on all of those comments.

4. Synchronously, remember that less can be more in this modality as well. While a certain amount of instructor talk must be dedicated to asking contextualizing questions and teaching the needed lesson, the interaction is most valuable to students when they're invited to write in response to the lesson and independently of the instructor.

Modeling by Proofing and Editing

I have often heard that it is not an instructor's job to proofread and edit for students. In fact, instructors get into some really heated discussions about this aspect of their work. As Chapters 4 and 5 show, particularly in online settings, educators tend to worry about doing too much for students, "fixing" their writing, giving them "the answer," and appropriating by assuming they know what students wanted to say. While few would argue that it is actually our job to teach the skills of proofing and editing to online students, simply posting an online proofreading or editing handout is not sufficient. Neither is referring students to a handbook section or telling them to edit and proofread. If these methods worked, we could expect polished writing from all our students. Therefore, especially in online settings where we use text to do the teaching, we must *show* students how to proof and edit in addition to telling them. And that generally means being a bit more hands-on—like being willing to experiment with using the word processor's track changes feature in students' own texts to demonstrate what they need to be looking for and to help them make critical choices in their proofing and editing. If this level of teaching about editing and proofreading presents philosophical problems in online writing centers, administrators can consider this book's advice relative to their guiding epistemologies and determine helpful teaching strategies for their tutors to use with students online.

In effect, while it is not the online instructor's job to do the proofreading or editing for students, I maintain that it is the instructor's responsibility to teach them how to proofread and edit—and then to remind them when and how to use these skills. Traditional classroom teachers and tutors frequently provide strategies for proofreading, such as reading aloud slowly, reading from the printed page, reading silently while moving the lips to enact reading every word, or reading each sentence from the end of the paper back to the start. In online settings, video or audio clips (with written scripts for those with audio disabilities) can be helpful in teaching these strategies, but they work best when combined with some kind of personalized lesson.

This finishing-up process is important for all writers, of course, which means that what is good for students is good for us. Teachers/tutors alike ask students to proofread and edit their writing before making it public. Therefore, as a model of good writing, online instructors should always proofread and edit their asynchronously written commentary about student writing—whether it is in a letter, on the essay, or in an email. We expect students to write complete sentences and not use comma splices. Online instructors should do the same. To make this point (since writing instructors can be exceptionally observant of these issues <wink>), I have not corrected any existing instructional errors and infelicities in the conference examples presented in this book. Two of those follow.

Example 5.1B provides one instance where the instructor should have proofed his asynchronous comments. In comment 3, he says: *"Also, it seems to me that duplicating an image is much different then duplicating a person."* The difference between *then* and *than* confuses many students, but it should not confuse instructors. Most handbooks address frequently misused words; online instructors, whose words often take on the power of a textbook when they become archived and used by students, should become familiar with them. Most likely, the words themselves did not confuse Michael's instructor; a slip of a finger on the keyboard can create such a problem. Nonetheless, spelling and usage errors need to be corrected before sending the conference to the student.

Another example can be found in Example 5.2A when Robin's online instructor talked about sentence clarity. In comments 1 and 2, the instructor said: *"This sentence is a little unclear to me, can you revise?"* This comma splice is especially egregious because it links a declarative sentence and a rhetorical question. I suspect there is a bit of indirection going into the blended clauses, which may have complicated an otherwise simple writing issue for the online instructor. A more direct comment would eliminate the problem: *"This sentence needs to be revised. Specifically, make XYZ clearer by doing ABC or DEF."*

Whether we teach in a classroom or virtually, we inevitably model behaviors for our students. Thus, all online instructors need to know enough about English and instructional strategies so that each student's conference is as accurate and strong as possible. We can get some help either by asking a supervisor for occasional review or by peer reviewing for one another. Often, another experienced reader will make us more aware of our strengths and weaknesses and can lead to fruitful collegial dialogue and professional development opportunities.

My thinking about how we model proofing and editing changes significantly when teaching synchronously. For example, "errors" take on a different meaning in a synchronous conference. First of all, synchronous conferences happen dynamically in real time. Given the circumstances, there is little time for proofing or editing. Second, a different culture of writing surrounds chat: Both parties are more understanding of infelicities and goofs than in static asynchronous conferences (i often write without capital letters in a chat, but i never would do that in formal email or other writing). Indeed, speedy interaction, which can keep participants affectively connected in synchronous settings, more than compensates for not actively proofing.

Aside from speed, which certainly can be slowed by conference participants, the platform makes a difference in how error may be perceived. In a whiteboard setting, for example, one's typing often is view-

Example 7.4
Partial Synchronous Conference

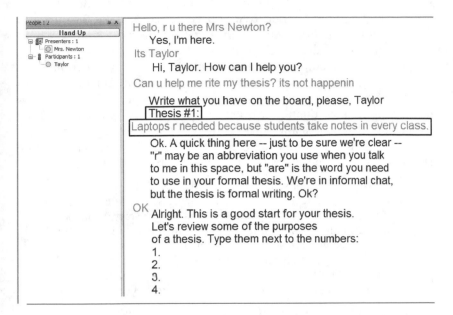

Hello, r u there Mrs Newton?
Yes, I'm here.
Its Taylor
Hi, Taylor. How can I help you?
Can u help me rite my thesis? its not happenin
Write what you have on the board, please, Taylor
Thesis #1:
Laptops r needed because students take notes in every class.
Ok. A quick thing here -- just to be sure we're clear --
"r" may be an abbreviation you use when you talk
to me in this space, but "are" is the word you need
to use in your formal thesis. We're in informal chat,
but the thesis is formal writing. Ok?
OK
Alright. This is a good start for your thesis.
Let's review some of the purposes
of a thesis. Type them next to the numbers:
1.
2.
3.
4.

able to both parties with minimum time lag—as it is being typed—and usually there is no need to click "send." That means students get the full benefit of watching an expert writer in process—and they learn that even their instructors misspell or incorrectly punctuate while in a drafting, freeflow invention, or question/response mode.

Like uncorrected misspelling in synchronous conferences, IM-ular abbreviations and shortcuts also have their place because the chat itself can be informal—just like an oral conference. For example, when chatting, a student might say "r u there?" for "Are you there?"; I often will say "brb" or "ttyl" ("talk to you later") as ways of conveying presence. Nonetheless, given scholarly debate about the potential transfer of such abbreviated language into more formal writing, it is helpful for online instructors to clarify their expectations about language formality during an early conference. As Example 7.4 shows, it is wise to hold a middle ground, remaining mindful of the purpose, audience, and context.

Addressing Sensitive Issues

Sometimes communicating in writing—whether online or handwritten—can be downright dicey. We might want to address some specific concerns, issues students should know about in their messages or essays, or perhaps something about their attitudes that is best addressed orally. Talking face-to-face about sensitive issues with a reassuring nod, a gentle touch of the hand, or a softening of tone can make potentially bad news or negative criticism easier to take. We need to consider how to address delicate writing concerns, which emerge both in students' online discussion tone and essay content.

As we have seen, we can use direct speech to offer our comments, suggestions, instructions, and criticisms overtly. Written language does not have to avoid directness to teach kindly and well. In fact, providing one's comments in digital form can be beneficial in terms of enabling instructors to rehearse and review what they want to say before sending the message. As Ginnie, a veteran teacher of distance-based online classes since 1998, observes about giving bad news online:

> [In providing a digital response,] I will first of all just say what I want to say, then I'll look at what I've said and say, "Now, this is going to be too painful." And I can edit my comments and be more tactful and be encouraging and so forth. And you just don't get the opportunity face-to-face to soften and you don't have the commitment to writing out [by hand] what you're trying to say fully and you try to talk it through [orally] and people can't listen; they're too emotionally distressed by what they thought was [a] "wow!" [paper] and you're like, "No, no, no, it's really not."

In a handwritten essay response, we do not often have the opportunity to take thorough notes about an essay, write out complete thoughts, and then to edit them for clarity, focus, and sensitivity. Online, we can edit our comments. Similarly, in face-to-face conferences, once we have orally spoken these concerns to students—however softly—we cannot easily edit them or call them back. In using digital media to type and then convey responses, which is one of the ways that we are defining a one-to-one online conference, we have the opportunity to write first and then to "soften," as Ginnie says, while still being straightforward. And, although many instructors do that softening through indirect language choices, here I talk about how we can be both direct and respectful of student's feelings while not falling into the traps of potentially haunting accusatory statements or of missing the point altogether.

Instructors encounter a variety of sensitive scenarios that require necessary or advisable discretion. One example is politically incorrect or offensive speech. The online class discussion forum is ripe for poorly expressed ideas that can be insulting or demeaning, however unintentional. Such cases are prime opportunities for engaging the involved students in private conferences about appropriate public language uses particularly in educational forums—a subject that students used to openly negative speech in gaming and social networking forums may need to learn more about.

While speaking with discretion is important, it is equally critical to be straightforward so students do not misinterpret an online instructor's message or intentions in raising the sensitive issue. *"You probably didn't mean to hurt anyone, but it is not always a good idea to use that kind of language in our class' chat room because it might hurt someone's feelings"* may be kind, but its indirectness does not adequately express how unacceptable certain language choices are; in fact, it suggests that using such language sometimes is appropriate. A more straightforward response is: *"Our chat room is a public, educational forum. It is unacceptable to use stereotyping or hateful language here. Put yourself in your reader's place and find another way to express your thoughts."* These statements may produce momentary embarrassment in the average student, but they are not inappropriately damning and they give students a clear message.

Another sensitive issue is plagiarism, especially "secondary" or unintentional plagiarism when students do not know how to integrate quotes, paraphrase, and cite sources properly. In Chapter 5, Example 5.1B (repeated below as Example 7.5) offered a glimpse into likely plagiarism.

Example 7.5
Student Michael (Three Paragraphs and Embedded Commentary)

So because people don't know about cloning does it make it okay? Is cloning not bad as it seems? **[1] Missing word.** Is it just another experiment that needs to be done for glory? To me cloning is definitely wrong, trying to duplicate an image or person is wrong. **[2] Run-on sentence. [3] Also, it seems to me that duplicating an image is much different then duplicating a person. [4] What do you mean by image?** Only the man upstairs is allowed to make or create people, by giving Adam, and Eve and all other humans and animals privates to reproduce. **[5] Consider using a different word than "privates." [6] It seems a bit informal and slangy for an article.**

But because of confusion outside the scientific community concerning the differences between human cloning and embryonic stem-cell research, the study also will explain the distinctions between these two endeavors. **[7] Are you referring back to the previous study here? [8] Consider making that clearer. [9] Also, consider mentioning the difference between these two things so your reader has some idea what you're talking about.**

It will assess the current status of animal cloning, including outcomes of previous trials whether knowledge of assisted reproductive technologies can be applied to cloning a human criteria that should be used to evaluate the safety of human cloning and public policy issues, including responsible conduct of research. **[10] A paragraph should never be one sentence long. [11] Consider splitting this sentence.**

Presumably, Michael's online instructor did not notice that the second and third "paragraphs" of this example had vocabulary and syntax markers indicating a different author, which I interpret as the student's lack of facility with outside sources. Regardless, the likely plagiarism presented a communication challenge. The reality of digital text, which is fixed, archivable, and in that sense unchangeable, could be especially intimidating when addressing possible plagiarism. Not only might students interpret the comment as an accusation, but any authoritative reader such as a classroom teacher or an administrator could take the online reader's statement very seriously, and such statements could be used in disciplining students.

Perhaps such concerns explain why I have observed some other online instructors—particularly in tutorial settings—skirting the source use and citation issue. In one case, an instructor said: "*This sounds a little too textbooky—plus the British spelling of 'colour' above suggests you might be relying too much on another's words.*" The student's revision response was merely to change the spelling of *colour* to *color*, demonstrating that he did not understand the hints about sounding "textbooky" or "relying too much on another's words." He needed specific instruction about paraphrasing, quoting, citation, and attribution.

In Example 7.6, the online instructor used in comment 2 a yes/no rhetorical question to obliquely inform Tyrone he was using more "technical" language than we normally find with a novice writer.

The combination of Tyrone's word choices specific to aircraft along with the sentence's relative sophistication strongly indicates that he has copied rather than paraphrased here. At best, he has not attributed the information to a source; at worst, he has used someone else's words as if they were his own. But the online instructor's indirect way of addressing apparent plagiarism by using a rhetorical question did not elicit any revision from Tyrone. Tyrone's next draft contained the exact same language and the instructor's implied message apparently went over his head.

Example 7.6
Student (Tyrone) Paragraph and Embedded Instructional Comment

Their training facilities, located at J. Hughes Technical Center near Atlantic City, New Jersey, consists **(1) [subject verb agreement]** of a B-727 retired narrow-body aircraft computer controlled targets, and a bullet proof observation platform, and indoor laser disc judgment pistol shooting interactive training room, and a close-quarters countermeasures/personal defense training room with protective equipment and dummies. **(2) [Is this a bit too technical for the average reader?]**

What could the instructor have written? First, she needed to decide whether she was in a formative or a summative teaching mode. She could have taken the rhetorical question and turned it into a declarative statement: *"This language is a bit too technical for the average reader."* Then, she could have explained that it also is not language that matches Tyrone's typical language: *"In fact, Tyrone, the language is too technical for what you've been writing in this essay and in this class all semester."* After that, the instructor could have given the student a task and required a conference to follow up: *"Please go back to your original source and either photocopy it or copy/paste the text into a blank document. If it is available on the Internet, please provide me with the URL. Have these materials and this essay available to meet with me during my office hours on Tuesday."* In a formative mode, she could have added, *"Our job is to work with paraphrasing other people's words."* If they were assigned to a networked classroom, their conference could have been orally conducted in the classroom after class or in the instructor's office. If they met in a fully online setting, it could have been scheduled synchronously, which would have given the instructor an opportunity to determine whether Tyrone understood the problem and its solution. An asynchronous conference most likely would take more interactions to satisfy the instructor's goals, so a phone call could also be planned.

It is our responsibility as instructors not to sidestep such delicate issues especially in online settings. Indeed, we do not need to duck or evade these issues if we use problem-centered teaching strategies that involve direct speech acts. Example 7.7 offers one case where the online instructor used direct speech with a student and taught a lesson about plagiarism; the student subsequently addressed this issue in a revised draft.

Example 7.7
Online Instructor Response to Possible Plagiarism

Online Instructor: I'm concerned about the possible plagiarism I mentioned on the marked copy [of your essay]. I'm not at all saying that you're trying to cheat on this paper, but I'm suggesting that you don't fully understand the rules about plagiarism. If I quote someone, or use information from someone, I must give credit to the original author. If I give credit to an author but don't use quotation marks, then I'm telling my readers that this section of my paper uses summaries or paraphrases, not direct quotations. If I do quote but don't use quotation marks, then I'm plagiarizing even if I give the author and a page number. If you'll look at what [your handbook] *Keys for Writers* says on plagiarism, you'll save yourself a lot of grief.

This commentary is a good example of addressing a delicate issue head-on. One of the wise choices this online instructor made
was to use first-person "I-language" to talk the student through the
situation rather than second-person "you-language," which could be
considered more confrontational or accusatory. In this case, the instructor did not accuse the student of plagiarizing, which might have
caused a self-defensive response or could have provided language to
be used against either the instructor or the student by other parties.
The online instructor maintained politeness and clarity while being
straightforward and informative. Such direct expression offers clues
for dealing with meaty and substantive, but ultimately sensitive, issues like primary and secondary plagiarism, politically incorrect or
offensive speech, and similar concerns.

Conferencing Action Plan for *addressing sensitive issues*

1. When you find yourself wondering whether a paper has been
   plagiarized or feeling offended by the speech used, wait a few
   minutes before responding. Think about what your major concern is. If you aren't sure how to handle the problem, ask a
   supervisor or colleague for advice.

2. Decide what you want to achieve through your response. How
   can you best benefit the student in this sensitive situation?
   How can you maintain your own integrity as an educator and
   as an employee of a particular institution? What are the possible repercussions of straightforward speech? What are the
   possible educational benefits of such speech?

3. As you draft your response, be as straightforward, direct, and
   nonconfrontational as possible. If the content is particularly
   sensitive, have a supervisor or colleague read your response
   before sending it to the student.

Chapter Eight

Having Effective Conferences

Learning from Student Progress

The feedback we give to online students helps them grow as writers, students, and human beings. Similarly, we need their feedback to grow as online instructors. This chapter is about asking students "how's it going?" in regard to their learning based on our interactions with them. While there may be as many ways to do learning audits as there are online instructors, we'll look at five basic methods here: (1) instructional rubrics, (2) interactive journals, (3) spontaneous or scheduled chats, (4) midterm and end-term surveys, and (5) self-audits. Any of these options can be refocused and revised to meet the needs of individual teachers, tutors, courses, programs, and institutions.

Instructional Rubrics

Instructional rubrics as mentioned in Chapter 7 can help determine how and where to spend precious time with students. Online teachers/tutors likely will have their own favorite rubrics that emphasize what students need to know about their writing with respect to their assignments, courses, and individual development. Example 8.1, for instance, uses a most-to-least-important organization with content as the most important factor followed by organization, style, and correctness. In other words, when content is lacking, it does not matter much that sentence correctness is weak; my goal for the conference needs to be content focused. It is presented here for an online argumentative writing class. In its earliest iteration, this impressionistic rubric originated from the State of Maryland "C" standards for first-year English composition. It is within the vertical structure of importance, the line items being assessed can be changed to meet the needs of different levels, courses, and assignments—both for course-based and tutored students. The rubric is impressionistic in that (shown horizontally) there is space for using a check to indicate below-average, average, or above-average achievement at any stage in the writing process.

Example 8.1
Essay Rubric and Global Commentary

Essay 3 Argument Assessment Rubric

Student Name: Bob D.

	Competency	Fails to Meet Competency √–	Meets Competency √	Exceeds Competency √+
Content (Fluency)	▪ Essay meets requirements: subject, organization, and length (7–8 pages total body w/ separate title page and references page, 9–10 pages total).	√	X	
	▪ Essay presents a clear assertion, which is stated at the end of the introduction.		√	X
	▪ The first paragraph defines the issue and introduces background, or reasons, for the assertion, including why this issue is important and why it is arguable.		√	X
	▪ The essay provides 3–5 good reasons why the assertion is credible.			√ X
	▪ Each reason is supported by evidence, such as facts, figures, examples, quotations, and field research.	√		X
	▪ The reasons are organized in a logical manner, such as strongest to weakest or cause to effect.	√	X	
	▪ The essay presents 1–2 counter-arguments.		√ X	
	▪ The evidence comes from 4–6 credible, reliable sources.			√ X
	▪ Conclusion paragraph/s summarize/s the issue and re-asserts the argument made. It may include questions that the argument leaves unanswered and that readers might want to explore further.		√	X
Organization (Form)	▪ Essay is unified in support of a central idea, or assertion.		√	X
	▪ Paragraphs are unified in support of subordinate points (reasons).	√	X	
	▪ Each paragraph has an appropriate transition to guide readers.	√ X		
Style and Expression	▪ Sentences are clear and precise.		√ X	
	▪ Tone & approach are interesting & engaging.		√	X
Grammar and Mechanics (Correctness)	▪ Substantially free of major errors in grammar, spelling, punctuation, and mechanics. Completely free of distracting errors (e.g., run-ons, comma splices, fragments, tense/number shifts, s-v disagreement).		√ X	
	▪ Introduces and explains paraphrases and quotations correctly and completely.	√	X	
	▪ Correctly uses MLA or APA guidelines for in-text citation.			√ X
	▪ Correctly uses MLA or APA guidelines for *Works Cited* or *References*.		√	X

√ Preliminary draft

X Presentation draft

Example 8.1 *continued*

Preliminary Draft Comments: Bob, I'm very excited about this essay! Your topic is pertinent to firefighters and housing contractors alike. The essay has great potential and the essential parts exist and are ready for you to begin to revise. Below, I'll give you steps that will help you make your argument work.

1. First, read the arguments that I've provided as models and example arguments from your textbooks. Notice that quotations are introduced and explained. They (and paraphrase) are used as support for main points—not as the main points, but as support. In your essay, I see the following:

   a. Paragraph 2: much of this paragraph's primary information can go into paragraph 1 as contextual material that will make the introduction deeper and clearer.

   b. Paragraphs 3–5 actually present background material to the problem: how and why lightweight structures burn quickly and dangerously. More about these in a minute.

   c. Paragraph 6 actually contains your main points. They are highlighted in green. Each of these points needs its own fully fleshed-out paragraph complete with supportive evidence (including, perhaps, anecdotal stories about how such codes would have saved a home or people).

   d. Paragraph 7 is your counterargument, which also needs fleshing out.

   e. Paragraph 8 is your conclusion, which you'll be able to flesh out better upon having revised the rest of the essay. Here is where you really hit hard on the importance of following through with writing the code.

   If you do as I suggest here, your essay will have the necessary depth of detail.

2. The following is an example way of incorporating quotes into your own arguments and material from paragraph 2; use a similar method for paragraphs 3–5, which may end up becoming 1–2 paragraphs total depending on how you choose to revise them:

   Manufactured wood I-joists are one of the most commonly used lightweight building materials. **According to the American Forest and Paper Association (2006),** "I-joists are composed of two horizontal components called flanges and a vertical component called a web." **This means that XYZ.** Flanges, **on the other hand,** "are manufactured from sawn lumber or structural composite lumber, while webs typically consist of plywood or oriented strand board" (Wood I-Joist Manufacturers Association, 2001)**; this quality of flanges suggests that XYZ. The International Association of Fire Chiefs (2008) e**xplains that essentially a manufactured wood I-joist it is one piece of particle board or glued wood in the center of two thin pieces of lumber. Another common type of lightweight building materials used is pre-made wood trusses attached by metal gusset plates. A gusset plate is a plate that attaches two to three sections of wood together and are be embedded into the wood by 3/8ths of inch metal prongs. Due to the small amount of depth that the gusset plates are inserted into the wood they are **prone** to quick failure under fire conditions (p. 169). **These lightweight building materials do XYZ (or are ABC, or something).**

How does the incorporation of your sources help to distinguish between your words and those of the sources? How should you add to the sources by explaining what the material you're presenting means with respect to your assertion? One reason you have to argue the assertion is that not everyone will understand what is so obvious to you given your profession and professional knowledge and experiences.

The rubic competencies are marked with a checkmark. Let me know if you have any questions, Bob. I look forward to the next draft!

Presentation Draft Comments:

Bob, this essay is one of the most improved essays I've ever seen! You've got a good introduction and assertion, a series of good reasons for your assertion, as well as suggested code changes that are convincing. The conclusion is effective, too. I see a need to work on the depth of some paragraphs, as indicated in the essay, as well as your counterarguments. But overall, you can be proud of your work here.

Also note the kinds of edits I made as a model for what you can do to clarify sentences and punctuation. Don't forget commas after introductory clauses and the kinds of errors that we've talked about and I've highlighted in yellow. The checkmarks with the line through them concern the graded, or presentation draft.

A rubric like this meets several needs. First, it is a time-saver. Second, it offers students impressionistic and ungraded feedback, which teaches them to look at writing as a process that is improved over time. Third, when used as shown here, the rubric also offers feedback to online instructors. The first set of checks and commentary were made in response to the student's earliest, or preliminary, draft. The second set of checks (with a line through them) and italicized commentary (which I usually present in colored font) concern the graded, or presentation, draft. Not only does the student see progress or lack thereof, but so do I. When a pattern emerges of many students similarly failing to meet specific competencies, I have evidence that something I am teaching is not working. The rubric helps me monitor my teaching effectiveness.

Interactive Journals

Interactive journals offer both instructors and students the opportunity to create and continue ongoing conferences. Although these might sound time consuming, in reality, a teacher could spend less than thirty minutes on an entire class' journals each week. In the rare tutorial setting where ongoing journals between tutor and writer can be sustained, they take only the amount of time that tutors set for themselves.

Co-journaling about writing/reading experiences reinforces relationships and also is a crucial way to receive feedback. When introduced early in the conferencing process and appropriate levels of discussion are taught, students learn that the journal is a safe place to ask for specific kinds of help, blow off steam to the instructor, and respond to the feedback and conferences they are receiving. Instructors, on the other hand, can use these journals to ask specific kinds of questions that provide a weekly accounting of the students' learning and needs, allowing the instructor to make immediate changes and adjustments. For a successful journal experience, I recommend using a workspace within the CMS or tutorial management system that is private rather than email. A private, centralized work space enables private journaling boundaries that email, with its ease of forwarding to other parties, does not.

The journal can include:

- Questions that concern how students are adjusting to a course: *How was this first week of class? What would you like to get out of this course? What parts seem like they may be extra challenging? What parts seem like they may fit your writing abilities at this point? How can I best help you as a writer?*

- Questions that address students' writing processes:
  - *Please write a journal entry explaining how you used my comments and your peers' comments (if, indeed, you did so) in your revision of the summary for Essay 1. What was difficult about the assignment? What was easy? What would you like to learn from it? This is a good opportunity to reflect on your writing process and to share with me some challenges you've had.*
  - *Please explain your revision process for Essay 2 beginning with when you first read the returned Preliminary Draft rubric and listened to my oral comments. Name any tools you've used in this revision, such as computer tools, dictionaries, peer response, and the like. What questions, if any, do you have for me as I grade these essays?*

- Questions that allow focused self-reflection and provide encouragement: *Please discuss in what ways you are changing as a writer as a result of our work in this course. How are other courses you're taking and/*

or the professional work that you're doing influencing your writing? By the way, I appreciate your hard work!

- Questions that specifically address student discussions: *Which of our discussions have been useful? What different activities or topics (if anything) would you like to see in future discussions?*

- Especially helpful are questions that can lead to an instructor's mid-course correction regarding any aspect of the online instruction: *We are halfway through the course. Although we have been communicating frequently through conferences, writer's journals, essay drafts, discussions, and chat, this is a good time for you to evaluate the course according to what you like, don't like, need, or don't need. My goal is to see whether I should make any adjustments that will better meet your needs for the last half of the course.*

  ☐ What do you like about the way this course is set up? What don't you like about it?

  ☐ What is your opinion about the readings in general? About the writing assignments in general?

  ☐ What would you change about this course if you could? What would you keep about this course if you were advising me about a future semester?

  ☐ What would you change about your own participation in the course, if anything at all?

  ☐ What else would you like to share about your experiences of this online writing course?

These journal questions, while helpful, do not end the instructor's responsibility. Each student who provides journal responses deserves response from us. Responses could be as short as a few sentences (*"I'm glad you're finding that some suggested revision changes are useful, Tina. I'll respond to your question about aspects of writing that need help when I grade your essay because then I'll know more."*) or as long as two paragraphs in response to queries and concerns:

> *Commas can be a problem for many writers. I'm glad you're using the handbook. There are guidelines for when/how to use commas. They are always used: (1) in a list, (2) after introductory clauses, (3) before and after nonrestrictive clauses, (4) after—but not before—subordinate clauses, and (5) before coordinating conjunctions. There are, of course, other times commas are used, but the ones listed here are fairly frequently needed. Notice that I just created a list for you and how I used the commas. I also used a comma before the coordinating conjunctions* and *and* but *in previous sentences. The coordinating conjunctions are: FANBOYS (for, and, nor, but, or, yet, so). Let me know whether this answers your question. Have a great week!*

To be fair, it is a sign of caring to reveal something personal about our own writing processes or difficulties; co-journals are best when they are real:

- Student: *I posted my first draft for essay 1. I cannot stop reading it and making changes. I chose to write on children who experience illnesses, which to me is a very intriguing subject. I enjoyed it. I need to make sure I stay on top of my reading. Feeling rushed is not a good feeling. :-)*
- Instructor: *Hi, Russ! Boy, do I know how hard it is to stop fiddling with a piece of writing! Sometimes I have a hard time putting it down, too. No worries on this preliminary draft, though, as you'll also be revising to a presentation draft before it's graded. Keep up the good work!*

Ultimately, interactive journaling is a matter of give-and-take. Students who give more may naturally receive more from us. But sometimes it is the quieter students who write less who need more from us. Over time, online instructors will learn when and how to adjust their journaling as both a relational and a feedback mechanism.

Spontaneous or Scheduled Chats

IM-like chats often are used for synchronous conferencing. In this case, I am not referring to teaching conferences but to chats for the purpose of interacting, whether spontaneous or scheduled. Online instructors often worry that if students feel free to contact them at all times of the day or night—whenever their CMS reveals their presence online—then they will never have peaceful moments online. My experience, however, is that students are cautious about bothering the instructor outside of online office hours or are hesitant to make contact altogether. Either way, it is useful to set early expectations (and invitations) for when we are available to chat. In my case, I choose to ping each student I see online at some point early in the semester. I keep a checklist to make sure I have spoken to everyone. I risk interrupting them when they are working—not the best thing—but I also make clear that I am available to them when online. I usually begin with a greeting like: *"Hi, Sam. I just wanted to pop my head in and see how you're doing."* In these chats, I apologize for any interruption and we talk briefly about subjects such as their overall experiences with online instruction (*"I've never had a teacher talk to me online before."*), our pets (*"You have two dogs, too?"*), the next assignment (*"I'm working on it, but I don't like my writing very much"*), or an upcoming break (*"Not much of a break. I'll be writing papers."*). Then, I quickly end the chat if there are no questions. The point is to use chats as a way to let each student know he or she matters to me, that I'm available when the software shows my presence online, and that I am always looking for feedback about how things are going.

Midterm and End-of-Term Surveys

Informal evaluations when offered in the midterm can help us to correct our conferences and strategies midstream—before they become so set that we fail to meet particular students (or entire classes) at their points of need. When offered at the end of term, we can write our own questions, avoiding administratively driven surveys that do not respond to our particular settings and epistemological assumptions. Other advantages include gaining a sense of what students might reply in more formal evaluations and using the surveys to build our own files of online conference-based information. These files, which may be good for promotion and salary raise purposes, can drive well-considered changes in our online pedagogy and they offer useful data for an ongoing investigation into student comprehension and uses of online instructional interactions in particular institutional settings and modalities.

Online instructors might ask of students the following kinds of survey questions found in Example 8.2.

Example 8.2
Sample Feedback Survey for Tutorials

The Online Tutorial Website/Platform

1. Please think about online tutorial website/platform.

   a. Evaluate the following features of the online tutorial website/platform using a scale of 1 to 5 (where 1 means "Poor" and 5 means "Excellent").

      ◆ Overall design (e.g., colors, layout, etc.): 1 2 3 4 5
      ◆ Ease of finding what you are looking for: 1 2 3 4 5
      ◆ Clarity of WHICH services are available: 1 2 3 4 5
      ◆ Clarity of WHEN services are available: 1 2 3 4 5

   b. Overall, how satisfied are you with the online tutorial website/platform (where 1 means "Not at all satisfied" and 5 means "Extremely satisfied")?: 1 2 3 4 5

   c. Were you able to submit your essays and/or questions without difficulty?

      ☐ Yes
      ☐ No
      ☐ Somewhat _____
      ☐ Not sure/Don't know _____

   d. Were you able to access your returned essays or archived conferences without difficulty?

      ☐ Yes
      ☐ No

□ Somewhat _____

□ Not sure/Don't know _____

Asynchronous Essay Conferences

2. Have you submitted an essay for online instruction?

   □ Yes

   □ No

   □ Not sure/Don't know

   a. If yes, why did you submit your essay/s?

   _____

   _____

   b. If no, why didn't you submit your essay/s?

   _____

   _____

3. About how many total essays have you submitted for online instruction?
   1 2 3 4 5 6 7 8 9 10 (or more ___)

4. About how many essays have you submitted more than one time (e.g., in more than one draft) for online instruction? 1 2 3 4 5 (or more ___)

5. Think about the last essay you submitted for online instruction.

   a. On a scale of 1 to 5 (where 1 means "Poor" and 5 means "Excellent"), how helpful were the comments that you received? 1 2 3 4 5

   b. Evaluate the following features of the online instruction using a scale of 1 to 5 (where 1 means "Poor" and 5 means "Excellent").

   ◆ The overall helpfulness of the instructor's comments: 1 2 3 4 5

   ◆ The clarity of the instructor's comments: 1 2 3 4 5

   ◆ The instructor's responsiveness to your needs: 1 2 3 4 5

   ◆ The instructor's friendliness: 1 2 3 4 5

   ◆ The time it took an instructor to return your essay: 1 2 3 4 5

   c. Did you use some or all of the instructor's advice to develop or rewrite your essay/s?

   □ Yes

   □ No

   d. If yes, which advice did you use? Why?

   _____

   _____

   e. If yes, how did you incorporate the advice into your writing? _____

   _____

   _____

f. If no, which advice didn't you use? Why not? _____
_____
_____

g. Were you satisfied with the advice you received?
    □ Yes
    □ No

h. If no, how could the advice have been more helpful? _____
_____
_____

Synchronous Conferences

6. Have you used the synchronous, or "real-time" writing assistance of an online instructor to ask a question?
    □ Yes
    □ No
    □ Not sure/Don't know

a. If yes, why did you asked question/s of a synchronous online instructor?
_____
_____

b. If no, why didn't you ask questions of a synchronous online instructor?
_____
_____

7. About how many total real-time conferences have you had this semester?
1 2 3 4 5 6 7 8 9 10 (or more _____)

8. For about how many different essays have you talked with an online instructor? 1 2 3 4 5 (or more _____)

9. Think about the last time you asked a question in a live conference session.

a. What was the purpose for asking the question? [CHECK ALL THAT APPLY]
    □ Preparing for a test or exam
    □ Brainstorming ideas for an essay
    □ Organizing an essay
    □ Learning grammar and/or mechanics
    □ Other _____
    □ Don't know/not sure

b. What question/s did you ask? _____
_____
_____

c. Was/were your question/s answered?
    □ Yes

❑ No

❑ Don't know/not sure

d. Did you use the online instructor's advice in developing or revising your writing?

❑ Yes

❑ No

❑ Don't know/not sure

e. Did you use some or all of the instructor's advice to develop or rewrite your essay/s?

❑ Yes

❑ No

f. If yes, which advice did you use? Why? _____
_____
_____

g. If yes, how did you incorporate the advice into your writing? _____
_____
_____

h. If no, which advice didn't you use? Why not? _____
_____
_____

i. How could the advice have been more helpful? _____
_____
_____

j. Please evaluate your last conference using a scale of 1 to 5 (where 1 means "Poor" and 5 means "Excellent").

- The instructor's responsiveness to your needs: 1 2 3 4 5
- The instructor's supportiveness: 1 2 3 4 5
- The instructor's friendliness: 1 2 3 4 5
- The instructor's knowledge of English language: 1 2 3 4 5
- The instructor's ability to motivate you to learn: 1 2 3 4 5
- The instructor's availability when you needed him/her: 1 2 3 4 5
- The privacy of the session: 1 2 3 4 5
- The instructor's pace in helping you: 1 2 3 4 5

k. How helpful was your last session on a scale of 1 to 5 (where 1 means "Not at all helpful" and 5 means "Extremely helpful")?: 1 2 3 4 5

10. Overall, how satisfied are you with the synchronous conferencing you received (where 1 means "Not at all satisfied" and 5 means "Extremely satisfied")?: 1 2 3 4 5

11. How could an online conferencing session improve the synchronous inter-action to meet your needs better? _____

_____

_____

Undoubtedly, we can gather useful information about how our students are learning from such surveys. For example, from reviewing several sets of anonymous questionnaires along with student writing from the classes, a trend emerged in that students' comments did not always match the actions demonstrated in their writing—suggesting that they were not always consciously aware of their writing choices with respect to their thinking about writing. It was not uncommon for them to say that they used "all of the advice" they were given, although careful comparison of their revisions to the conferences revealed that no student applied *all* of the commentary when revising.[1] My point is that while students' beliefs about their experiences do not reveal everything about the strengths and weaknesses of an online conference, they can tell us a lot. Undoubtedly, such feedback provides necessary information for online instructors to improve their skills and performances.

Self-Audits

Finally, there is the self-audit. We have seen a kind of self-audit on the part of students from questions asked of them in their interactive journals. They can be asked to complete similar self-audits before they post any revised essay, which enables them to reflect meta-cognitively on their own writing processes and idea development. Online instructors also benefit from self-audits. I recommend that online teachers/tutors audit themselves at least three times a semester—in the beginning, middle, and end. Our focus should alternately be (1) what we hope to learn about online instruction, (2) what we are learning midstream from our activities and conferences with students, and (3) what we have learned at the end of the term from interacting with students online about their writing. We should write for our own files (also good for teaching/tutoring philosophy statements and promotions/raises) what has worked well, what has not and why—as well as what we think we will do differently and what kinds of professional development or training we would like to engage.

---

[1]Similarly, in another study, students in an interactive CMC-based peer group study actually used *more* advice from their peers then they did, also revealing a disconnection between their perception and the textual evidence (Hewett 1998, 2000).

Another important way to conduct a self-audit of our online instruction is similar to looking for patterns in the rubric discussed earlier. For at least two essays, we should look at three different students and carefully compare whether and how they used the writing instruction provided to them in conferences. Because textual teaching is what primarily happens online, it is important to measure what is taught against what has been learned through a more empirical lens. Students may say they have done XYX in light of a conference, but have they done it? If so, was it done well? If not, what could we as teachers/tutors have done differently? Students may not "listen" or demonstrate that they care about our working with them. Ultimately, however, online instructors have the responsibility to create conferences that help students learn and improve. Careful self-audits are a critical key to knowing how well we are doing that job.

Conferencing Action Plan *for having effective conferences*

1. Use your own concerns, those of your department or program administrator, or some of the ideas presented in Chapter 7 to develop a few research questions relevant to the online instruction that you are providing. Those questions can form the basis for either informal or formal research about your practices—and online instructional theory and practices overall.

2. Depending on your online setting, decide whether seeking feedback through online (asynchronously or synchronously), voice (telephone), or face-to-face interactions would work best. Remember that it might be beneficial to seek feedback in the same medium in which your primary teaching occurs. One advantage to seeking feedback online, for example, is the archival nature of the medium. Another advantage is that talking or writing online can help bring to students' minds the challenges and benefits that they experience in that instructional setting.

3. Test and refine your feedback tools with a small group of students before using it with larger groups. Once you think you understand the feedback, check out your understanding with your students (a few or all, depending on the setting) to learn whether you need to synthesize the information differently.

4. Consider collaborating with another online instructor for the development, use, and analysis of the feedback that you seek.

5. Don't hesitate to ask for instant feedback after any online interaction or to initiate a spontaneous chat, so that you can do an immediate course correction if necessary or otherwise reinforce the instruction.

Postscript

Toward a Theory of Conference-based Teaching

According to Stuart Selber, at a minimum, efficacy in online settings involves the concept of computer literacy among student users, who either "*can control* their online environment or *be mediated* by it" (2004, 476; italics in original). The same thinking applies to educators and OWI pedagogy. Beyond their obvious needs for functional computer literacy, without adequate preparation and understanding about OWI, educators do not control the most basic of their own online pedagogies; instead, their teaching is mediated by the online environment. As a result, their instructional choices diminish.

Despite the popularity of the de-centered classroom, which attempts to equalize authority among teacher and students and is especially valued in online settings, students come to writing courses expecting their instructors to teach and guide them and to do so overtly. In the case of OWI, this expectation supposes functional expertise in the basics of online-based pedagogy and one-to-one instruction beyond the technology itself. Thus it is critical that educators understand their OWI pedagogy at the practical, experiential level. This book has been about such understanding.

In addition to answers for questions about efficacy, educators need solid descriptions and analyses of online instructional commentary: how instructors talk online, so to speak, and how students revise in response. Conducting writing instruction solely through text—particularly in online settings where students and instructors may never meet in real time—is challenging even for experienced teachers. This is one reason that we badly need deeply descriptive, yet reflective research into instructional commentary and revision that occurs in both asynchronous and synchronous settings.

For example, the research that grounds this book considered the language used in both asynchronous and synchronous conferences.[1] I studied sixty-three asynchronous teaching interactions from thirty-three first-year English students and twenty-two from seven developmental students, as well as fifty-three conferences from thirty-four high school students. I examined the linguistic functions of the online instructors' commentary and then, using textual analysis, considered whether and how a portion of those conferences were used in the students' writing and revision after the conference. I learned that the asynchronous conferences primarily were:

- Conducted by the online instructors as the main speakers in the context of student-initiated requests;
- Focused on informing, asking few questions;
- Both imperative- and suggestion-oriented, depending on the students' levels;
- Minimally phatically oriented;
- Used by students to develop and revise their writing;
- Used to address a wide variety of writing concerns,
- Of generally correct, yet moderate helpfulness for the writing;
- Not used to effect either positive or negative change where praise was concerned; and
- Potentially more frequently used when the comment was made locally within the text rather than globally placed at the beginning or end of the text.

In terms of synchronous conferences, I studied fifty-two online whiteboard interactions from twenty-three of the developmental and first-year English students. I examined the linguistic functions of the participants' talk together and then, using textual analysis, considered whether and how those conferences were used in the students' writing after the conference. Specifically, these conferences were primarily:

- Dialogic;
- Varied in terms of linguistic function types;
- Focused on informing, asking very few questions;
- Response-based rather than providing problem-centered instruction;
- Focused on idea development over stylistic or mechanics-based concerns;

---

[1]See Hewett 2004–2005 and 2006.

- Task-focused to retain connectedness between participants;
- Used by students to develop and revise their writing;
- Used for developing discrete areas of the writing like thesis sentences or transitions;
- Of moderate overall effect on the writing; and
- Highly collaborative.

From these studies and other research, this book is grounded in the reasonable presumption that online conferences can be efficacious: students can and do use them to revise and to improve their writing. However, there is much upon which online educators can improve. Teaching through text is the essence of teaching in online settings. Some technology, like synchronous whiteboards, provides the ability to use graphics and symbols while talking in real time. Other technologies enable voice and video recordings and live interactions. By and large, however, online educators likely will continue to rely on text as their primary conference mode for conveying asynchronous and synchronous instruction in online settings. Therefore, I contend that we need more research to learn how to teach through text in effective, thoughtful, respectful, and efficient ways. The research report in Appendix 1 stands as one example.

To teach textually in an online conference is not a static act. It is not a matter of posting digital handouts or of creating an online textbook for students to read. Online conferences are dynamic, individualized to the writer, and contextualized by the writing in progress. They are different from the idea-generating nature of online group discussions. Online writing conferences have their own dynamism inherent in the act of sharing and talking about writing, whether asynchronous or synchronous. Such conferences are held with the explicit intent of helping students to improve as writers, so generally they have a broader goal of attending to the formation of drafts rather than to the summative evaluation of writing.

Teaching through text is not an easy task. It challenges experienced and novice educators alike to use their instructional voices fully, freely, and with focus on the writer's needs as revealed by the writing. It requires that we admit to and own our authority as educators, and to use it on the student's behalf. It requires semantic integrity.

I suspect that teachers and tutors who typically instruct orally will find themselves eventually teaching textually online and will face the kinds of issues that the online instructors exemplified in this book have faced. Whether that instruction is connected to a single email commentary about a student's draft, a hybrid networked classroom, a distance-based writing course, or a supplementary tutorial setting, if an

Internet connection is available, the teaching can occur as a text-based one-to-one conference.

To teach effectively online, we need a consciously held, eclectic understanding of our instructional theories. Better, though, would be a theory that addresses the dynamic nature of an online commentary and the textual essence of its communicative nature. Thus, future theoretical and pedagogical research needs to consider the online conference-based instructional environment as one that requires its own theories and practices—attentive to, but distinctive from, contemporary writing instruction theory and practice developed for traditional settings. OWI, particularly in the form of online conferencing, has reached a stage where researchers and educators need to reconsider how instructional theory and practice actually converge in online settings, and we need to investigate and develop new theory that sufficiently addresses the textual nature of the online instructional environment.

Appendix 1

A Study of Online Writing Instructor Perceptions

Christa Ehmann Powers

Introduction

This study explores online writing instructor attitudes and experiences to gain a deeper understanding of how instructors' affective and cognitive concerns and priorities lead to particular pedagogical decisions in online environments. Of particular interest are: instructors' beliefs about online strategies, meanings online instructors wish to convey to students, instructors' attempts to guide student writing while preserving student authority, and how issues specific to online instruction can inform training and professional development. Phase One of this empirical investigation, reported here, was undertaken with consenting, professional writing instructors who worked with writing students via an Online Writing Lab where participants "meet" for one-to-one asynchronous and synchronous conferences.[1]

Background

Many online writing instructors enter online arenas having knowledge of "computer-assisted learning" or "online learning" but little actual experience with asynchronous or synchronous instructional methodologies. They typically come to positions with educational backgrounds in face-to-face classrooms; they often are selected for online positions based on traditional classroom performance. Ability to address student writing *in text*, rather than through oral or blended[2] instructional conversation, is oftentimes de-emphasized or unaddressed in selection and training processes for online positions. Directors of online departments

---

[1]Asynchronous and synchronous conferences occur on a web-based platform. Synchronous tutorials consist of student-tutor whiteboard interaction. Asynchronously, students send a writing project to a tutor who downloads it, inserts global and local comments, and returns the document.

[2]"Blended" is defined as learning situations that include multiple teaching and learning modes—both face-to-face and online.

or programs may attempt to recruit faculty or tutors with online instructional experience. In practice, however, the relative newness of online instruction often means that applicant pools with online writing instruction (OWI) experience are shallow. Further, although there is foundational research addressing OWI pedagogical approaches and strategies(for example, Hewett, 2004–2005, 2006; Cargile Cook and Grant-Davie 2005; Ehmann 2001; Hewett and Ehmann 2004; Conrad 2004), practice is often based on "assumptions" about what seems to work for OWI. To a degree, face-to-face instructors are accustomed to variations of text-based instruction that share characteristics of online asynchronous communication. Indeed, instructors write global and embedded comments when addressing student essays; these comments, however, are written in the context of previous *oral* instruction and future *face-to-face* communication to clarify comments or address student questions. Hence, there is often a significant period of transition and acclimation when instructors begin working with students solely online.

A growing body of literature addresses training approaches and professional development for instructors transitioning into online settings (for example, O'Quinn and Corry 2002; Pelz 2004; Maguire 2005; Morris, Haixia, and Finnegan 2005; Conrad 2004; Joy 2004) and specifically OWI settings (Hewett and Ehmann 2004, Hewett and Ehmann Powers 2005; Coppola 2005; Rude 2005; Grady and Davis 2005; Cargile Cook 2005). Missing, however, is an in-depth, empirical consideration of instructor perspectives regarding online experiences: transition challenges (particularly for completely new online instructors); approaches to online practices; and views about influences of online instruction on face-to-face practices. Specifically, what happens when educators accustomed to face-to-face instruction become immersed in OWI? How do past classroom experiences affect perceptions of OWI? How does teaching/tutoring online teacher/influence educators' face-to-face instruction, and vice versa? In undertaking theory-generating research to address these questions, the intention is to gain insights about improving instructor training and professional development and how writing instruction may be affected in this "digital age."

This appendix: (1) provides brief contextual background for the study, (2) presents components of Phase One research regarding preliminary themes emerging from respondent data, and (3) considers methodological implications for future phases of the study and practical implications for instructor training and professional development in light of these findings.

Methodological Context

The purpose of Phase One research is to: (1) explore respondent perceptions of student revision after a student has engaged in an asynchronous conference and after the online instructor has opportunities for reflection, (2) explore pedagogical approaches to conveying instructional information online, and (3) hone data collection tools and analysis frameworks for a broader survey. A randomly selected group of ten online writing instructors from a larger instructional pool of 160 completed a semi-structured online email survey. Although researchers and respondents were employed by online learning provider Smarthinking, Inc., participation was voluntarily. Consenting respondents understood that their engagement in this study did not affect employment. Survey items were framed around respondents' views of OWI qualities and challenges with teaching online. Grounded in actual experience, the first questions asked respondents to review their final asynchronous essay conference of 2004 and examine the conference's strengths and weaknesses. Respondents were then asked to discuss the strengths and weaknesses of OWI more generally. Prompts were designed as open-ended and geared to elicit a range of responses. The survey asked respondents to address other issues they believed were important. The respondents also were prompted to discuss experiences with OWI in the context of their asynchronous interactions.

The conference that the instructor discussed was chosen not because of a desire to study particular conference types or demographics. Rather, the intent was to ground instructor responses in specific instances to elicit meaningful responses rather than lofty notions about what OWI *should* be. Selecting the most recent tutorial helped facilitate this. Cohen and Manion, Oppenheim, Powney and Watts, and Foddy support this survey design and sampling. Further, the survey questions were designed to elicit a wide range of responses. Suggestions for survey design changes are noted in this appendix's conclusion.

Instructor Perceptions: Preliminary Themes

This section presents preliminary findings: (1) pedagogical challenges of OWI for instructors, (2) distinctiveness of OWI as a teaching and learning modality, (3) attitudes toward OWI, and (4) claims of student benefits. These key areas as well as other areas will be explored further when the main survey instrument is revised and administered to a larger set of online instructors.

Pedagogical Challenges

Instructors reported on their approaches to OWI and the strategies that they used in particular conferences. A significant feature of the reports is the respondents' unsolicited references to perceived pedagogical challenges. Although one question in the survey prompted respondents to address challenges directly, throughout the survey individuals shared perceptions about difficult aspects of working online. For all but one individual who mentioned that he felt more comfortable expressing himself via text than verbally, the biggest challenges involved: (1) teaching in text and (2) the lack of immediate student feedback. Individuals noted in great detail the difficulty experienced in moving from the identification of particular student weakness to the *written instructional expression* of how to address said weaknesses. Concerned with both clarity and precision of their written communication, respondents expressed early frustration with knowing how to address a problem face-to-face while having difficulty translating those strategies in asynchronous conferences. Regardless of experience level, all respondents raised concerns about the lack of immediate student feedback within asynchronous conferences. Such concerns fueled questions about whether students understood their comments. For example, one respondent reported that OWI was viewed to a degree as an exercise based on "assumptions" about how students would understand his written instructional cues. Further, all but one respondent noted degrees of discomfort with the absence of cues received in face-to-face contexts (no eye contact, gestures, or expressions to help convey meaning). The overriding discomfort of most was emphasized by the views of the single respondent for whom such verbal, face-to-face cues were characterized as "distracting." Specifically, that respondent reported that such face-to-face, nonverbal interactions were diversions in identifying student understanding. For him, understanding was demonstrated in what students wrote on the page. Hence, the online environment allowed him to identify the "bottom line" of what students were trying to convey and the exact level of their writing. Respondent notions of OWI as a practice based on assumptions and their concerns with the lack of nonwritten cues warrant further exploration.

Distinctiveness of OWI

Respondents also identified OWI elements that they viewed as distinctive compared to other pedagogical experiences. Claims of perceived distinctiveness fall into one of two categories: (1) instructor's opportunities for self-evaluation and (2) students' cognitive processing during OWI. The majority of respondents reported OWI provided opportunities for self-evaluation unavailable in other contexts. Aside from standard employment practices specific to Smarthinking, Inc., respondents indicated there was a self-reflective process of evaluation inherent to OWI. According to respondents, the permanence of archived conferences allowed them to take greater, actionable interest in their craft. In considering the perceived strengths and weaknesses of their electronic episodes, respondents claimed they changed elements of their practice in future online conferences and even face-to-face conferences.

Interestingly, only two respondents actually characterized OWI as a distinctive form of learning for students. Both reported that OWI was distinctive because it involved cognitive processing mechanisms that were not employed by students in other instructional writing contexts. It was their belief that students learned writing differently from face-to-face contexts because all of the instructional commentary was written. Similarly, these respondents characterized how they were instructing and guiding students as unique and different from other experiences. Because instructors could not rely on potential face-to-face interactions to supplement written comments, they indicated that written text needed to be more methodical and more meaningful than, for example, typical marginalia written on students' physical essays for a traditional class. Interestingly, in highlighting these issues, these two respondents did not place value judgments on which approach they perceived as more "effective." Hence, these respondents were focused on differences with OWI, student learning, their own teaching, and process, rather than on overall claims of efficacy.

The notion of OWI as a distinctive way of learning is an intriguing proposition. Additional exploration into how instructors perceive OWI as fostering particular cognitive processes in composition students will shed light on the ways in which OWI may be a distinctive instructional endeavor for participants. Further investigation into the relationship between instructors' tendency for self-evaluation and their involvement with OWI is also needed. A deeper understanding of instructors' need for self-evaluation could provide further insight into professional development needs—thereby helping to alleviate and/or leverage perceived challenges associated with OWI.

Attitudes Toward OWI

Despite claims of enthusiasm about working online, the majority of respondents approached OWI with skepticism. For all but two, these attitudes were characterized by: (1) concerns about the pedagogical validity of OWI itself and (2) politically focused concerns about the use of online instruction within educational institutions more generally. Specifically, a distinguishing characteristic of the survey responses was the majority of respondents' perceptions that face-to-face teaching environments were superior to online environments. It is not surprising, therefore, that most comments about OWI were couched in comparison to traditional brick-and-mortar conferencing. Respondents explained their detailed methodology and approach to OWI and the care given to all students; they reported their general enthusiasm for working online. Nevertheless, all respondents save two stated that they believed OWI was an inferior teaching medium for writing. Their primary reason was the perceived lack of in-person, human touches that most considered could not be conveyed online. Despite respondents' detailed statements about steps they took to create personal, human touches in asynchronous conferencing, the majority of respondents characterized OWI as overall less personal and intimate than face-to-face writing instruction. For this main reason, respondents perceived OWI to be overall less effective than teaching writing face-to-face.

Skepticism about OWI and online learning more generally was also manifested in respondents' concerns about the "institutional politics" of adopting online programs. For those who voiced such concerns, OWI was perceived as a strategic move by institutional administrators to cut costs and appeal to student tendencies of "consumerism." Respondents considered cost cutting and a focus on efficiency as unsavory in academic contexts. OWI, therefore, seemed to evoke strong, sometimes conflicting reactions from individuals. Given the strength of these reactions and their potential influence on approach to OWI, such views will be explored in this study's later stages.

Student Benefits

Respondents shared perceptions relating to claimed benefits of OWI for students. Given individuals' attitudes toward OWI as well as the pedagogical difficulties they encountered, it is not surprising that respondents tended to assert that sometimes OWI was more valuable than other times and that in some circumstances, OWI was of no value to students at all. Further, all respondents save two reported that if students were not "hardworking" and "motivated," OWI would be of no value. When respondents did refer to benefits, all mentioned gains in terms of students' understanding of the drafting and revision process and strengthened writing skills. Claims of improved writing skills were substantiated for respondents in that they referred to demonstrated improvement in students' subsequent drafts. In acknowledging the perceived skill-level and substantive benefits of OWI, all respondents couched their claims in terms of the: (1) affective qualities of working online and (2) practical utility of working online. Because writing instruction was conveyed via text, respondents claimed the relative anonymity of the asynchronous conference allowed students to "save face." Minimizing fears of looking stupid, respondents perceived that "saving face" afforded students affective security, thereby helping students focus on writing. Further, respondents were unanimous in perceiving that student writing improved because there were few practical limitations to gaining access to the actual instruction. Although respondents did not have direct data to substantiate claims, they perceived that students saved travel time and they accessed instructor critiques "around the clock." Hence, claims tended to focus on utility and affect, thereby highlighting the situational benefits of working online.

Concluding Implications

Although broad conclusions about instructor perceptions cannot be made given the small scale of this Phase One research, practical suggestions about preparing educators for OWI-based interactions emerge.

- Instructors' reports of OWI's perceived pedagogical challenges reinforce the notion that training is essential to instructors' successful transitions into online environments. Further, instructors need specific strategies for teaching in text. More research is needed, however, on specific training methodologies and orientation frameworks that address instructors' concerns and preconceptions.

- Despite engaging OWI, individuals may still have pedagogical and political biases against this type of teaching and learning—as seen by most instructors' efficacy comparisons with face-to-face instruction. Addressing these preconceptions in training might foster greater comfort with OWI.

- Instructors might not conceptualize OWI as an opportunity for students to learn writing in cognitively different ways. Specifically, the majority of instructors did not indicate that OWI's text-based nature helps students learn in new ways. Further, it was also the instructional means of teaching through text that caused the most tension for instructors. Teaching through text was viewed by most as a potential inhibitor to student learning, rather than an opportunity to reach students in new ways. Addressing OWI as a potentially distinctive teaching and learning phenomenon may help instructors negotiate aforementioned challenges and embrace the full potential of OWI.

- Phase One research suggests important methodological points. First, the pilot survey questions elicited responses that addressed the broad research themes. Respondents also reported on other issues and areas they believed important. An online survey, therefore, can be deemed an appropriate data collection method. Preliminary results also highlight additional themes that warrant further exploration. Phase Two will involve piloting revised probes and open-ended online chats. A more precise, close-ended survey eventually will be developed and administered to hundreds of OWI instructors.

- Findings about instructors' perceptions will complement sister research on OWI processes and student perceptions. Valuable insights will be gained in exploring how participants view OWI in light of what actually occurs in an online conferencing episode. Ultimate outcomes will further theoretical frameworks for training and professional development and highlight practical implementation steps necessary to these activities.

References

Cargile Cook, Kelli. 2005. "An Argument for Pedagogy-Driven Online Education." *Online Education: Global Questions, Local Answers*. Eds. Kelli Cargile Cook and Keith Grant-Davie. Technical Communications Series. Amityville, NY: Baywood. 49–66.

Cargile Cook, Kelli, and Keith Grant-Davie, eds. 2005. *Online Education: Global Questions, Local Answers*. Amityville, NY: Baywood.

Cohen, L., and L. Manion. 1994. *Research Methods in Education*. London: Routledge.

Conrad, Dianne. 2004. "University Instructors' Reflections on Their First Online Teaching Experiences." *Journal of Asynchronous Learning Networks* 8.2.

Coppola, Nancy. 2005. "Changing Roles for Online Teachers of Technical Communication." *Online Education: Global Questions, Local Answers*. Eds. Kelli Cargile Cook and Keith Grant-Davie. Technical Communications Series. Amityville, NY: Baywood. 89–100.

Ehmann, Christa. 2001. "Exploring New Territory: Developing a Research Agenda for Online Tutoring and Instruction." *Journal of the National Tutoring Association—Inaugural Edition*. Spring: 69–86.

Foddy, W. 1996. *Constructing Questions for Interviews and Questionnaires: Theory and Practice in Social Research*. Cambridge: Cambridge University Press.

Grady, Helen M., and Marjorie T. Davis. 2005. "Teaching Well Online with Instructional and Procedural Scaffolding." *Online Education: Global Questions, Local Answers*. Eds. Kelli Cargile Cook and Keith Grant-Davie. Amityville, NY: Baywood. 101–22.

Hewett, Beth L. 2004–2005. "Asynchronous Online Instructional Commentary: A Study of Student Revision." *Readerly/Writerly Texts: Essays in Literary, Composition, and Pedagogical Theory.* 11 & 12, 1 & 2: 47–67.

———. 2006. "Synchronous Online Conference-Based Instruction: A Study of Whiteboard Interactions and Student Writing." *Computers and Composition* 23.1: 4–31.

Hewett, Beth L., and Christa Ehmann. 2004. *Preparing Educators for Online Writing Instruction: Principles and Processes.* Urbana, IL: National Council of Teachers of English.

Hewett, Beth L., and Christa Ehmann Powers. 2005. "IIow Do You Ground Your Training: Sharing the Principles and Processes of Preparing Educators for Online Writing Instruction." *Kairos* 10.1 Fall.

Joy, Donna. 2004. "Instructors Transitioning to Online Education." Virginia Polytechnic Institute and State University.

Maguire, Loréal L. 2005. "Literature Review—Faculty Participation in Online Distance Education: Barriers and Motivators." *Online Journal of Distance Learning Administration* 8.1.

Morris, Libby V., Ju Haixia, and Catherine L. Finnegan. 2005. "Roles of Faculty in Teaching Asynchronous Undergraduate Courses." *Journal of Asynchronous Learning Networks* 9.1.

Oppenheim, A. N. 1996. *Questionnaire Design, Interviewing, and Attitude Measurement.* Second ed. London: Pinter.

O'Quinn, Lisa, and Michael Corry. 2002. "Factors That Deter Faculty from Participating in Distance Education." *Online Journal of Distance Learning Administration* 5.6.

Pelz, Bill. 2004. "(My) Three Principles of Effective Online Pedagogy." *Journal of Asynchronous Learning Networks* 8.3.

Powney, J., and M Watts. 1987. *Interviewing in Educational Research.* London: Routledge and Kegan Paul.

Rude, Carolyn. 2005. "Strategic Planning for Online Education: Sustaining Students, Faculty, and Programs." *Online Education: Global Questions, Local Answers.* Eds. Kelli Cargile Cook and Keith Grant-Davie. Technical Communications Series. Amityville, NY: Baywood. 67–87.

Appendix 2

Direct and Indirect Speech in Writing Response: What, Why, How

What Direct and Indirect Speech Acts Are

Table 1: Direct Speech Acts

Category	Form	Function	Example
Inform	Declarative (subject + verb order)	Assertion, statement	*Your paragraph needs to be expanded.*
Direct	Imperative (no overt subject)	Order, command, or request	*Expand your paragraph.*
Elicit	Interrogative (verb + subject order, with some exceptions)	Question	*How can you expand your paragraph?*

As Table 1 shows, when linguistic form and function match in a communicative utterance, a *direct speech act* exists. This book advocates using direct speech for OWI.

Table 2: Indirect Speech Acts

Category	Form	Function	Example
Suggest	Declarative, Imperative, or Interrogative. Form and function do not match.	To inform, question, or direct by mentioning, introducing, prompting, or proposing an idea or thought. To address specific actions in an indirect manner and without plain expression.	*Is it possible to expand your paragraph?* Or, *You might expand your paragraph.*

As Table 2 shows, when linguistic form and function do not match, an *indirect speech act* exists. Indirect speech acts can work only "by virtue of a basic, shared assumption that when people speak and listen to each other, they normally do have the intention of accomplishing purposeful and effective communication in the context" (Traugott and Pratt 1980, 237). In other words, interlocutors "work together to accomplish shared, mutually beneficial goals" and the Cooperative Principle, above all others, is "crucial to all communication" (1980, 237). An indirect speech act violates the Cooperative Principle because, by definition, it relies on a disconnection between linguistic form and communicative function, creating a situation whereby *any* function can be the purpose of a particular form. Characteristics of indirection include:

- A tendency to disguise a command as a request or information (for example, "*Could you reorganize this paragraph in chronological order?*");

- Modals and conditionals (for example, "*You may want to send that new draft back.*");

- Rhetorical and leading questions (for example, "*You make several claims about your mother here that you don't necessarily prove in your essay. Do you show how she is respected in the community? Do you show her child-rearing ability?*");

- Stacked verbs (for example, "*In addition, you'll want to learn how to use 'who' and 'whom' correctly.*"); and

- Tangled or tortured syntax[1] (for example , "*My recommendation is that you NOT try just to tinker with the language in the last paragraph to make it clearer . . .*").

Why Online Instructors Use Indirect Speech

The study of pragmatics considers that a successful linguistic communication occurs when the listener "recognizes the speaker's communicative intent" (Akmajian et al. 1997, 352). Such recognition represents cooperation between the speaker/writer and listener/reader; the listener/reader uses "inferential strategies" to decode "the speaker's communicative intent" (1997, 352). The utterance's context provides clues for solving the problem of meaning (1997, 353).

---

[1] I thank Laurie Johnson for coining this apt characterization of indirection in instructional language.

Context

Communication tends to occur "within the context of a fairly well-defined social situation" (Akmajian et al. 1997, 345) and provides context clues to assist interlocutors in offering and assessing meaning. In an online setting, the communication occurs in the margins. In most cases, both online instructors and students are more familiar with traditional oral writing instruction. Students are more familiar with using computers for recreational purposes, Google-based "research," or informal chats than with *instructional* communications. Yet, many students—especially traditional ones—may be familiar with more or varied forms of technology than the average educator who began teaching without computers. For many novice instructors, the online environment is a hybrid setting with a less familiar educational context. Since any form of indirectness requires interlocutors to infer meaning (Grundy 1995, 7–9), indirect speech necessarily requires a high level of inferential skill. Both parties should be *competent* in the rules of language use—not of grammar necessarily, but of conveying meaning—and both should be able to infer the intention of an indirect statement when there is no intonation, other vocal patterns, or body language to help. However, *the general communicative competence levels among students and instructors naturally differ in any environment.* Students do not have as well developed a lexicon as their instructors, and even in face-to-face settings, they do not have the same facility with discussing and identifying writing and its qualities. They also have experiential differences that may be exaggerated in the online environment. Where intention and inference do not agree, as Chapter 6 demonstrates, opportunities for communicative misfires abound.

Pedagogical Intention to Avoid Directness

Attempting to avoid appearing directive or to avoid any directness also accounts for indirect instructional language. As Chapter 4 explains, expressivism, social constructionism, and postprocess theories often lead to instructional indirection and nondirectivity. If one believes philosophically that *any* direction or directivity is improper—a position that many traditional and online instructors apparently hold—then suggestions become a potentially acceptable way to urge discovery, foster understanding, or construct knowledge with students while not "taking over," or appropriating, their texts. The tension between contemporary instructional theory and practice thus leads to a perceived need for indirect instructional language.

Another philosophic reason for indirection includes personal or institutional ethical concerns and honor code proscriptions against "giving answers" or offering too much help (Ehmann 2003, 11–12, 225).

For example, some online instructors are involved in high-stakes environments, such as certain kinds of gateway testing, where it is critical to avoid potential impropriety. Thus, indirection may be used to intersect "appropriate" kinds of online commentary with the theoretical and practical premises that guide the online instructors. The result, at times, can be ambiguity that puzzles or confuses students.

Finally, indirection also may stem from a philosophical belief that instructional commentary is a form of the epideictic genre, leading instructors to equate indirection with ways to avoid hurting students' feelings. Using epideictic thinking, one might praise students for strong writing while wanting to avoid the appearance of blaming them for weaker or poor writing. Therefore, one might praise using direct speech, but note weaker writing indirectly to avoid the act of "blaming." Unfortunately, this thinking does not take into account the *teaching* aspect of a written conference; it considers only opportunity for responsive/critical feedback, which automatically sets up a feedback dichotomy: positive = praise for strong writing // negative = blame for weak writing. As an example of this reason for indirection, Thomas Batt explains that in his study the teacher's praise is intended to emphasize first the student's progress, not the product—a result of both expressivist thinking and process theory:

> The epideictic rhetoric continues in the fourth paragraph, but the "blame" here—pointing out where the fault lies—is indirect, couched in either the passive voice ("these ideas could have been divided into multiple paragraphs") or targeting subjects other than the student writer: "The *essay* could have slowed down and explained ideas more carefully" [Batt's emphasis]. . . . The indirect constructions reduce the possibility that the student will feel that she has failed, especially in this case, when she probably realizes that her essay is not unequivocally successful. . . . One effect of Margaret's rhetoric is to allay the student's fears about Margaret's evaluation and to promote in the student a positive mindset with which to read the rest of the comment. (2005, 217)

While I empathize with this strategy's kind goal, it is not necessarily successful, particularly where indirect, suggestive comments are concerned. Indeed, as even Batt notes and Richard Straub (1997a, 1997b) supports, savvy students recognize some statements of praise as a setup to prepare them for the pain of the "blame." However, when overt teaching is the second part of the conference, the weaker writing in a student's essay need not be construed negatively as blame or as something to fear as hurtful to the student. It presents a teaching moment in which both student and online instructor can participate toward writing development.

Susan Blau, John Hall, and Tracy Strauss, in discourse analysis of oral tutor-tutee conversations at their writing center, identify three "rhetorical strategies" that participants used: *questions, echoing* (inform-ing), and *qualifiers* (suggesting). Even though they clearly advocate social theory in their article, the authors find it problematic that "an un-due—or misdirected—emphasis on the collaborative approach resulted in tutorials that seemed to waste time and lack clear direction" (1998, 38). They indicate that their consultants responded in nonstraightfor-ward ways, using qualifiers and conditional language to "be kind and to keep the discussion collaborative" (1998, 37); as a corrective, they recommend that the collaborative approach be "used judiciously and appropriately" (1998, 38). In favor of "an informed flexibility," they indicate that studiously avoiding overt instruction (informing and di-recting) does not always make sense: "We saw too many examples of tutors dancing around a direct question, when they clearly knew the answer, wasting the already too-short time they had to spend with their clients" (1998, 38). As a result, they recommend a more directive approach for essay content and formal concerns and a nondirective approach for process (see also Clark 2001, 38). Such an approach has particular benefits in OWI, as this book has argued.

Politeness Intentions

Politeness softens messages and is found linguistically in certain speech patterns. In English, the phrase *"Can you x?"* is an idiomatic way of commanding *"Do x"* (Grundy 1995, 97). In fact, the indirect interroga-tive *"Can you pass the salt?"* has almost the same function as the impera-tive *"Pass the salt"* or *"Please pass the salt."* These utterances convey the expectation that the listener will pass the salt. The small difference is important, however—especially online. *"Can you pass the salt?"*—a *rhetorical question*—conveys politeness in ways that a mere command cannot (1995, 100), and it softens the written command like a nod or a smile can in face-to-face settings.

How Online Instructors Use Indirection

Encoding Distance

Politeness strategies encode "distance between speakers and their ad-dressees" (Grundy 1995, 127). Because overcoming distance is chal-lenging in online settings, using politeness to encode distance rather than to eliminate it might seem odd. Ironically, although it is natural to think of distance in terms of moving *away*, the online instructional setting may require encoding distance to seek *closeness*. In this environment, the distance between speaker/writer and listener/reader exists on several levels. First, there is the geographic distance between instructors and students that exists through the computer medium either asynchronously or synchronously. In either modality, the reality of typing rather than orally talking is never fully breached. Second, distance is created by various levels of sophistication in communication, skills, and knowledge. Third, distance is inherent in the online instructor's empowered role of teaching through feedback and instructional advice; the student's role is naturally less empowered. Written politeness strategies attempt to reduce distance by bringing participants closer— creating, in effect, a socially constructed equality. Our politeness to students offers a surface impression that we are equals in the conference; however, as Chapter 1 indicates, conferences are task-based encounters, and there never exists a genuine leveling of roles.

Etiquette

Politeness also is a form of etiquette. Peter Grundy explains:

> . . . politeness phenomena are a paradigm example of pragmatic usage. Among the aspects of assumed external context that are particularly determinate of language choice in the domain of politeness are *the power-distance relationship of the interactants and the extent to which a speaker imposes on or requires something of his/her addressee* [italics added]. In being "polite," a speaker is attempting to create an implicated context (the speaker stands in relation X to the addressee in respect to act Y) that matches the one assumed by the addressee. (1995, 127)

Not surprisingly, "linguistic politeness phenomena are predictable in relation to the contexts in which they occur" (1995, 128), such as in any relationship where different power levels exist. The person in the superior position may try to eliminate the distance for politeness sake; yet, the attempt to eliminate distance *reinforces* its reality. In the case of indirect speech in online instructional settings, the instructor anticipates what the student writer should know or do next but uses indirection to deflect that anticipation and assert a false equality of standing. The online instructor may address unasked questions that the student chooses not to ask or does not know to ask. Additionally, the instructor may try to forestall an obvious mistake or a logical error by indirectly trying to lead a student away from a particular course of action: *"Would it be more logical to put all the description together . . . ?"* Such a suggestion results from the "do not give the answer" rule, and it leads to an ambiguous comment that may, ironically, result in the student doing nothing.

Superiority Lowering

Regardless of their attempts to change the instructional setting to one of equality, online instructors remain in a superior position to their students. Elizabeth Traugott and Mary Louise Pratt consider superiority levels:

> The basic rule of politeness seems to be: Regardless of the reality, act as if the addressee is superior. One of the most obvious effects of this norm is that it rules out speech acts that require the speaker to be in authority, namely, commands. If one is being polite, one always phrases directives as requests, not commands, and makes them very indirect: not Hand me that phone book not even Will you had me that phone book, please? but Could I ask you to hand me that phone book? or Would you mind handing me that phone book? (1980, 246)

When people are offered the linguistic option of merely answering the question rather than doing the request, the surface situation is that they can refuse this request. Contextually, however, people generally know that this option is a pretense and that they are expected, if not required, to follow through with the request (1980, 247). I have observed both online and traditional instructors using indirect or "suggestive" language that creates the *pretension* that students can say no; however, the implied *expectation*—even in a tutorial—is that students should act on the advice. In traditional settings, moreover, observation reveals that such language often is accompanied by nods or other positive head movements, facial expressions like smiles, and other positive body language. Online students, especially, can be confused because they not only do not receive these physical cues, but they also are less familiar with how to respond to written instructional text that suggests or leads them.

The rhetorical question lowers superiority by anticipating particular answers from those who know how to respond, and it creates similar confusion. Instructors know that the answer to a rhetorical question always is implied and expected. However, a rhetorical question can misfire when the recipient has limited linguistic competence with its conventions, limited experience reading written teaching interactions, or actually presumes he or she may say "no" when "yes" is the expected response. Many contemporary students are not well versed in the convention of rhetorical questions even when those questions are offered orally with intonation, physical, and facial gestures that hint at the expected response. When online instruction removes aural and body language cues, unsophisticated student writers probably will not understand how to respond to written rhetorical questions.

Face-Saving

"Saving face" is a concept not unlike self-esteem. A positive face is "a person's wish to be well thought of. Its particular manifestations may include the desire to have what we admire admired by others, the desire to be understood by others, and the desire to be treated as a friend or confidant" (Grundy 1995, 133). Conversely, a negative face involves "our wish not to be imposed on by others, and to be allowed to go about our business unimpeded with our rights to free and self-determined interactions intact" (1995, 133). In short, people want to feel good about their writing—to have positive face. Whenever we need to perform a face-threatening act as speakers, we have one of three strategic choices. We can "act on-record," or overtly; "act off-record," or covertly; or choose not to "act at all" (1995, 134). Covert communicative strategies, despite their indirect nature, are successful whenever the listener/reader recognizes and understands them. Online instructors responding to Ehmann Powers' survey expressed a belief that students saved face via online anonymity, which "afforded students affective security, thereby helping students focus on writing" (Appendix 1). This belief helps to explain why online instructors would employ face-saving strategies regardless of their potential to produce ambiguous communication. Beyond student benefit, face-saving also serves instructors, who may experience themselves as constrained by theoretical requirements—using indirect language to practice a pedagogy of noninterventionism and/or nondirective teaching in a setting where they may suspect that straightforward, directive language would accomplish the job better.

Semantic Results of Politeness Intentions

Semantically, online politeness strategies in instructional settings can lead to especially challenging and ambiguous sentences, such as: *I wonder if you couldn't capture attention even more strongly immediately by dropping some hints about your possible solution toward the beginning, rather than leaving it all until the end?* This sentence has a particularly tangled and tortured syntactic structure with the declarative form and interrogative punctuation, as well as qualifiers and modals that obscure meaning. H. P. Grice's maxim of "manner" supposes that in cooperative communication, the interlocutors will be clear, unambiguous, brief, and orderly (Akmajian et al. 1997, 382). Yet, according to Grundy, "it is very often the case that politeness phenomena depart from the principle of maximal economy of utterance, if by maximal economy we mean uttering only the proposition to be conveyed . . ." (1997,

128). This departure from economic statements—which can be said similarly of the maxims of clarity, non-ambiguity, and orderliness—makes sense because politeness requires more indirection to move the listener in the desired direction. The general result is a somewhat odd-looking exchange "from a linguistic point of view, because it means everyone is treating everyone else as his or her superior, that is, everyone pretends equally to be unequal to everyone else" (Traugott and Pratt 1980, 247).

As an illustration, in his rhetorical analysis of two letter-length end-comments from one teacher in a traditional setting, Batt notes a shift to passive voice as the teacher (Margaret) being studied moves into the "business-like rhetoric" of the "imperative mood," which he supposes that the student would "more likely try to implement." He states: "Rather than write, 'Do more research,' Margaret offers, 'Some research might have been needed here, since the first anecdote is personal experience and the second is not'" (2005, 215). This indirect, passive-voice comment, which Batt suggests is motivated by a desire to critique the student "obliquely," creates potential miscommunication. That the student *might have done* more research does not necessarily convey that he *should do* that research for this essay or future ones. Passive comments thus become easy to ignore.

In a way, rhetorical questions and other indirection strategies provide hints and clues like that of a wink of the eye—written expressions that convey a "here you go" or "secretive" stance to account for loss of physical cues. Yet, such hints and clues do not always provoke the desired revision. For instance, an instructor probably would recognize this polite comment as one that corrects: "*Actually the word* media *is plural (the singular is* medium*), so* "Do the media . . ." *is correct, but I must admit that some writers just don't want to be quite that correct.*" The student, who made other revision changes responsive to instruction, did not change "media does" to "media do." In terms of response, it is possible to be too polite—and too indirect—by offering students "choices" where they need to learn to make changes.

Works Cited

Ahrenhoerster, Greg, and Jon Brammer. 2002. "What's the Point of Your OWL? Online Tutoring at the University of Wisconsin Colleges." *The Writing Lab Newsletter* 26.2 (February): 1–5.

Akmajian, Adrian, Richard A. Demers, Ann K. Farmer, and Robert M. Harnish. 1997. *Linguistics: An Introduction to Language and Communication, 4th ed.* Cambridge, MA: MIT.

Anderson, Carl. 2000. *How's It Going?: A Practical Guide to Conferring with Student Writers*. Portsmouth, NH: Heinemann.

Ascuena, Andrea, and Julia Kiernan. 2008. "The Problem of Email: Working to Decentralize Consultant Authority in Online Writing Centers." *Praxis: A Writing Center Journal* (Spring). <http://projects.uwc.utexas.edu/praxis/?q=node/199>. Accessed July 10, 2009.

Batt, Thomas A. 2005. "The Rhetoric of the End Comment." *Rhetoric Review* 24.2: 207–23.

Black, Laurel Johnson. 1998. *Between Talk and Teaching: Reconsidering the Writing Conference*. Logan, UT: Utah State UP.

Blau, Susan R., John Hall, and Tracy Strauss. 1998. "Exploring the Tutor Client Conversation: A Linguistic Analysis." *The Writing Center Journal* 19.1: 19–48.

Boquet, Elizabeth H., and Neal Lerner. 2008. "Reconsiderations: After the Idea of a Writing Center." *College English* 71.2: 170–89.

Bruffee, Kenneth A. 1984. "Collaborative Learning and the 'Conversation of Mankind.'" *College English* 46.7 (Nov.): 635–53.

———. 1985. *A Short Course in Writing Instruction*. Boston, MA: Little.

———. 1993. *Collaborative Learning: Higher Education, Interdependence, and the Authority of Knowledge*. 2nd ed. Baltimore: Johns Hopkins UP.

Burnham, Christopher. 2001. "Expressive Pedagogy: Practice/Theory, Theory/Practice." Eds. Gary Tate, Amy Rupiper, and Kurt Schick. *A Guide to Composition Pedagogies*. New York: Oxford UP. 19–35.

Clark, Irene. 2001. "Perspectives on the Directive/Non-Directive Continuum in the Writing Center." *The Writing Center Journal* 22.1 (Fall/Winter): 33–58.

Clark, Irene L., and Dave Healy. 1996. "Are Writing Centers Ethical?" *WPA: Writing Program Administration* 20.11-2 (Fall/Winter): 32–48.

Cooper, George, Kara Bui, and Linda Riker. 2000. "Protocols and Process in Online Tutoring." *A Tutor's Guide: Helping Writers One to One*. Ed. Ben Rafoth. Portsmouth, NH: Boynton. 91–101.

Duch, Barbara. 1996. "Problems: A Key Factor in PBL." University of Delaware Center for Teaching Effectiveness. <www.udel.edu/pbl/cte/spr96-phys.html>. Accessed May 31, 2006.

Ehmann, Christa. 2003. *A Study of Peer Tutoring in Higher Education*. Diss. Oxford U.

Faigley, Lester. 1990. "Subverting the Electronic Workbook: Teaching Writing Using Networked Computers." *The Writing Teacher as Researcher.* Eds. Donald A. Daiker and Max Morenberg. Portsmouth, NII: Boynton. 290–311.

Flower, Linda. 1979. "Writer-Based Prose: A Cognitive Basis for Problems in Writing." *College English* 41 (September): 19–37.

———. 1994. *The Construction of Negotiated Meaning: A Social Cognitive Theory of Writing.* Carbondale, IL: Southern Illinois UP.

Flower, Linda, and John R. Hayes. 1980. "The Cognition of Discovery: Defining a Rhetorical Problem." *College Composition and Communication* 31: 21–32.

———. 1981. "A Cognitive Process Theory of Writing." *College Composition and Communication* 32 (December): 365–87.

Flower, Linda, et al. 1986. "Detection, Diagnosis, and the Strategies of Revision." *College Composition and Communication* 37 (February): 16–55.

Fulkerson, Richard. 2005. "Composition at the Turn of the Twenty-First Century." *College Composition and Communication* 56.4 (June): 654–87.

George, Ann. 2001. "Critical Pedagogy: Dreaming of Democracy." *A Guide to Composition Pedagogies.* Eds. Gary Tate, Amy Rupiper, and Kurt Schick. New York: Oxford UP. 92–112.

George, Diana, and John Trimbur. 2001. "Cultural Studies and Composition." *A Guide to Composition Pedagogies.* Eds. Gary Tate, Amy Rupiper, and Kurt Schick. New York: Oxford UP. 71–91.

Greenhalgh, Anne M. 1992. "Voices in Response: A Postmodern Reading of Teacher Response." *College Composition and Communication* 43.3 (October): 401–10.

Greening, Tony. 1998. "Scaffolding for Success in Problem-Based Learning." Medical Education Online [serial online]: 3,4. <www.utmb.edu/meo/ f0000012.htm>. Accessed May 31, 2006.

Grice, H. P. 1989. *Studies in the Way of Words.* Cambridge, MA: Harvard UP.

Grundy, Peter. 1995. *Doing Pragmatics.* New York: St. Martin's Press.

Harris, Muriel. 1992. "Collaboration Is Not Collaboration Is Not Collaboration: Writing Center Tutorials vs. Peer-Response Groups." *College Composition and Communication* 43.3 (October): 369–83.

Haswell, Richard H. 2006. "The Complexities of Responding to Student Writing; or, Looking for Shortcuts via the Road of Excess." *Across the Disciplines, 3* (November). <http://wac.colostate.edu/atd/articles/ haswell2006.cfm>. Accessed May 13, 2009.

Hawisher, Gail, and Charles Moran. 1997. "Responding to Writing Online." *New Directions for Teaching and Learning* 69: 115–25.

Hewett, Beth L. 1998. *The Characteristics and Effects of Oral and Computer-Mediated Peer Group Talk on the Argumentative Writing Process.* Diss. Catholic U of America.

———. 2000. "Characteristics of Interactive Computer-Mediated Peer Group Talk and Its Influence on Revision." *Computers and Composition* 17: 265–88.

———. 2004–2005. "Asynchronous Online Instructional Commentary: A Study of Student Revision." *Readerly/Writerly Texts: Essays in Literary, Composition, and Pedagogical Theory* (Double Issue) 11 & 12.1 & 2: 47–67.

————. 2006. "Synchronous Online Conference-Based Instruction: A Study of Whiteboard Interactions and Student Writing." *Computers and Composition* 23.1: 4–31.

Hewett, Beth L., and Christa Ehmann. 2004. *Preparing Educators for Online Writing Instruction: Principles and Processes.* Urbana, IL: NCTE Press.

Hewett, Beth L., and Russell J. Hewett. 2008. "IM Talking About Workplace Literacy." *Handbook of Research on Virtual Workplaces and the New Nature of Business Practices.* Eds. Kirk St. Amant and Pavel Zemliansky. New York: Information Science Reference. 455–72.

Hobson, Eric H. 2001. "Writing Center Pedagogy." *A Guide to Composition Pedagogies.* Eds. Gary Tate, Amy Rupiper, and Kurt Schick. New York: Oxford UP. 165–82.

Horner, Winifred Bryan. 1988. *Rhetoric in the Classical Tradition.* New York: St. Martin's Press.

Howard, Rebecca Moore. 2001. "Collaborative Pedagogy." Eds. Gary Tate, Amy Rupiper, and Kurt Schick. *A Guide to Composition Pedagogies.* New York: Oxford UP. 54–70.

Kastman Breuch, Lee-Ann M. 2003. "Post-Process 'Pedagogy': A Philosophical Exercise." *Cross-Talk in Comp Theory: A Reader,* 2nd ed. Ed. Victor Villanueva. Urbana, IL: NCTE. 97–126.

Kent, Thomas (Ed.). 1999. *Post-Process Theory: Beyond the Writing-Process Paradigm.* Carbondale: Southern Illinois University Press.

Kestner, Mike. "Why Problem-Centered Learning?" *Learn NC: K-12 Teaching and Learning.* The University of North Carolina at Chapel Hill School of Education. <www.learnnc.org/articles/dpi_probmath>. Accessed May 31, 2006.

Lindemann, Erika, with Daniel Anderson. 2001. *A Rhetoric for Writing Teachers.* New York: Oxford UP.

Martin, Kenn. 1996. "Problem Based Learning." University of Western Australia, Centre for Staff Development. <www.uwa.edu.au/csd/newsletter/issue0496/pbl.html>. Accessed May 31, 2006.

Moran, Charles. 2001. "Technology and the Teaching of Writing." *A Guide to Composition Pedagogies.* Eds. Gary Tate, Amy Rupiper, and Kurt Schick. New York: Oxford UP. 203–23.

Mortensen, Peter L. 1992. "Analyzing Talk About Writing." In *Methods and Methodology in Composition Research.* Urbana, IL: Southern Illinois UP. 105–29.

Newbold, Webster. 1993. "Strategies for Computer-Based Distance Writing Courses." Paper presented at the Conference on College Composition and Communication. ED377476. (April): 1–14.

North, Stephen M. 1982. "Training Tutors to Talk About Writing." *College Composition and Communication* 33.4 (Dec.): 434–41.

————. 1984. "The Idea of a Writing Center." *College English* 46 (Sept.): 433–46.

Onore, Cynthia. 1989. "The Student, the Teacher, and the Text: Negotiating Meanings Through Response and Revision." Ed. Chris M. Anson. *Writing and Response: Theory, Practice, and Research.* Urbana, IL: NCTE. 231–60.

Peterson, Patricia Webb. 2008. "The Debate About Online Learning: Key Issues for Writing Teachers." *Computers in the Composition Classroom: A Critical*

Sourcebook, Eds. Michelle Sidler, Richard Morris, and Elizabeth Overman Smith. New York: Bedford/St. Martin's. 373–84.

Prensky, Marc. 2001. "Digital Natives, Digital Immigrants." From *On the Horizon.* NCB UP, 9.5 (October). <www.marcprensky.com/writing/ Prensky%20-%20Digital%20Natives,%20Digital%20Immigrants%20 -%20Part1.pdf >. Accessed May 29, 2007.

Ryan, Leigh, and Lisa Zimmerelli (Eds.). 2006. *The Bedford Guide for Writing Tutors,* 4th ed. New York: Bedford/St. Martin's.

Selber, Stuart. 2004."Reimagining the Functional Side of Computer Literacy." *College Composition and Communication* 55.3 (February): 470–503.

Sidler, Michelle, Richard Morris, and Elizabeth Overman Smith (Eds.). 2008. *Computers in the Composition Classroom: A Critical Sourcebook.* New York: Bedford/St. Martin's Press.

Smith, Ernest. 1989. "'It Doesn't Bother Me, But Sometimes It's Discouraging': Students Respond to Teachers' Written Responses." *Journal of Teaching Writing* (Special Issue): 253–66.

Sommers, Nancy. 1982. "Responding to Student Writing." *CCC* 33.2 (May): 148–56.

———. 2006. "Across the Drafts." *College Composition and Communication* 58.2: 248–56.

Spiegelman, Candace. 1998. "Habits of Mind: Historical Configurations of Textual Ownership in Peer Writing Groups." *CCC* 49.2 (May): 234–55.

———. 2000. *Across Property Lines: Textual Ownership in Writing Groups.* Carbondale: Southern Illinois UP.

Straub, Richard. 1996. "Teacher Response as Conversation: More Than Causal Talk, an Exploration." *Rhetoric Review* 14.2 (Spring): 374–99.

———. 1997a. "Response Rethought." *College Composition and Communication* 48.2 (May): 277–83.

———. 1997b. "Students' Reactions to Teacher Comments: An Exploratory Study." *Research in the Teaching of English,* 31.1 (February): 91–119.

———. 2000. "The Student, the Text, and the Classroom Context: A Case Study of Teacher Response." *Assessing Writing* 7: 23–55.

Thonus, Therese. 2001. "Triangulating the Key Players: Tutor, Tutee, and Instructor Perceptions of the Tutor's Role." *Writing Center Journal* 22.1: 59–82.

Traugott, Elizabeth Closs, and Mary Louise Pratt. 1980. *Linguistics for Students of Literature.* New York: Harcourt, Brace, Jovanovich.

Tremmel, Robert, and William Broz (Eds.). 2002. *Teaching Writing Teachers of High School English and First-Year Composition.* Portsmouth, NH: Heinemann.

Walvoord, Barbara E. Fassler. 1986. *Helping Students Write Well: A Guide for Teachers in All Disciplines.* New York: MLA.

Welch, Nancy. 1997. *Getting Restless.* Portsmouth, NH: Heinemann.

Williams, James D. 2003. *Preparing to Teach Writing: Research, Theory, and Practice,* 3rd ed. Mahwah, NJ: Erlbaum.

Zoellner, Robert. 1969. "Talk-Write: A Behavioral Pedagogy for Composition." *College English* 30.4 (January): 267–320.